BLACK ROBE

and

TOMAHAWK

BLACK ROBE
and
TOMAHAWK

The Life and Travels of
Father Pierre-Jean De Smet, SJ (1801–1873)

George Bishop

GRACEWING

First published in 2003
Gracewing
2 Southern Avenue
Leominster
Herefordshire
HR6 0QF

ISBN 0 85244 576 8

Typesetting by Action Publishing Technology Ltd,
Gloucester GL1 5SR

Printed in England by
Antony Rowe Ltd
Eastbourne BN23 6QT

Contents

Note on Text

A particular feature of George Bishop's presentation of the life of Father De Smet is the use of so much of De Smet's own letters – themselves one of the richest sources of material for the early history of the American West, particularly during the critical period of the Indian wars.

Previously the detail provided by these letters has only been available in the magisterial four-volume *Life, Letters and Travel of Father De Smet* (Francis P. Harper, New York, 1905) edited by Chittenden and Richardson. George Bishop has done the general reader an invaluable service by taking pertinent extracts from this vast corpus of letters to provide the core of his exciting presentation of this heroic and inspiring life in the missions – a life of tireless activity to promote the spiritual and material welfare of the Native American peoples that Father De Smet encountered in his work.

At times the language of Father De Smet's letters may seem flowery or hyperbolic to the modern reader, used to a more restrained style. The English of the published texts is almost throughout a nineteenth-century translation from Father De Smet's letters, originally written in French, and none of it apparently his own work. When Chittenden and Richardson were compiling their original edition they found the translation full of clumsy renderings of French phrases and more particularly of geographical names, which showed a lack of familiarity with the subjects treated. These problems still lurk in the extracts from the letters presented in this volume, but it seemed important, as the text of Chittenden and Richardson has provided a definitive text for scholars, not to try to re-revise their presentation.

Nonetheless, the use of so much of Father De Smet's own words gives a gripping immediacy to the work, and the idiosyncratic style of the translation adds a period flavour, even at times a personal charm, to the text.

William G. Hewett, SJ

Chapter 1

A Novice-Ship

The congregation of the small church in Termonde, in Belgium, watched as a grey-haired man climbed slowly into the pulpit. His knuckles showed white as he gripped the lectern.

'Napoleon!' he bellowed. The voice boomed around the church; all eyes were on the origin of the deafening sound. Hardly had the echo died down when another shout of 'Napoleon!' thundered again.

'He had only to lift his left eyebrow,' the old man continued, 'and a whole troop of young men followed to join his army. For what? To expand his empire, to win more land. For what? For himself, for his own glory.' He pulled a white kerchief from his sleeve and wiped his face. 'I do more than he. I shout. I badger. I plead – also for an army, also to win new empires. For what? To bring the knowledge of Jesus to men and women and children who, in their ignorance, in their paganism, have never heard of the Redeemer. "Go; teach all nations," He said. These children of the desert live in darkness, waiting to hear the Good News. But who will give it to them? I shout, I cajole. Not one young man flocks to the banner.'

Father Nerinckx introduced himself. He was a missionary in Kentucky. He held the audience captive as he told them of his life and its rigours in the New World of the Rocky Mountains, of the burning Great Plains, where thousands of unlettered Indians eked out a living hunting the bison.

'The harvest is rich ... the labourers few.' He paused. 'Yes, few,' he reiterated. 'Very few indeed.'

The white knuckles released their grip on the pulpit. Slowly the venerable old man, his silver grey hair falling across his forehead, wound his way down the spiral wooden stairs. He prayed his

1

exhortation would fall on fertile soil; that his message would resonate with some over-generous hearts.

A month later, there was a knock on the old man's door at the Seminary of Malines.

'I'm Pierre-Jean De Smet,' a burly young man said, holding out his hand.

'Oh, yes,' Father Nerinckx replied.

'I listened to your sermon some weeks ago.'

'Oh, yes,' the missionary replied again.

There was a pause.

'I would like to join your army,' Pierre-Jean smiled.

'Oh, yes,' Father replied, raising his right eyebrow. 'Come in. Let us talk.'

The old missionary from Kentucky peered carefully at the attractive, thickset young man of twenty in front of him. He was about five feet six inches tall and had piercing blue eyes. His face was full and frank in its expression, beaming with the natural buoyancy and good humour of his temperament.

Would he make it? the old man wondered to himself. It was a tough, dangerous life among the Indians. Nerinckx pointed out all the disadvantages, discomforts and dangers of a missionary's life in the wilds.

'You must have heard of Isaac Jogues?'

He told the story of the martyrdom of the Jesuit by the Iroquois Indians of Canada 300 years ago. 'That is the kind of life we have to face.'

Pierre-Jean's eyes matched those of the old man's impassively.

Another martyrdom might quench the young man's flame, thought Father Nerinckx. He told the story of the martyrdom of Jean de Brébeuf by the same Iroquois in 1649, dwelling on their barbarous ingenuity familiarised by centuries of practice.

The two men just looked at one another. After a long pause the old man smiled. Pierre-Jean joined him.

'Go home and think about it,' Father Nerinckx said as he let the young man out of the building.

It was 15 August 1821 and the American brig the *Columbus* was setting sail from Amsterdam. The captain strode to the rails. There was nothing to mar the blackness, only the orange light at the masthead and the two lights, one at the prow, and one at the stern, of the bucking craft. He looked at his watch. He stayed awhile, staring into the black. Presently a prick of light, like a firefly, pierced the night. He breathed a sigh of relief.

'It must be them.'

The light grew larger with time. Slowly the fishing vessel hove to. The first officer joined the captain. Instructions were shouted between the two vessels.

A huddled figure clambered up the rope ladder. He was followed by another, and another. The first officer led them down to their cabin.

De Smet ducked his head as he stepped into the tiny sleeping quarters. He threw a small bundle containing his few belongings onto a narrow bunk. This was what he had pawned his few possessions for – a passage to the New World. He could not have asked his parents for the cost. Indeed, they did not know he was on his way there. Pierre-Jean knew they would never approve. It was all right for someone else's son to brave the world of the barbarous Indians, but not *their* son. His colleagues, five of them, squeezed into the tiny space that was to be their home for the next six weeks.

Father Nerinckx had arranged with the captain of the *Columbus* to wait off Texel Island after he had set sail from Amsterdam. Protestant Holland would not allow any Catholics passage to the United States. So a rendezvous had been arranged with a fishing vessel carrying the six young men who had volunteered to join the missions in the New World.

Forty-two days later the *Columbus* sailed up the Delaware River and moored at Philadelphia. De Smet was glad to be on dry land. The buildings, the houses, were all fine, modern and elegant; there were even steam streetcars. It was surprisingly civilised. He had been expecting to find Red Indians with tomahawks and bows and arrows, uttering their chilling war cries. Here, he might just as well be back in Belgium. He was a little disappointed.

The young men went by steamer to Baltimore, and from there to Washington and Georgetown by a stage with six horses. A man was on the box, the reins between his fingers and one foot teetering on the brake. Another man rode shotgun guard. The stage lunged on its fore and aft springs as it rocked across the flat earth, from town to town, its big, heavy wheels slamming through the road ruts and whining on the curves. They were glad of the halts when their legs, tired and stiff from the shaking, touched ground. Their final destination was the Novitiate at Whitemarsh, fifteen miles from Annapolis, where Pierre-Jean and his five companions joined the Society of Jesus. They remained at the novitiate for eighteen months.

In the spring of 1823 the six novices, with their novice master, Father Quickenborne, began the move to St Ferdinand, near St Louis, 1500 miles further west in the heart of the United States, to found the first Jesuit establishment in the western part of North America since the suppression of the Society in 1773. St Louis was the gateway to the West. On 10 April 1823, they began the long journey from the Chesapeake to the Mississippi. At Baltimore they procured a decrepit two-wheeled cart to convey their heavier articles to the Ohio River. Ohio country was the wild west, the wilderness. They pushed and wheeled the cart for 300 miles to the Ohio. They passed along unpaved streets, between wooden houses and saloons with false fronts. All the way they travelled '*pedibus apostolorum*, staff in hand'. They cooked their own food. They slept in the outhouses of farms. Failing that, they curled up into their blankets under the sky. Sometimes they built a lean-to, a windbreak, to protect them when the weather was wild. From a forked tree to a forked branch, its other end thrust into the sodden earth, they placed a branch. This formed a ridgepole. They placed other branches, slanting to the ground, against the ridgepole. They made a roof and a back wall for the lean-to. At intervals, as when it drizzled or rained, they would cut more branches to add to the roof. At night they might hear the bark of a coyote, the braying of wild jackasses, or the plaintive howl of a wolf. On the way they met poorly fed, poorly clothed vagabonds, thieves and renegades, outlaws on the dodge, hiding out in caves, barns and shacks, suspicious of each other and everyone else. One even boasted of holding up the Santa Fé express and was now 'vanishing' into the 'badlands'. They crossed the Potomac River at Cumberland. The creeks and the rivers were flowing with melted snow water. Brown hills still carried dark patches from dampness left by melting snow.

After a march of eighteen days they reached Wheeling on the shores of the Ohio River. The swollen river swept down in a broad expanse of turbulent green and yellow flood. They had no money either to purchase steamboat tickets to travel down the Ohio or to buy a boat. So they set to making their own – a flatboat, or raft, made of logs lashed together by cord.

Making the raft took some days. Necessity forced the intrepid band of young adventurers to become inventors. [In the Jesuit Archives in the Foley Centre at Gonzaga University in Spokane, Washington, is a steel knife made by one of the group from a wagon wheel.] They had a chance to observe life in a 'wild west' town. The town had one street, half a mile long. For a quarter of a mile on either side it was built solid, with shops, blacksmith shops, a bank, a saloon, and an undertaker's mortuary. After that the street tapered off with scattered buildings, 'honky-tonks', adobe and frame houses, gambling bars, warehouses, sheds for storing timber etc.

The main shop, floored with split pine logs, was a low building with a shade roof and canvas awning that provided shade from the sun. It sold the usual wares – bright calicos, gumdrops and chocolate.

The blacksmith shops were working overtime, hammering out shoes for horses, shoeing them or doing bits of ironwork for wagons. Their anvils clanged under the blow of the hammer, the forges glowed with their fires and the soot-begrimed faces of the smiths reflected the red of the fires on their faces and bodies. Half a dozen rigs stood in the street. Huge drays rumbled past drawn by huge horses – Percherons and Clydesdales.

At last the raft was ready. It was twenty feet long and about fifteen feet wide. In the centre of the raft the novices erected a hut, about seven feet by six, which was essentially just a frame covered with tent canvas. Behind was a space for their goods, covered with another canvas.

Piloting a flatboat down the Ohio was not a task for inexperienced hands because of the treacherous hazards on the way. But they couldn't afford to hire a professional pilot. So the Master of Novices bought a book about the Ohio River and Brother Strahan offered to do the piloting.

The water lapped against the riverbank, and slapped against the raft. There was a splash as Brother Strahan dipped the steering oars of the raft into the water; the ripples moved outwards in ever-widening circles. He gave a push with the oar and the raft drifted into the main stream. The river was rushing swiftly. They could feel the pull of the current against the raft, against the oar. The water was green and brown and black, flecked with foam, as it took them towards the heart of the great continent. The distant forests spread like a verdant carpet of dark green. The landing stage, so full of bustling activity a few minutes ago, slowly diminished in size. The only sounds now were the shrill piping of some of the bigger boats. Periodically these would be drowned by the drawn-out blaring of the horn of a riverboat.

5

The novices tried their hand at fishing but this proved unsuccessful. The early frosts had driven the fish down to deeper water.

Before sunset, they beached their raft on the shore. The long branches of the trees stretched out like snakes over the water. They built a fire to cook their meal and to keep warm.

They gathered together broken branches and debris cast up by high water. Near the roots of a great tree they put together the wood for a fire. Tearing the bark from a tree, they got at the dry inner bark and shredded it. Then, with a little dry moss found high up on the side of a tree, they had the tinder for a fire. The fire felt good against the raw, cold wind that blew in chill and damp off the water. They dug a trench round the fire so that it could not spread. They fed the fire continually with shredded bark and then with twigs until it was blazing brightly. The crackle of the fire sounded loud, drowning the ceaseless whisper of the wind in the trees and the steady croak of frogs. The glassy expanse of water glittered with a thousand reflected stars. They would try to sleep – if the mosquitoes would let them.

Day after day they floated down the big river that soon began to seem endless. In the morning a river fog would settle in a thick blanket of white over the water. But then the sun would struggle through the misty atmosphere, disperse the fog, and climb high over them. They waved as a 'fire canoe', a steamboat, with its huge paddlewheels churning up the water, passed them. It was the *Sacramento Queen*. There were people on the deck – some waved back, others just laughed and jeered. A band was playing, while in the saloon the card sharks were relieving their clients of their money. Some Indians swept past in their light canoes made of the bark of the Canada balsam, of the thickness of pasteboard. On occasions the daylight would be turned to darkness as fog closed in over the river and its valley, blanketing the surrounding flatness of the countryside.

'Look out!' someone shouted, as a boat, riding low in the water, suddenly appeared, drifting towards them. There was no one in it. It must have been abandoned. One thought gripped the group immediately: why travel balancing precariously on a raft when you could ride more comfortably in a boat? Brother Strahan, with a sweep of his paddle, swung nearer the boat. He feathered the blade as he approached, letting the raft glide under the impetus of the blade. There was a paddle tied to the stern of the boat, covered with sewn deerskin. The oarsman stopped suddenly, frozen with horror, as he stared down the barrel of a large Colt revolver. A man stood up from the boat. You couldn't see his face. It was masked by a bandanna from the nose down. Narrow snake eyes shone from below his worn Stetson. He wore a check cowpuncher's shirt. A pair of bandoliers were coiled around his shoulders, one holding pistol bullets, the other rifle cartridges. As he pulled himself erect, he showed two guns, strapped against his thighs so that he could pull them free of their scabbards without getting the long barrels caught in the leather.

'Right! Your money!' he drawled. 'And be quick!'

Father Quickenborne, the Novice Master, stepped forward.

'We have no money. If we had we wouldn't be travelling like this, on a home-built raft.'

That reply disappointed the river pirate. He paused. 'What's that you got in there?' he asked, pointing with his left hand at the canvas-covered pile on the raft.

'That's our clothes,' the priest replied.

He paused again. Meanwhile a second body sat up in the boat. He also had his face covered with a bandanna.

'Right!' the first desperado said at length. 'Let's have your liquor. And quick!'

Father Quickenborne replied, 'We have no liquor.' To give substance to his remark he added, 'We don't drink.'

'Your baccy then,' the man demanded angrily.

Father Quickenborne was about to reply when the man stopped him.

'Don't tell me,' he said, pointing his left forefinger at the priest, 'you don't smoke.'

'I was just about to say that,' replied the Novice Master.

'Jesus,' the man blasphemed as he pulled down his bandanna in disgust and looked up to the heavens. 'Jake. We have all the boats on the Ohio to hold up and we pick on a bunch of penniless tinhorns.'

His partner forced a smile as he twirled his pistol's chambers.

'Buzz off,' the first man said, dismissing the raft with an angry motion of his hand.

After that the travellers kept a careful lookout for river pirates and also for the main hazards of the river – rapids. They had been warned of the many rapids on the fast-running stream. They were told they would see no white water, not until it was too late; and that the rapids would seem anything but alarming. Only those who had navigated those waters knew the danger; it all looked so easy, so smooth.

'Look out!' There was panic in the voice. In front of them was a huge rock, the water boiling over it. Beyond it, another. The strong current was sucking them towards the rocks. The raft was no longer simply swept along by the current, it had become like a living thing, plunging and bounding, flung into a cavernous upsurge of water. Everyone held on for dear life – and prayed. Suddenly the bow of the raft was lifted on a swell of rushing water and swept into the icy water. There was a crack like a pistol shot as one of the logs was smashed and snapped some of the binding cord. Flying wooden chips and shards struck them in the face. On the shore lay the smashed wooden logs of a previous wreck. They steered ashore to inspect their raft closely, and dragged it up onto the bank. After some repairs, patching the raft with birch bark peeled from a nearby tree and rebinding the loose logs with raw thongs, the fortunate mariners continued down river. Silent, subdued, they descended the Ohio to Shawneetown, Illinois. At Louisville was another set of rapids. Their voices were drowned out by the ominous roar of a cascading waterfall, like the rumbling of distant thunder, threatening catastrophe. A tower of spume hung above the falls. They decided not to take any more chances with their lives. They would portage, that is carry the raft overland to avoid the falls. Knee-deep in water they dragged the raft over the slippery rocks. Then they had to carry it on their shoulders, through knee-high grass. From a distance they watched the waters of the cataract descend from cascade to cascade, through whirling eddies and whirlpools.

Beyond the falls they continued by their flatboat raft down the Ohio. On reaching the Mississippi their river travel came to an end. The raft was not able to go up the great river. They continued the rest of their journey to St Louis, 150 miles to the north-west, on foot. It was still early in the spring, and the ground was soaked with rain, and in many places covered deep with water. The mosquitoes persecuted them all the way.

Finally, on 31 May, they reached the east shore of the Mississippi, opposite the city of St Louis, exhausted, having travelled nearly the whole length of the Ohio River, as well as more than 400 miles on foot, since leaving Whitemarsh six weeks earlier. They rested for several days at the house of the Bishop. They then moved on to St Ferdinand, fifteen miles from St Louis, which they reached after three days. Here, at a farm at Florissant, which was to serve as the Novitiate of St Stanislaus, they were to spend two years completing their probation, and their studies in philosophy and theology.

Florissant was near the confluence of the Mississippi and Missouri rivers. The farm was tumbledown. Their accommodation was a rude, log structure, in the low loft of which seven of them crowded together on pallets of straw in a single room. The walls of the building were of logs, plastered with mud; the roof was of oak shingles. And 250 acres of arable land needed ploughing and cultivating. The first spadeful of earth was dug on 31 July 1823, the feast of St Ignatius. By combining hard physical labour with their studies, serviceable buildings soon took shape. De Smet's Herculean strength enabled him to do the work of three men. 'Samson', as he came to be known, became both architect and builder. De Smet later recalled cutting down and moving thousands of logs for building purposes.

De Smet made good progress in his studies. In due course he completed his novitiate and was ordained priest in 1827. A great day, but saddened because his parents and family could not be there to share in his happiness.

By 1828 St Louis College had been established with 'Professor' De Smet as Director. This was the founding institution of what was to become the great University of St Louis.

In 1833 Father De Smet's health was in a bad state. He was sent to Europe for treatment. He travelled by way of Washington to New York, where he embarked for his second crossing of the Atlantic. He landed at Le Havre in France later in the year and proceeded from there via Paris and Rouen to Belgium.

He visited his home in Termonde, where he had been born on 30 January 1801, together with his twin sister Colette, the twelfth of a family of sixteen (his father had seven children from his first wife, and nine from his second). He had kept in close contact with his family through letters. He met a friend who pulled a half-broken coin from his pocket. De Smet pulled the other half from his own pocket. They laughed. Before his departure for the New World his friend had asked for a souvenir. In those days parting from family and friends was usually final. There was little hope of meeting them again face to face in this life. Reunion had to wait for the life to come. The burly De Smet had pulled a coin from his pocket, put it between his teeth, bent it and broken it in two.

'You keep one half, I'll keep the other,' he had said.

During his stay in Belgium in 1834 Father De Smet persuaded three brave young souls to return with him as missionaries. They had succumbed to his infectious enthusiasm. He also managed to collect an important set of scientific instruments for the new University of St Louis.

They set sail from Antwerp for America, but, during the turbulent passage of the North Sea, Father De Smet became dangerously ill with seasickness. The doctor advised he should not continue his journey. He landed at Deal in Kent and returned to his native Termonde. Father De Smet spent the years 1835–1836 traversing the principal cities of Belgium, Holland and France. He devoted his time to recruiting selfless young people like himself for the missions and obtaining further equipment for the University of St Louis. He sent several thousand books and a large number of fine church pictures.

In 1837, however, Father De Smet set out for America once again, along with three candidates for the priesthood, and some Poor Clares and Carmelite nuns. They crossed the Atlantic on an American packet in thirty days. Landing at New York, De Smet went by rail and canal to Pittsburg and from there by steamboat to St Louis. On 27 November 1837 he was back in Florissant, with the three candidates for the novitiate. He had been away from America for four years.

Chapter 2

A First Mission – The Potawatomies

In the spring of 1838 Father De Smet was sent, along with Father Verreydt and two lay brothers, to found a mission among the Potawatomies, near today's Council Bluffs in Iowa. On 10 May 1838, he left St Louis by the steamboat *Howard* in the company of the Father Superior (Verhaegen), who wanted to visit the Kickapoo Indians near Fort Leavenworth, and Father Helias who was going to found a new mission around Jefferson City. The rest of the party was to follow a few days later by another boat, the *Wilmington*.

He was enraptured with the size and magnificence of the Missouri River with its many islands, formed by sediments, which from a distance resembled a flotilla of boats, their sails entwined with garlands of green and festoons of flowers. The Missouri (or Muddy) River is 3,000 miles long from the clear waters of its sources in the Rocky Mountains to the muddy waters of its mouth, the junction with the Mississippi at St Louis. The Missouri, as Father De Smet was later to show, merited the title of the largest river in North America, by virtue of the abundance of its waters and the length of its course. This title is usually given to the Mississippi but only because the Missouri was not explored until after the Mississippi and hence came to be considered its tributary.

The flat country or valley of the Lower Missouri was covered with dense forests extending from the bank of the river to the high hills that skirt it on either side some four to six miles away. The prodigious length of its course, its wildness and the force of its current induced the Sioux to call it the 'Furious'. Its width varies from one to three miles and its length up to the Three Forks is 2,546 miles.

In a letter dated 20 July 1838 to the Father General, De Smet said he wouldn't bore him with descriptions of the towns on the

11

Missouri, the vertical cliffs, several hundred feet high, the caverns, the forests and the immense prairies, with their thousands of buffalo, or of the river's numberless islands, up to twelve miles in length and filled with every kind of game. But he did describe the dangers of steam navigation on the Missouri, 'one of the most dangerous things a man can undertake', on his journey of 800 miles up the 'muddy water'.

> In my opinion, the sea despite its storms and the tribute which one is compelled to pay [seasickness], is much to be preferred. The current of this river is of the swiftest; high pressure is therefore required to overcome it, and hence the continual danger to which the traveller is exposed of finding himself overturned, and even, as happens only too often, of having his limbs shattered and hurled here and there to a terrible elevation. Add the sandbars with which the river is filled, and upon which one is always being cast, and the innumerable snags and sawyers upon which boats are often wrecked; all these things brought us several times within a finger's breadth of our destruction. Snags are trees whose roots are imbedded in the mud at the bottom of the river, with their branches spreading on all sides below, above and at the water level.
>
> With the exception of the snags ... and the sandbars ... our journey was pleasant enough. The boat has to be lifted over these bars, which is not any too easy. Two heavy timbers (spars) are set in the water in front of the boat and made fast to them. Then the engine is started full speed, and by means of posts it lifts the stern and shoves the boat forward a yard or two or three. Then the same thing is done over again, and so on until the bar is crossed. This often takes a whole day.
>
> *Chittenden and Richardson (C and R), pp. 161, 153.*

Often the entire crew of the boat was put on the towrope to overcome the current.

During the delays Father De Smet took the opportunity to leave the boat and make excursions into the woods and prairies to collect minerals, fossils and rare and new plants.

> While the boat was stranded on a big sandbar ten miles below the mouth of the Platte, I had a chance to explore the rocks, and found a great number of petrifactions [fossils] scattered along the

bank, among them fine specimens of the pretended vegetable-animal, the polyp, tubipores, encrini, trachitae, columnar asteria, etc. I filled my handkerchief to send to you. I unluckily forgot on board the *Howard* the stones and minerals I had picked up below the fort.

... The Devil's Rake, which has to be passed through, is a place much dreaded by the river-men. It has the appearance of a whole forest, swallowed up by the immense river. Gigantic trees stretch their naked and menacing limbs on all sides; you see them thrashing in the water, throwing up foam with a furious hissing sound as they struggle against the rapid torrent. Add to these inconveniences the fear of the boiler exploding, which often causes loss of life among the unhappy travellers. At the same time the weather was excessively hot: the warm, muddy water of the Missouri was our only drink, and myriads of mosquitoes, fleas, and other insects were our travelling companions. I fear the seas, I will admit, but all the storms and other unpleasant things I have experienced in four different voyages did not inspire so much terror in me as the navigation of the sombre, treacherous and muddy Missouri.

C and R, p. 154.

Whenever the steamboat stopped to cut or load a supply of wood, Father De Smet would take the opportunity to minister to the inhabitants of the region who came down to the woodyard or wharf. He married couples; he baptised a great number of children and several adults. The Indian life was a hard one; the climate very severe. A great number of children died very young, unable to resist the fatigues, privations and maladies and diseases, such as malnutrition, cholera, smallpox, whooping cough and measles, for which they had no remedies.

Father De Smet stayed at the village of the Kickapoos for three days. On 25 May he left for Fort Leavenworth to await the *Wilmington* which would take him to the new mission station among the Potawatomies, and which was carrying Father Verreydt and Brother Mazelli. But when he reached Leavenworth he found the *Wilmington* had left the place two hours before. He describes what he did.

Arming myself with a good switch, I applied it to the sides of my poor Rozinante, and galloping, galloping, we made together

seven miles in half an hour. I reached the path where the boat
was taking on wood in time.

C and R, p. 150.

He describes the rest of the journey up the Missouri.

The first night we stopped two miles from the village of
Pashishi. Here the captain bought some twenty cords* of wood,
cut by the Indian women. The passengers amused themselves
with putting up small coins on sticks to test the skill of the little
Indians in shooting with the bow: one especially, only seven or
eight years old, handled his bow and arrows with admirable
dexterity, for though the distance was considerable he never
missed, and he always went promptly to put the little piece of
money into his poor mother's hands. I rejoiced in his good
success: he was the only one who had a chaplet and medal about
his neck, and I learned that he had earlier been baptised by the
Rev F Van Quickenborne.

Father Quickenborne had died the previous year. The first Jesuit to
enter the Mississippi valley after the re-establishment of the
Society in 1814, he had been one of De Smet's teachers at
Whitemarsh and had brought him to Missouri.

One day when the boat had stopped and the crew landed to cut
wood, which generally took one hour, I walked back from the
river quite a distance alone in search of rare plants. I had seated
myself on a rock when a Negro of about eighty years came up to
me. He seemed to stare at me attentively and with astonishment
because of my black coat, and asked me if I was not a Catholic
priest? Having replied that I was, he said to me with tears in his
eyes 'I too have the happiness of seeing a priest of my religion.
Often have I said my prayers that I might have the consolation of
confessing once more before I die. Sir, would you not have the
kindness to hear and help me?' I made him sit down beside me,
and I had hardly uttered the words of absolution when the steamboat bell gave the signal for starting. The poor man wept with
joy and pressed my hand, unable to speak a word. I cannot
express to you the consolation that this little meeting yielded me.

* A cord of wood was eighteen feet in length, four feet in depth and four feet in height

Two days' journey further north lived the Sauk Indians. They lined the riverbank, chiefs, warriors, women, children, and dogs, to see us pass. The chief, who knew Father Verreydt and Brother Mazelli, saluted us very cordially with shouts of joy and wished us a pleasant voyage.

We stopped several hours at the village of the Iowas. There I talked with our former disciple Francis, called White Cloud, who since his father was killed has become chief of the nation. I made him a little present of tobacco, which he accepted with much pleasure. It seems that these Indians are very much dissatisfied with their present minister and they expressed to me their wish to have us among them. They seem poor and very drunken, sell everything they have to obtain the unlucky stuff, the great scourge of the Indians. Some days before we were there an Indian had been killed in a drunken row and several mortally wounded. I noticed among them certain young men well dressed, with silk ribbons of all colours entwined in their hair, a profusion of porcelain beads hung about their necks, and wolf-tails and little bells attached to their heels, knees and arms. Their faces too were painted with great care, in red, black, green, grey, yellow and brown according to the taste of each. In Belgium they would have been taken for fine Harlequins from the fairs. All these young men were playing on a sort of flageolet or flute. I addressed a young Indian who spoke English well to learn the reason of this distinction. He laughed and told me: 'those gentlemen are in love. When any one among us desires to wed, he makes his inclination known by playing the flute, and passes whole days, and often nights too, in serenading around the girl's cabin. When the parents have arranged the affair, he passes his flute on to another comrade who has been taken with the notion.' This custom seems quite general among all the tribes.

Another of the customs of courtship among the Indians was to send a gift of horses to the girl's brother and to bestow much buffalo meat on the mother.

Father De Smet's description of his journey continues.

I visited the village of the Otoes who dwelt near the mouth of the Platte; they seem poor and miserable; steal when they can and get drunk when they have a chance. A visit to an Indian village is worth a few words of description. Some of the interesting peculiarities that I observed among the Otoes were as follows. Groups of naked children were amusing themselves on all sides at various games, and painfully lean dogs without end were frolicking with these young *sans culottes* [without breeches]. The village consisted of a number of large earthen huts, containing some ten families each, and a few tents of tanned buffalo hides sewed together. The women whom I met presented an appearance of the utmost misery. Some were blind, others one-eyed, and all extremely filthy and disgusting to look at. They were clothed in petticoats of deerskin, reaching to the knees, jackets, leggings and shoes of the same material, all as dirty and black as if they had been their towels for the last century. Bracelets of polished metal were worn at the wrists by both sexes, and around their necks they had five or six yards of porcelain or glass beads.

I was introduced into the largest cabin, that of the first chief, his queen put a cushion, shining with grease, upon a still more greasy mat, and made me the sign to be seated. She then presented me a rudely made wooden dish (for everything here is done with the hatchet and knife) and a pot-spoon of the same material, which seemed not to have been washed since the day of their manufacture. Then she served me with a stew of her own compounding and a pie of a grey colour and sufficiently disgusting in appearance. To refuse an Indian who offers you food in his own cabin would be considered a grave affront. 'Well, well,' I said to myself, 'you are not in Belgium; let us begin our apprenticeship in earnest, and so long as we are in the woods, howl heartily with the wolves.' A dozen or more dogs, sitting on their hams in front of me, with their eyes fastened on my dish, seemed really to envy me my happiness as I approached my spoon to it, and to be offering their aid and assistance in case of need. But it was not necessary to have recourse to my canine company; I had a good appetite and the stew was excellent, a buffalo tongue with a good gravy of bear fat, mixed with flour from the wild sweet potato. I thanked my hostess, and handed her dish back much cleaner than I had received it.

It is sorrowful to see the neglected condition of the little children in all the Indian villages. Their hair seems never to have undergone the operation of the brush, so that their heads look like masses of cobwebs. Many have eye trouble, and their faces and all their limbs look as if water had never touched them. The younger ones are generally naked, and great was the alarm that my presence occasioned among this juvenile portion of the community, wherever I presented myself without warning. The dogs in these villages (all belonging to the wolf family) are the greatest torments to a stranger, the barking of one brings all the others together, of all sizes; they form a chorus, utter piercing yelps and roars and follow you in all directions.

The men seem to pass their time in complete idleness: playing cards and smoking are their only amusements. They subsist the greater part of the time on a small quantity of dried meat and a mush of roasted and pounded corn. But this temperance and frugality are the result of necessity, not of choice, for when they have abundance you will see them thrust their whole hands into the pot and eat incessantly like starving wolves until they are ready to split; then they lie down and go to sleep. All their wealth consists of a few horses, which graze at large in the uncultivated prairie. It is truly a melancholy sight to see these desolate villages surrounded by such fine country and such fertile virgin soil. The Indian at his birth is wrapped in rags; he grows up in buffalo-skins; he is raised in idleness, and industry has no attractions for him; he never tries to improve his condition, and in fact were one of them to aspire to higher enjoyments and to raise his fortune by his efforts and activity, he would soon find himself the object of universal hatred and envy, and whatever he had gathered together would speedily be pillaged or sacked.

C and R, pp. 150–7.

The journey continued through plains and prairies, often filled with flowers. These were interspersed with volcanic areas, where nothing but cactus, Adam's needle (*yucca*) with their pretty flowers, and sagebrush grew. On the open prairies the long winds blew the rolling waves of grass from horizon to horizon.

On the last day of May the party arrived at the site of the proposed mission of St Joseph, near the site of the modern city of Council Bluffs. However none of the 2,000 painted Potawatomies who had come to meet the boat showed the slightest interest in them. Out of a family of some thirty French half-breeds only two came to shake hands with them. De Smet and his companions repaired to the tent of the great chief, a half-breed, called William Caldwell. He offered them three tents.

It was for the priests to make themselves 'all things to all men', to win them over to Jesus Christ, according to the beautiful maxim of the apostle. Slowly they began to break down the barriers of indifference, to get to know the Indians better. Father De Smet began catechising and teaching in a school that they had built. He learned to adapt himself to the habits and customs of the people, to close his eyes to the filth of their lodges, to relish their food. It was often impossible to discover what went into the cooking. The ingredients would be placed in something like a fish-kettle, made of osier, and smeared with gum. To boil this kettle stones were heated red hot and then thrown into it.

In a letter to his Superior Father De Smet described his day-to-day work:

I spend the greater part of my time in a tent, eating whatever comes, sometimes in abundance, sometimes in penury, performing my spiritual exercises as best I can, regulating my time by the sun and the stars when the weather is clear, otherwise by the occupations that offer.

C and R, p. 802.

The bison, or buffalo, was the mainstay of Indian life. It supplied almost all the necessities of life. Its skin was used for lodges, as well as for clothing, litters, bridles, saddle coverings, vessels to hold water, and boats to cross lakes and rivers. With its hair the Indians made rope; with its sinews, bowstrings and thread for clothes. Its shoulder blade was used as a spade and pickaxe. The bison provided the Indians' chief food, and its dung abundant fuel.

In course of time Father De Smet carried out a few baptisms. Success was modest. There were great obstacles to overcome in converting a pagan nation. One was language, very difficult to acquire. Another was the practice of polygamy: 'They change wives as often as the gentlemen of St Louis change their coats.' Yet another was the superstitious beliefs.

There is a tradition among the Potawatomies that there is in the moon an old woman, always busy at the making of a big basket. If she succeeds in finishing her task the world must perish, but a great dog is watching her continually, and destroys her work as often as she has it nearly done. The fight between the dog and the woman takes place at every eclipse of the moon.

18

The big dog is the black spot that appears on the south of that luminary.

C and R, p. 1094.

The Indians believed in a Great Spirit, and lived in dread of the unknown befalling them. It was in their power to avoid this evil by sacrifice and penance, to an unknown, incomprehensible power, which they knew from actual phenomena had an existence.

They believed that when they died their spirits went to the setting sun, across the great waters, to the happy-hunting grounds. In speaking of the departed a Blackfoot never said such a one is dead, but was gone 'to the Sand Hills'. The voices in the wind were the spirits of his ancestors.

Each Indian had his *manitou* (tutelary, guardian, spirit or divinity). To his *manitou* he addressed his prayers or supplication and offered his sacrifices. When he was in danger, when he set out for war or went fishing or hunting as well as in every other enterprise he was about to engage in, he invoked his *manitou* for success or some extraordinary favour.

The young man, after making deep incisions in the fleshy parts of his body, or after a vigorous fast, was believed to see in his dreams, the form or resemblance under which the *manitou* manifested itself. During his whole life he was bound to wear the image or mark of it, for example if he selected a bird as his *manitou* he would wear a talon suspended round his neck. The object, whatever it was, was enveloped in several folds of skin, with a lock of some deceased relative's hair and a small piece of tobacco and the whole placed in a *parfleche* sack ornamented and fringed, and this comprised the arcanum of his medicine sack.

And there were the medicine men, or jugglers, who held the people in their hand. These *wah-kons*, as they were called, naturally resented the pale-face Black Robes moving into their monopoly with their new notions of God and redemption. The word 'medicine' in their case had nothing to do with the use of drugs for treatment; it meant all that was incomprehensible, supernatural, all-powerful, everything that could not be explained by ordinary means. The medicine men were adept conjurers or jugglers. They needed to be to retain the belief of the people in their supernatural powers. They professed to heal diseases by witchcraft; they predicted the outcome of wars and hunts; they boasted of knowledge of the future. They began their ceremonies by beating a drum, shaking a gourd rattle, or blowing a flute. Sometimes, they operated in collusion with deceitful accomplices. The medicine men were visited secretly by night by these accomplices, who carried all the news of the village and its neighbourhood. By these means the jugglers, on leaving the forest and returning to the village, easily imposed on the credulous. The first part of their predictions consisted of giving an exact account of all the events of the village since their departure – marriages, deaths, returns from the war or the hunt, and all other remarkable items.

Rufus B Sage, in his *Life in the Rocky Mountains 1820–1875*, mentions some remarkable examples of the craft of the medicine man. One claimed he could cure illnesses by imbibing them and discharging them through his eyes and nose in the form of live snakes. He would dress up in a bear skin and then after the usual fasting and praying, he would produce live snakes hidden about his body.

Another difficulty posed to the evangelisation of the Indians was their inclination to a nomadic, wandering life. 'This inclination is so strong,' wrote Father De Smet, 'that they became melancholy and morose if they stay three months in the same place.' At each campsite the village remained till the grass and firewood was consumed. The chiefs then met in council and on the basis of reports of bison brought back by scouts, they moved to another location. They found 'meat that turned the hunger of the winter into the feast of the summer. But generally deprived of agricultural instruments and firearms the Indians were always in want, and kept a perpetual Lent'.

The principal obstacle to conversion was, perhaps, liquor. Father De Smet was scathing about the whisky traffickers.

Whisky traffickers, who seem void of all conscience, rob and murder many of these Indians; I say rob – they will get them drunk, and then take their horses, guns, or blankets off their backs, regardless of how quick they may freeze to death; I say they murder – if not directly, then indirectly, they furnish the weapon – they make them drunk, and, when drunk, they kill their fellow-beings. Some freeze to death when drunk; several drunken Indians have been drowned in the Missouri River this season, aiming to cross when drunk.

When drunk – and now they get drink in large quantities – all the good qualities of the Indian disappear, and he no longer resembles man; one must flee from him. Their cries and howls are terrible; they fall upon each other, biting noses and ears, mutilating each other in a horrible manner. Since our arrival, four Otoes and three Potawatomies have been killed in these drunken orgies.

A few extracts from the Mission Diary illustrate the problem.

May 30th. Arrival of the steamer *Wilmington*. Quarrel succeeded quarrel. Blows followed blows. The club, the tomahawk, spears, butcher knives, brandished together in the air. I shuddered at the deeds. A squaw offered her little boy four years old, to the crew of the boat for a few bottles of whisky. No agent here seems to have the power to put the laws against alcohol in execution.

May 31st. Drinking all day. Drunkards by the dozen. Indians are selling horses, blankets, guns, their all, to have a lick at the cannon.

June 5th. A drunken Potawatomi killed a Sauk. The murderer, after the perpetration of the deed, was mortally stabbed by his own father-in-law. The Indian way of redressing wrongs.

June 19th. A monster in human shape. On the Mosquito (Creek), a savage returning home from a night's debauch wrested his infant son from the breast of his mother and crushed him against a post of his lodge.

August 20th. Since the day of payment, drunkards are seen and heard in all places. Liquor is rolled out to the Indians by whole barrels; sold even by white men even in the presence of the agent. Wagonloads of the abominable stuff arrive daily from the settlements and along with it the very dregs of our white neighbours and *voyageurs* of the mountains, drunkards, gamblers, etc., etc.

C and R, pp. 173–5.

Father De Smet continued:

Whisky traders flocked faster and faster into the neighbourhood; fur traders, also, found it much more in their interest to trade with drunken Indians than sober ones, and the Indians grew rapidly demoralised – money, goods and provisions soon squandered for whisky.

C and R, p. 146.

The Government prohibited the introduction of whisky into the Indian Territory under penalty of the law, but no agent respected the law, and brandy, too, arrived in shiploads. De Smet wrote a strong letter to the Government in Washington denouncing this abuse as being both criminal and illegal. But little heed was given in high places to these complaints; and some Americans looked on with satisfaction at the self-destruction of a race they detested.

One day Father De Smet saw a barrel of whisky being rolled along the ground. He went up to investigate.

'Paul, what are you doing? Don't you know that's whisky, gut-rot poison?'

The tall Indian uncurled from his stoop and stood erect. Paul was a lean, wiry Indian, about fifty, his black hair streaked with grey.

'Yes, Father, I know it's the fire-water,' he answered somewhat sheepishly.

'That poison is forbidden here. You know that.'

'The white man asked me to take it to the chief's *tipi*,' he answered as if in mitigation.

The blood boiled in the Fleming's veins. He leaned forward toward his neophyte, took the war-hatchet from Paul's belt and stepped back. He whirled it as far above his head as it would go and then brought it down on the wooden cask with all his strength. The oak splintered; the amber liquid gushed out, flowing over the green grass. He handed back the hatchet. Paul watched the liquid gurgle out with unbelieving eyes. After a long pause, his hatchet in the palm of his hand, he said.

'The chief will kill me for this. So will the white man.'

'No, they won't,' Father De Smet reassured him.

A crowd soon gathered around the rapidly emptying barrel of liquor.

Father De Smet returned to his lodge. Some hours later he looked up from reading his Breviary. A heavy, powerfully built man, with a steady intensity of purpose, was swaggering up the hard-packed earth path, swept clean of dust, which led to the lodge. His arms hung on either side of him, like a gunman waiting to draw. It was a man named Duke. He had a reputation as a skilled duellist and noted pistol shot. He was a drifter who lived footloose and would go on so living until a rope or a lead bullet put him under the sod. His buckskin jacket was open. Tied loosely round his neck was a tattered old bandanna. His leather hat was tilted at a cavalier, daredevil angle. Revenge was not a perquisite only of the Indian. Duke was coming to get his.

He stopped at the entrance to the lodge. He rolled up the hide awning from its pegs. He lowered his head and entered.

'You done a bad thing, today,' the ruffian began. 'You broke a cask of my whisky. That be a lot of money to me.' He paused, menacingly.

'You know it is illegal to bring whisky into the camp,' the priest stated.

'Illegal?' The big man gave a quiet smile that is the universal emblem of scorn, in between chewing his tobacco. 'You know there is no law west of Pecos. Even the lawman, the Agent, sells the stuff.' He paused again. 'How else we gonna live? Eh?'

'I will see that the law is not broken,' Father De Smet replied, as he pulled himself up. He stood opposite the gunman, the whisky contraband dealer.

They stood like two duellists, facing each other, each with their arms by their sides. Except that one had Colt revolvers in his belt, the other had no weapon.

'So you're gonna keep the law?' He laughed derisively. 'You ain't gonna live long enough for that.' He paused.

Here was a crisis. Action was required more than words. But what action? De Smet wondered to himself.

'But first,' the outlaw said, spitting out a trajectory of tobacco juice, which Father De Smet side-stepped. 'First,' he continued, 'you gonna pay me a lot of money for my whisky.' He smirked again.

'I have no money. You know that,' Father De Smet replied.

'Oh, no? No money to pay with!' He paused. 'Then you gonna pay with your life,' he smiled.

There followed a profane and ominous silence.

Duke pulled aside the skirt of his coat so as to clear the holster of his gun, placed with the butt forward. He coolly fastened the flap of his belt holster. His right hand then moved to the butt of his Colt, dangling in its holster below the shell belt. His fingers clasped the walnut hog-leg of the revolver. There was a squeak from the gun scabbard as he grasped the handle of the six-shooter. At the same time there was a twang from a cord and a hiss – like a rattler skimming through the grass. Suddenly the big man lowered his tall form into a crouching position. His left arm moved to his right that hung limp, a vibrating arrow in the flesh. The right arm suddenly blossomed bright crimson as blood spurted out.

23

Father De Smet moved forward and picked up the loaded Colt, which had fallen to the floor. He removed the second Colt from the waist of Duke who tried to kick him away; he removed, too, a Bowie knife that was tucked into the top of his trousers.

Paul appeared at the lodge entrance. In his hand he held a man-size bow of horn. He was smiling, his bosom swelling with pride. He had seen the white man moving to Black Robe's lodge. He suspected trouble. He had observed events through a chink in the wall of the lodge. He plucked an arrow from the quiver on his hip, fitted it to the string, and then pointed the flint head at his target. At the critical moment, he twanged the bowstring and shot the arrow.

'That was a good shot, Paul,' Father De Smet said, thankful his life had been spared.

It was a good shot, indeed, especially as Paul had the first joints of the fingers of his right hand cut off. As a sign of mourning Indians would cut off the first joints of their fingers. But never of the first two fingers, since these were critical to shooting an arrow or a bullet.

Arrow wounds often go septic, causing blood poisoning. Father De Smet tied a ligature of bark as a tourniquet round the bleeding arm. He wrapped the wound in a bandage.

'Now, you go back to your friends and tell them there will be some law here. Especially as I am keeping your guns – loaded. Paul, help him back to the trading post. The doctor there will deal with the arrow.'

The gunman, still bent, slouched out of the lodge, and holding on to the Indian's arm, slowly made his way down the path, like a wounded animal returning to its lair.

The weeks and months passed by. Father De Smet was in no doubt about the problems that lay ahead.

The conversion of the Indians is altogether a work of God. This portion of the divine Master's vineyard requires from those who tend it, a life of crosses, privations and patience. Still, we hope that aided as we are by grace, and assisted by your prayers and those of all our brothers, the Lord will grant some measure of success to our feeble labours.

Letter to Father General, 20 July 1838.
C and R, p. 163.

They struggled on. Spring went by, summer blossomed into blazing autumn, winter melted into spring, spring followed into summer, summer withered into autumn. In course of time they had constructed a chapel, the Lodge of the Lord as they called it, twenty-four feet square, surmounted with a little belfry. The massive timbers supporting the altar were from larch trees five feet in diameter and were raised to their positions by the Indians, with the aid simply of a pulley and a rope. Some years later Bishop Miège lived among the Potawatomies for four years. So this humble temple, constructed of logs, became a cathedral. They trained an orchestra of flutes, horns and tambourines. What Father De Smet does not mention in his accounts of his travels, is that he was an accomplished clarinet player. The instrument is still preserved in the Jesuit Archives in the Foley Centre at Gonzaga University in Spokane, Washington, together with the remnant of his buffalo robe on which he slept during his endless journeys through the prairies and mountains. The missionaries also had four poor little cabins, made of rough logs, fourteen feet each way, with roofs of rude rafters, which, unfortunately, protected them neither from rain nor hail nor later, snow in winter.

The missionaries never went out without a good knife, a tomahawk or a sword cane. In a letter to his Superior, dated 28 July 1838, Father De Smet explained why.

> It is not uncommon to meet bears in our neighbourhood, but this animal will seldom attack a man first, though he will defend himself when wounded. Wolves come very often to our very doors; quite lately they have carried off all our chickens. They are of all kinds; prairie wolves, small and timid; black mountain wolves, large and dangerous. There are snakes too, among which I might name the copperhead, the garter snake, blacksnake and rattlesnake. Field, forest and cabin swarm with mice, which gnaw and devour the few fruits that we possess. Insects, butterflies especially, are very numerous here, and very variegated and very large. Night-moths are of all colours and of a prodigious size; they are no less than eight inches in length. We also live in the midst of horseflies and mosquitoes; they come upon us by thousands and give us no rest day or night.
>
> *C and R, p. 167.*

The Mission was very poor. The brothers and fathers were often without even the bare necessities of life. By spring of 1839 the distress of the missionaries was extreme. Their entire nourishment for weeks had been acorns and wild roots. For weeks De Smet had been without shoes. He improvised with boots made from hessian. At last, on 20 April 1839, the provision boat from St Louis arrived. There was great rejoicing. But not for long. At the very moment of mooring the boat struck an obstruction and was wrecked. De Smet watched it sink before his eyes. Only a saw, a plough, a pair of boots and some wine were saved.

'At least,' said De Smet, 'with the boots I can tramp the prairies and woods without being bitten by snakes, which throng there; and the wine will be offered in the sacrifice at the Mass.'

But an even greater suffering than poverty was loneliness. News from St Louis arrived only two or three times a year. On 18 December 1839, De Smet wrote to a colleague:

Reverend Father,

Since the month of June, I have filled up a score of sheets; I have written to fathers and brothers whom I cherish most in the world, at St Louis and round about. Well, I have received, in return, aside from your letter, *five lines*.

I will tell you plainly, every letter that we receive makes a great feast-day for us. Ah! If they knew the joy and consolation, which news from them brings us, and how, after we have received them, our ardour and zeal revive, in the most arduous functions of the ministry.

He kept in touch with his family. In the summer of 1839 he wrote to his brother Francis:

When I think of what my life was with you during four years, I often smile at my present condition. My only shelter is a little hut fourteen feet square, constructed of trunks of fallen trees covered with a rough shingle roof that protects me from neither snow nor rain. The other night, during a downpour, I was obliged to open my umbrella to protect my face from the rain that fell on it and awakened me. My furniture consists of a cross, a small table, a bench, and a pile of books. A piece of meat, or some herbs and wild roots, washed down by a glass of fresh spring water, is about my only food. My garden is an immense forest bordering on the largest river in the world; the huge prairie resembles a vast sea, where gazelle, deer, roebuck, buffalo, and the bison graze at large.

My gun is my constant companion. One must go about armed to defend one's life from the red bear and the starved wolves that prowl about here. Our situation is rendered even more precarious by the war that is going on between the Indians. Bands of Otoes, Pawnees, and Sioux roam in every direction seeking scalps, and every day we get fresh news of their atrocities.

The Potawatomi and Sioux tribes were always at war with each other. In 1839 Father De Smet made a trip up the Missouri, alone and unprotected among the Indians whose friendship was doubtful, on a mission of peace from the Potawatomies to the Sioux. On 29 April, he set off by the American Fur Company's steamboat, *St Peter*, that was going up the Missouri. He travelled up to the Sioux post at the mouth of the Vermillion River, a short distance above where Sioux City stands today. Progress was slow because of low water, contrary winds, sandbars and underwater obstructions. On board he met a gentleman from St Louis who, when he heard the missionary was working on a map of the Missouri, gave him his instruments for measuring heights and making observations. On the way the boat passed near a village of the Omahas, composed of about 1,400 souls. The huts of the Omahas were built of poles, covered with bark over which they plastered earth, with turf over the whole. They looked like small conical mounds. A large hole in the top allowed light to enter and smoke to escape. But no one came to the shore. Two years previously the Omahas had been ravaged by smallpox, introduced by the steamboat, the *St Peter*. Thirty thousand or so Indians in the country had perished in a few weeks. A great many committed suicide in despair, some with their lances or other warlike weapons; many flung themselves off a high rock which overlooks the Missouri. They did not want another infection.

On 11 May, Father De Smet reached his destination. In a letter to the Mother Superior of the Orphanage of Termonde, dated 28 July 1839, he wrote:

On my arrival among the Sioux, the chiefs and warriors of the tribe of Yanktons invited me to feast. All were seated in a circle in a grand lodge or tent of buffalo hides. Each one rested his

27

chin on his knees; the legs drawn close up to the body, a position that my corpulency would not allow me to assume. I therefore seated myself like a tailor on his table, with my legs crossed. Every one received a big piece of venison in a wooden trencher; those who cannot finish their portion are permitted to take away – it is their custom – the remains of the dish – I was among this number, and I had enough left for two days. I observed at this feast that when a savage had finished his dish, he rubbed his belly and breast with his two hands in sign of satisfaction, and thanked his host for having so well regaled him.

The repast concluded, I disclosed to them the principal object of my visit among them, viz: a durable peace between the Sioux and the Potawatomies, their neighbours.

C and R, pp. 182–9.

De Smet's engaging personality and persuasive arguments convinced the Sioux to make peace with their sworn enemies. The Sioux agreed to bury the hatchet and to make presents to the children of such Potawatomies they had killed, which was called 'covering the dead', and to smoke the calumet (pipe of peace), the emblem of brotherhood and union, with them. Smoking the calumet together is equivalent to a treaty confirmed by oath, which no one can contravene without dishonouring themselves in the eyes of all the tribe. Father De Smet presented the Sioux with a wampum (shell) sash and a tomahawk dipped in blood sent by the Potawatomies as a seal of their friendship.

After sowing the first seeds of faith in this tribe, he began his return to the Potawatomies on 15 May, to tell them of his peace negotiations.

This time my only means of transportation was a primitive canoe, a tree hollowed out, ten feet in length by one and a half in width. I could just seat myself in it. Before this, I had crossed the river in this sort of craft, but never without fear, it being evidently very dangerous: now I had 360 miles to descend on the most perilous and most impetuous of rivers, and it was necessary, for I had no other way. Happily I was accompanied by two very skilful pilots, who, paddling on the right and left, darted with the fleetness of an arrow through the numerous sawyers with which the river was filled, the frail bark which the slightest shock could overturn. Judge how swift its course is: in three days, sailing from four o'clock in the morning until sunset, we passed over 120 leagues. Two nights only I slept in the open air, having no bed but my buffalo robe, and no pillow but my travelling-bag. Yet I can assure you that my slumbers were as peaceable and profound as I ever enjoyed in my life.

Lavaille, p. 91.

On his return the Potawatomies greeted Father De Smet as the father and saviour of the nation.

Liquor, however, still threatened the very existence of the Mission. What could one do with 2,000 drunken Indians? Where would it end? But however dark the future appeared, the missionaries determined not to desert their post.

In a letter to a friend dated December 1839, Father De Smet wrote:

Dear Friend

You will gather that our prospects are not so very bright and flattering, surrounded as we are by so many evils and obstacles, which all our efforts to the contrary are not able to stem. Indians are weak, laws disregarded, money a powerful temptation for the wicked white man and half-breed.

. . . We have not lost courage, however.

In 1840 another famine threatened to destroy the mission. Occasionally the winter brought some rejoicing. When a hunt had been successful, bison and elk meat dripping from the bloody hides tied to their ponies, every lodge would celebrate with feasting; the women ceased the hunger chant of the tribe. Night and day the sound of the flute and the deafening clamour of the *teweêken* or drum would accompany their songs.

Provisions were desperately low. Father De Smet offered to go to St Louis, nearly 1,000 miles away, to get supplies. An intrepid traveller, loving adventure, Father De Smet could travel months at a time, eat all kinds of food, sleep in the open and share in every way the life of the Indians. He faced all hazards – hostile Indians, outlaws, floods, illness, his horse breaking a leg or putting its hoof in a gopher hole.

On 13 February 1840 he left Council Bluffs. The winter was a severe one. The temperature was several degrees below zero. The streams were frozen; sleet and snow whitened the forests and filled the trails. As the intense cold had suspended navigation, he was obliged to travel on foot, then on horseback, and at times in a cart, a distance of 900 miles with no other companion save his guide. The snow was so bright it dazzled their eyes.

> I suffered greatly during the journey, often sleeping in the open, in deep snow, with only two blankets for covering. A bitter north wind froze my cheeks and one side of my nose. Droves of famished wolves appeared from time to time and followed us howling, but as they kept at a safe distance we were not alarmed.
>
> The intense cold affected my lungs in such a manner that I found difficulty in breathing, and feared at one time that I could not continue my journey. Upon arriving in St Louis I was put under the care of a physician – I, who fear American doctors as I do the pest. This one hastened to employ the entire resources of the apothecary: bleeding and leeches were the first prescription, then followed baths, powders, pills, plasters, and every known *tisane*, sweet, bitter, hot, cold, and tepid; added to which a strict regime was ordered. Complete rest quickly restored my health and I immediately set about getting out of the hands of the doctor, who would soon have had all the flesh off my bones.
>
> *Lavaille, p. 94.*

No sooner was Father De Smet's health restored than he began to make arrangements to rejoin his post. He collected provisions: clothing, church ornaments, vestments, and agricultural implements, and was about to start back when he heard he was to be sent to another mission.

Chapter 3

The Flatheads

On 18 September 1839, two Iroquois Indians arrived at St Joseph's Mission in Council Bluffs. They had travelled 3,000 miles, over high mountains, across broad rivers, across arid plains and desert sands, from their home in the Upper Columbia valley, on the banks of the Bitter Root, beyond the Rocky Mountains in the Far West. And this through regions infested with their implacable enemies, the Blackfeet.

Indians have the extraordinary ability to find their way anywhere. They acquire their practical knowledge by long and close attention to the growth of plants and trees, and to the sun and stars. They know that the north side of a tree is covered with a greater quantity of moss than the other, and that the boughs and foliage on the south side are more abundant and luxuriant. Thus a rapid glance at the moss on the trees, with an occasional upward gaze towards the setting sun, or a steady but passing look at the direction of the numerous water courses through which they wade, will give the Indians their bearings. They measure distances by a day's journey. When an Indian travels alone, his day's journey will be about fifty to sixty miles, but only fifteen or twenty when he moves with the camp. They divide their journey into halves and quarters, as we do into hours. When they decide on a distant excursion they lay off these journeys with astonishing accuracy on a kind of map traced on bark or skins. They have no formal knowledge of geography yet they form with great accuracy maps of territory that they know.

The Iroquois were tall men, with lean, almost haggard faces, painted with streaks of black and vermilion. Their heads were shaven, except for their crowns where a small tuft of hair was left so that, in the event of death, the enemy could wrench it off the

31

scalp. The scalp was the only admissible trophy of victory. It was more important to obtain a scalp than to kill a man. Three faded feathers from a hawk's wing nodded above their heads. They wore buckskin leggings that laced up at the sides and which were gartered above the knees with the sinews of a deer. A girdle of wampum guarded their knives. On their feet they wore ornamented moccasins. Around their shoulders hung ragged calico mantles. A pouch and a horn completed their accoutrements.

'*Robe-Noire*,' one of them began. Holding up his four fingers in front of Father De Smet's face, he continued, in broken French, 'This is the fourth attempt our people have made to contact Black Robes to ask them to come to us.'

'Fourth attempt?' queried Father De Smet, surprised.

'Yes, Black Robe, four times our men have tried.' Again he held up his four fingers to ram home the point. 'Each time we are promised a *nepapayat tok* (Black Robe), but no one ever comes.'

In October 1831 the first delegation had arrived at the Florissant Mission, near St Louis. It consisted of four Indians of the Flathead tribe. (They were so called because of the artificial deformity they exhibited as a result of their heads' normal growth being constrained by a wooden board at birth.) They had come to ask for the services of a Black Robe.

The priests at the Mission wondered how the men had even heard of the Black Robes. In the seventeenth century the Iroquois Indians of North America had laid waste to the missions of the French Black Robes. In 1646 Isaac Jogues and in 1649 Jean de Brébeuf, along with Gabriel Lalemant and some others (now all proclaimed saints) were martyred by tomahawk. Little did they dream that the faith they had preached and sealed with their blood would one day be carried beyond the Mississippi to the Rocky Mountains and as far West as the Pacific Coast by the descendants of those same fierce Indians who had treated them so barbarously.

Between 1812 and 1829 a band of Iroquois, tired of seeing their lands being appropriated by the white man, left the Caughnawaga Mission near Montreal and headed west to make a home in the Rocky Mountains far beyond the white man's encroachments. The band was led by Ignatius La Mousse (Old Ignace), who had been baptised and married by the Jesuits. He had now passed the meridian of his days, and the term *ak-kee-wai-zee* ('one who has been long above the earth') applied to him. In the west the travellers met the Flatheads, a tribe of some 2,000 souls, who received them kindly. They intermarried with their new hosts and became members of the tribe. Old Ignace often spoke to the Flatheads about the Black Robes he had known. How could they now get a Black Robe again? To reach the Montreal and Quebec missions meant a journey of over 4,000 miles, during which they would have to run the gauntlet of their mortal enemies, the Crows and the Blackfeet.

Some fur traders mentioned to them that a few Black Robes had just arrived on the Missouri. Old Ignace assembled the tribe in council and proposed sending a deputation to St Louis in search of a missionary. The proposition was eagerly received and in the spring of 1831 four travellers set out for St Louis. Within a few days of their arrival in St Louis two of their members fell ill and died, worn out by a journey that had lasted several months. No one could understand the language of the surviving two. They journeyed home but never reached their tribes. They were not heard of again.

The Flatheads, despairing of again seeing their brothers who had left the camp four years previously, decided to send a second deputation to St Louis. This time Ignace offered to go himself. Taking with him his two sons, he left the mountains in the summer of 1835. After unspeakable hardships the deputation reached St Louis at the beginning of December. Having been taught French when a child, Ignace could explain the object of his journey. The bishop promised to send some priests. Cheered with this hope Ignace returned to his tribe.

Eighteen months passed and yet no Black Robe arrived. In the summer of 1837 a third deputation started out for St Louis. It was composed of three Flatheads, one Nez Percé (Pierced Nose) and Old Ignace. In traversing the country of their enemy, the merciless Sioux, they encountered a band of 300 Sioux warriors. Outnumbered, they were defeated and unmercifully massacred, offering their lives for the salvation of their brothers. Upon learning this crushing news the Flathead Indians wondered if they would ever obtain a Black Robe. Undaunted, they decided to send a fourth deputation to St Louis. Two Iroquois who had some knowledge of French offered to go. One was the Young Ignace. They left in 1839, joining a party of trappers travelling in the same direction. In the middle of September 1839 the deputation passed the St Joseph Mission, at Council Bluffs. So here they were.

In a letter to his brother Francis dated 29 October 1839, Father De Smet wrote:

With tears in their eyes they begged me to return with them. If only my health would permit it, I might have the luck this time to get further up the Missouri. Should God deem me worthy of the honour, I would willingly give my life to help these Indians.

This time the delegation's plea was answered. The Great Black Gown (the Bishop) in St Louis promised that a Black Robe would be sent to them. Father De Smet volunteered for the assignment and was accepted.

One of the two Iroquois, Peter Left Hand, started back to his tribe on 20 October 1839, to tell them that this time a Black Robe was surely coming. He arrived back in Bitter Root Valley, the home of the Flatheads, early in spring 1840. Young Ignace stayed to act as guide to Father De Smet.

On 27 March 1840, De Smet, accompanied by Young Ignace, left St Louis by steamboat for the Flatheads in the Rockies. They travelled 500 miles up the Missouri to Westport (Kansas City) on the Indian Frontier, from where they would strike out for the mountains.

In his *Voyages aux Montagnes-Rochenses* Father De Smet gives a colourful description of his journey to the Flatheads.

> The craft on which I had embarked was (like all of them in this land, where emigration and commerce have grown to such an extent) encumbered with freight and passengers from every state of the Union; I may even say from the various nations of the earth, white, black, yellow and red, with shadings of all these colours. The boat was like a little floating Babel, on account of the different languages and jargons that were heard upon it. These passengers drop off here and there on the river, to open farms, construct mills, build factories of every kind; they increase day by day the number of the inhabitants of the little towns and villages that spring up as if by magic, on both sides of the river.
>
> *C and R, pp. 198–9.*

He relates the experience he usually encountered when he found himself among a boatload of passengers.

> When the priest appears in the midst of such a throng he is critically scrutinised. He is measured from head to foot. He is like

a curious beast in a menagerie. He is regarded with surprise and people are slow to approach him. But once the ice is broken, he is overwhelmed with questions on all points of religion. These questions are quite often sensible enough, but generally they are odd and sometimes even indelicate and gross, denoting a profound ignorance which inspires only pity and compassion.

C and R, p. 93.

Father De Smet does not overstate the natural beauty of the Lower Missouri valley with its high bluffs of white limestone, its varied and luxuriant plants.

As we went on up, we found the country full of charm and interest, diversified with vertical rocks and very high clay hills, often cut-faced. The bottoms exhibit a great variety of trees and bushes, oaks, and walnuts of a dozen different species; the sassafras and the *Acacia triacanthus*, those flowers load the air with their delicious perfume; the maple, which is the first to clothe itself in the livery of spring; and the sycamore, king of the western forest, which erects itself in the most graceful forms, with vast spreading branches, covered with a brilliant white bark, and adds a distinctive note of grandeur to the imposing beauty of the woods. I have seen them fifteen feet and a half in diameter. The cottonwood, (*Populus deltoides,*) is another giant, growing to a prodigious height: the *Bignonia radicans* seems to prefer it to all others, climbs to its very top and lets loose a profusion of great flame-coloured trumpet-shaped blossoms. Here the traveller is struck by the thousand lofty columns of the cottonwood, enveloped, from the ground to the branches, by a drapery of dark green vines. It is one of nature's charms that one never wearies of contemplating.

The dogwood, (*Cornus florida,*) and the redbud (*Cercis canadensis,*) fill the gap betwixt tree and shrub. The first has a handsome heart-shaped leaf and spreads out its branches like an umbrella: in the spring they are covered with brilliant white flowers: in the fall they exhibit lovely scarlet berries. The other is the first shrub that one sees in blossom the length of the Missouri.

These shrubs are scattered everywhere throughout the woods, and in the earliest spring their masses of brilliant flowers form a delicate contrast with the dominant brown of the forest. The redbud gives to the landscape a charm that the traveller who sees it for the first time can never forget. The wild cherry, mulberry and ash are very common. In all these bottoms the soil is prodigiously rich, and strongly impregnated with saline substances and decomposed limestones.

The banks, however, are very unstable and crumble continually: which renders the river water, otherwise very pure and wholesome, muddy and disgusting to drink. Sandbars and submerged trees are so numerous that one becomes used to them and scarcely thinks of the risks that he is running every minute. It is interesting to observe how deep the roots thrust themselves into this fertile soil; where the bank has crumbled you may observe the whole length of them; as a rule there is only one main tap root, which penetrates ten or twelve feet, with other smaller ones round about it.

C and R, pp. 199–200.

Father De Smet mentioned the cottonwood tree. The bark of the cottonwood tree served as a useful substitute food for horses and mules. In fact, even in the summer, they prefer it to grass. Village squaws, armed with axes, would arrive at the trees, climb to the topmost branch of the tallest tree and then lop off the surrounding boughs. Then they would carry the enormous loads, lashed with cords and slung to their backs, back to their wigwams. When possible dogs pulling *travois* (sleds) would also be used for transporting the cottonwood horse food.

After ten days' navigation they reached Westport. On 30 April 1840, they set out by land with the annual expedition of the American Fur Company, which was on its way to the mountains via Green River, one of the branches of the Colorado. On the first day they moved scarcely more than eight or ten miles, just enough to break in the teams of oxen, including one or two Bramah bulls, and get them used to the work. It was customary to make the first day or two easy, till the stock were broken to the trail. Usually they would cover fifteen miles between the rising and setting of the summer sun. Before them the plains stretched wide and lonely. When there was water the wagons were drawn up for a midday rest. At night they would light a fire, using bison dung and what sticks came to hand. Once the fire was ablaze they took the animals to water, then turned them into a rope corral to be watched by the night guards. They followed the usual route west across the country to the Platte River. A rough path had been widened for the passage of wagons – and troops. They travelled over immense desert arid plains, where the grass was parched and the rivers and streams dry; the deer, bison, and roebuck sought refuge in the few oases where life still existed. Piles of stone, steep peaks, and deep ravines were encountered; and walls of rock, seemingly insurmountable, barred their progress. The heat of summer was already beginning to make itself felt; often the temperature would be as low as 27°F in the morning, though it might rise to 90°F by noon. The howling winds that prevailed unceasingly in these vast plains made the heat bearable.

The only people they met on this journey were some Kansas Indians, who lived in camps consisting of huts made of earth. The doors were so low and narrow that one could enter only by crawling.

After six days in the wilderness Father De Smet was seized with a raging fever and fits of shivering. He dismounted. Staggering from weakness he swayed against one of the wagon wheels. He hung over it while sweat dripped in tiny glistening beads from his chin on to the desert sand. In a letter to his colleague he describes the torment.

I cannot give you any idea of my deplorable state. My friends advised me to go back; but my desire of seeing the nations of the mountains prevailed over all their good reasons. I therefore followed the caravan as best I could, sticking on my horse as long as I had the strength; after that I would go and lie in a cart on the boxes, where I was jolted about like a malefactor; very often we would have to cross deep and perpendicular ravines, throwing me into the most singular positions; now my feet would be in the air, now I would find myself hidden like a thief between boxes and bundles, cold as an icicle or covered with sweat and burning like a stove. You might add that during the three days when my fever was at its highest, I had no water but what was stagnant and dirty.

C and R, pp. 202–3.

Following the general route of the Oregon Trail, which was the route of the vast emigration on its way to California and Oregon, on 18 May they reached the Platte or Nebraska River. Platte was the name given to the river by the French. The Indians called it

Nebra-ska (fine white sand). The Platte, two miles wide, was only two to six feet deep, and so unnavigable. The bottom is quicksand. The mouth of the river is 650 miles from St Louis by water, and forms the dividing point between the Lower and Upper Missouri.

Father De Smet wrote of the area:

> Antelope are very plentiful in the plains of the Platte; I have often seen several hundred in sight at one time. It is the most agile animal of the prairies. Hunters make use of a trick to come near him: they run at him full gallop, and the animal is off like a flash, leaving the horseman far behind; but soon it stops to look at him, being a very curious creature; meanwhile the hunter dismounts and lays himself flat on the ground; here he makes all kinds of flourishes with his arms and legs, now and then waving his handkerchief, or a red cap, on the end of his ramrod. The antelope draws slowly near, to watch and investigate him, and as soon as it is within gunshot, the hunter fires and lays it low.
>
> *C and R, p. 204.*

For several days' journey they found the whole plain covered with buffalo bones and skins. These weather-bleached bones were a welcome sight. It meant herds of buffalo were at hand.

> As we went on, we saw here and there the solitary burial-places of the Pawnee; probably those of some chiefs or warriors who had fallen in combat with their hereditary foes, the Sioux, Cheyenne or Osages. These tombs were adorned with buffalo skulls painted red; the body is put in, in a sitting position, into a little cabin made of reeds and branches of trees, strongly inter-woven to keep the wolves out. The face is daubed with vermil-ion, the body is covered with its finest war-ornaments, and beside it one sees provisions of every kind, dried meat, tobacco, powder and lead, gun, bow and arrows. For several years the families will come back every spring to renew these provisions. Their idea is that the soul hovers for a long time about the spot where the body reposes, before taking its flight to the land of souls.
>
> *C and R, p. 205.*

After marching for seven days alongside the Platte, they reached the plains inhabited by thousands of buffalo.

I left the camp alone, very early one morning, to see them more at my ease; I approached them by way of the ravines, without showing myself or allowing them to get the wind of me. This is the most keen-scented of animals; he will detect the presence of a man at a distance of four miles, and take flight at once. I looked with wonder upon the slow and majestic walk of these heavy wild cattle, marching silently in single file, while others cropped the short buffalo grass.

C and R, pp. 205–6.

As there was no wood on the banks of the Platte, they made use of bison dung as a source of heat and fuel. On the way they would collect this bison dung, chunks of wood and odds and ends of fuel and store them in a canvas ground sheet that hung under the wagon.

One night Father De Smet woke to the most frightful sounds – howling and barking. He thought they were about to be attacked by the wild Pawnee Indians. But it was wolves feasting on the carcasses of bison. According to the Indians wolves killed every year a third of the bison calves born. Often when they are in strong groups they will even attack a full-grown bison, which they have managed to separate from the herd, hurling themselves altogether upon one single animal and bringing it down. To prevent being kept awake all night, the travellers had to fire a few shots from time to time, to reduce the wolves to silence.

On 28 May they forded the South Fork of the Platte. Little islands gave the appearance of a labyrinth of groves floating on the water. They entered a desert region of vast undulating and treeless plains, intersected by ravines.

On 31 May, they passed the Chimney, a cone-shaped column of rock, 175 yards above the plain, which could be seen from thirty miles away. It appeared to be the remnant of a mountain which the winds and rain had worn down over the ages. They passed through a narrow passage between two perpendicular cliffs of rock 300 feet in height.

Although still three days' journey away, the Black Hills came into view.

Rattlesnakes and other varieties of poisonous snakes abounded in the area. Fortunately, also abundant in this region was the root that was an antidote against the poisonous snake venom. 'The remedy is truly side by side with the ill.' Blackroot, or snakeroot

(*Pterocanlon*) was used by the Indians as a sovereign remedy against the bite of the venomous rattlesnake.

> The plant has a very handsome flower, red and purple. It stands one to two feet above the soil; it has a long, slender, fibrous and blackish root. All that is needful is to chew the root (either fresh or dried) with the teeth, and to apply the saliva to the part bitten by the reptile. Immediately the subtle poison loses its force and the inflammation stops. Eye witnesses have assured me that they have seen the Indian jugglers (medicine men) play with and caress rattlesnakes with impunity, which they attributed to the Blackroot, which stupefies the reptile and deprives it of the power to bite; the medicine man holds the root in his hand, or rubs his hands with its juice, before going to work on the snake.
>
> *C and R, p. 663.*

On 4 June they crossed the Laramie River, a principal tributary of the Platte, in a bison hide canoe, called a bullboat. Fort Laramie (La Ramée) was at the foot of the Black Hills, so called because of the dark colour of the little cedars and pines that cover the slopes. From Fort Laramie the Rocky Mountains, forty miles away, were visible. Sagebrush which grew to a height of eight to ten feet made travelling inconvenient.

On 14 June 1840 they camped at the foot of the Red Butte, a high hill of a red ochre colour. Here the Platte turned south. From Red Butte they crossed over a high ridge to the Sweetwater River (so-called because of its purity), one of the most beautiful tributaries of the Platte, on which stood Independence Rock. Travellers inscribed their names on the Rock. Father De Smet added his, the first priest to have reached that remote spot.

Every day it got colder and colder. The wind off the snow-covered peaks was bitter. At night one needed a blanket over the shoulders against the chill. On 25 June they crossed plains covered with snow. The next day they passed South Pass, which lay between the source of the Sweetwater River in the Missouri watershed and Big Sandy, a tributary of Green River, the main tributary of the Colorado that flows into the Pacific Ocean. The Pass is twenty-five miles wide and eighty miles long. The mountains on either side were nearly 20,000 feet, blocking out the western sky. The party descended towards the Pacific, first by following, then crossing the Little and the Big Sandy Rivers.

On 30 June, having followed the right bank of the Platte for a month, they reached Green River, the Rio Colorado of the West, the Fur Company rendezvous, where every year Indians and Canadian beaver hunters assembled to sell their furs or barter them for goods. Hat makers were the chief buyers of beaver pelts. The trappers hunted for the skins of beavers and others that were highly prized. They would set traps in snow trails for the beavers. Even more valuable were the skins of the silver fox and marten. At Green River Father De Smet met the ten Flathead warriors who had been sent as an advance guard by the Great Chief to escort their missionary to their main camp.

> Our meeting was not that of strangers, but of friends; it was like children running to meet their father after a long absence. I wept with joy at embracing them, and they also, with tears in their eyes, welcomed me with tenderest expressions.
>
> *C and R, p. 220.*

While the horses were resting from their fatigue, cropping eagerly the rich grass, after which they would stand three-legged, heads down, dozing in the morning sun, Father De Smet spent several days conversing with the Indians assembled on the banks of the Green River. At the rendezvous were the Snakes, the Sampeetches, Utahs, Nez Percés (Pierced Noses), Cayuses, Walla Wallas, Paloos, Spokanes and Pondéras or Pend d'Oreilles (Earrings), also called Kalispels. Many of these he met for the first time, such as the Shoshones, or Root-diggers, also called the Snakes.
He wrote:

> Their population of about 10,000 souls is divided into several bands, scattered here and there over the barrenest country in all the region west of the mountains; almost all the surface is covered with scoria and other volcanic products. They are called Snakes by reason of their poverty, which reduces them to burrowing in the ground like those reptiles and to live upon roots. At the rendezvous they gave a parade to greet the whites that were there. Three hundred of their warriors came up in good order and at full gallop into the midst of our camp. They were hideously painted, armed with their clubs, and covered all over with feathers, pearls, wolves' tails, teeth and claws of animals, outlandish adornments, with which each one had decked himself

out according to his fancy. Those who had wounds received in war, and those who had killed the enemies of their tribe, displayed their scars ostentatiously and waved the scalps they had taken on the ends of poles, after the manner of standards.

After riding a few times around the camp, uttering at intervals shouts of joy, they dismounted and all came to shake hands with the whites in sign of friendship. I was invited to a council by some thirty of the principal chiefs. Just as among the Cheyenne, we had first to go through all the ceremonies of the calumet. To begin, the chief made a little circle on the ground, placed within it a small piece of burning dried cow-dung, and lit his pipe from it. Then he offered the pipe to the Great Spirit, to the sun, to the earth and the four cardinal points. All the others observed a most profound silence and sat motionless as statues.

C and R, p. 217.

Even more impoverished than the Snakes were the Ampajoots (Ampah Utes).

The country they inhabit is a veritable waste. They live in crevices in the rocks and in holes dug in the earth. These Indians wear no clothing, and their weapons consist of bow and arrow, and a pointed stick. They wander over the barren plains searching for ants and grasshoppers, which they eat; insipid roots and nauseous berries are regarded as a feast. Men, whose word I cannot doubt, have told me that they feed on the dead bodies of their relatives, and even eat their children.

C and R, p. 989.

Whilst the Indians of the plains, who lived on meat, were tall, robust, active and generally well-clad with skins, those who subsisted chiefly on grasshoppers and ants were miserable, lean, weak and badly clothed.

Father De Smet had the consolation of baptising several of the tribe and giving them a glimpse of eternal joys.

The Nez Percés, the Spokanes, and the Coeur d'Alènes (Pointed Hearts) were more human in their habits and customs. They inhabited a fertile country and their wealth consisted principally of horses, some of the tribes possessing five or six hundred. All manifested a great desire to have a Black Robe among them. The

Kalispels, or Pend d'Oreilles, resembled the Flatheads in character, language, and habits, and formed with them one people. Like the latter, they had led a wandering life, and merely awaited the arrival of the missionary to begin the cultivation of the soil, and to live according to the precepts of the Gospel.

C and R, p. 989.

After four days on Green River, on 4 July, he set off with the Flatheads. Ten Canadian trappers also accompanied him, trailing behind them their packhorses, carrying their winter catch of furs, as did a Fleming from Ghent, John de Velder, a beaver hunter, who had once been a grenadier in Napoleon's army. He had been taken prisoner in Spain but had managed to escape to America. He offered to stay with De Smet on his travels.

For three days they ascended Green River. On 8 July they crossed it and headed for an elevated plain, which separated the waters of the Colorado from those of the Columbia. On leaving the plain they descended several thousand feet by a trail to the valley called Jackson's Little Hole, on the head of the Hoback River.

Mountains of almost perpendicular cliffs rise to the region of perpetual snow, and often overhang a rugged and narrow path, where every step threatens a fall. We followed it for seventeen miles, upon a mountainside inclined at an angle of 45° over a torrent that rushed uproariously in cascades, hundreds of feet below our route. The defile was so narrow, and the mountains on either hand so high, that the sun could scarcely penetrate it for more than an hour or two of the day. Pine forests like those of Norway, balsam firs, ordinary poplars, cedars, mulberry trees and many other varieties cover the sides of the mountains.

On the 10th, after crossing the lofty mountain, we arrived upon the banks of Snake River, one of the principal tributaries of the Columbia River. The mass of snow melted during the July heat had swollen this torrent to a prodigious height. Its roaring waters rushed furiously down and whitened with their foam the great blocks of granite that vainly disputed the passage with them. The sight intimidated neither our Indians nor our Canadians; accustomed to perils of this sort, they rushed into the torrent on horseback and swam it. I dared not venture to do likewise. To get me over, they made a kind of sack of my skin tent; then they put all my things in and set me on top of it. The three

Flatheads who had jumped in to guide my frail bark by swimming, told me, laughing, not to be afraid, that I was on an excellent boat. And in fact this machine floated on the water like a majestic swan; and in less than ten minutes I found myself on the other bank, where we encamped for the night.

C and R, p. 222.

The next day they had another high mountain to climb through the Teton Pass. The Three Tetons are sharp-peaked mountains of a prodigious height, rising almost perpendicularly more than 10,000 feet and covered with perpetual snow. The principal summit, the Grand Teton, is 13,691 feet high. The camp of the Flatheads and Pend d'Oreilles was situated in a valley called Pierrés Hole (named after an Iroquois trapper who discovered it) at the foot of the Three Tetons. This is one of the most beautiful valleys of the Rocky Mountains. They descended into the great valley down a very steep and slippery trail. One day's travel in the valley would bring them to the camp. Here they were joined by a few Flatheads. One led a fine horse that was for the Black Robe, but with instructions that no one was to mount him till the warrior, Bravest of the Brave, was introduced to Black Robe. Soon after they were joined by the warrior himself, distinguished by his superior skill in horsemanship and by a large red scarf 'which he wore after the fashion of the Marshals of France'. He was the 'handsomest warrior of my acquaintance'. They all trotted towards the Flathead camp.

At the approach of the Black Robe, men, women and children came to shake hands and welcome him. Men of other tribes: Kalispels, Nez Percés, Snakes, Ampajoots, Spokanes, Coeur d'Alènes, had come from distances of up to 800 miles to meet him. There were about 1,600 people to welcome him. 'The elders wept with joy, while the young men expressed their satisfaction by leaps and shouts of happiness.'

De Smet was led to the tent of the great Flathead chief, a patriarch called Big Face, a warrior of lofty stature, who received him surrounded by his council.

'Black Robe, welcome to my nation. Our hearts rejoice, for today Kyleêeyou (Our Father, the Great Spirit) has granted our petition . . . Speak, Black Robe, we will follow the words of your mouth.'

Big Face was so named because he had a very long face. As well as in years, in stature and sagacity he had all the essentials of greatness. At birth he was left an orphan by the death of his mother, with no one to care for him. It was proposed that, in accordance with the brutal practice of the tribe, he should be buried in the same grave with his mother. He was rescued by a compassionate young woman who adopted him.

The Chief's chest was loaded with medals, some in silver, and one or two even in gold: gifts, during the long period of his life. He also wore armlets, and gold cinctures above his ankles. His head, on the whole of which the hair had been permitted to grow, since it was a long time since he had been active in war, was encircled by a sort of plated diadem, from which smaller, more glittering ornaments hung, that sparkled among three drooping feathers, dyed a deep black. His tomahawk was nearly hidden in silver, and the handle of his knife shone like a horn of solid gold.

Father De Smet explained the advantages of settling permanently in a fertile area. The Indians were nomadic hunters, but they agreed to exchange bows and quiver for spade and hoe.

During his stay with the Flatheads and the Pend d'Oreilles Father De Smet baptised many people, including the chiefs of the two tribes, who were both octogenarians – tired of seeing the sun rise and set.

After a short time in Pierrés Hole Father De Smet and his party proceeded into Flathead country. They ascended the Henry Fork of Snake River to its source in Henry's Lake (named after Andrew Henry, a fur trader) every day making camp nine or ten miles.

On the 22nd July the camp came to Henry's Lake, one of the principal sources of the Columbia; it is about ten miles in circumference. We climbed on horseback the mountain that parts the waters of two great rivers; the Missouri, which is properly speaking the main branch of the Mississippi and flows with it into the gulf of Mexico, and the Columbia, which bears the tribute of its waters to the Pacific Ocean. From the elevated spot at which I was I could easily distinguish Mosquito Lake, source of one of the main branches of the north fork of the Missouri, called Jefferson River.

The two lakes are scarce eight miles apart. I started for the summit of a high mountain, for a better examination of the fountains that give birth to these two great rivers; I saw them falling in cascades from an immense height, hurling themselves with uproar from rock to rock; even at their source they formed already two mighty torrents, scarcely more than a hundred paces apart. I was bound to get to the top. After six wearisome hours, I found myself exhausted; I think I must have climbed more than 5,000 feet; I had passed snowdrifts more than twenty feet deep, and still the mountaintop was at a great height above me. I therefore saw myself compelled to give up my plan, and I found a place to sit down.

C and R, p. 229.

On 24 July the party crossed the Divide and moved from Henry's Lake to Mosquito (Red Rock) Lake, the ultimate source of the Missouri. Until 8 August they travelled through a great variety of country, from open smiling valleys, to sterile lands beyond high mountains and narrow defiles, to extensive high plains, covered profusely with blocks of granite. Then down the Stinking Water River to its confluence with the Beaver Head, and down the latter to Jefferson Fork, which they descended to the junction of the Three Forks where the Missouri proper takes its source.

On 10 August they reached Jefferson River. They travelled down it, making twelve to fifteen miles a day. On 21 August they reached the Three Forks of the Missouri River, and camped on the middle branch (Madison Fork). Immense herds of bison roamed over the plain, and the Flatheads made use of this opportunity to replenish their food supply. Father De Smet accompanied them on their bison hunts to see how it was done.

A brave would ride into a herd of stampeding bison, the reins tossed loose across the arched neck of his horse. The pony needed no directing; it turned alongside the herd and kept going as a bison was shot. The pony immediately turned in towards the next bison, thus selecting the next target for the man on its back.

At other times they practise a still more cunning stratagem; they urge their prey up some steep place, beyond which lies a deep ravine or precipice. There they form a half circle about it, closing in continually and redoubling their threats and howls. The poor bison, placed between two fires, hesitates a moment at sight of the abyss; but soon, bewildered by the yelping and baying, it attempts the only to escape from its assailants, jumps off and falls crushed at the bottom of the ravine. Then our high-waymen also go down by the roundabout way, and partake together of the fruit of their industry.

C and R, p. 603.

The Indians had many ingenious ways of killing the bison. If the hunter could not avoid being seen, he drew a bison skin over his head, as a kind of hood, surmounted by a pair of horns. This deceived the herd. He could then get close enough to shoot them. But his aim had to be sure: when wounded the bison becomes furious, turns upon the hunter and pursues him in turn.

The braves would rapidly skin the still warm carcasses. They would peel the thick, supple hides and hand them to the squaws for scraping, cleaning and dressing, so that they could be turned into warm durable robes or *tipi* covers. The meat, smoked over herb-fed fires, would be eaten or prepared into pemmican (a small pressed cake of shredded dried meat) and other winter delicacies. The horns and hooves of the bison would be saved for making powder flasks, drinking vessels and ornaments. Not even the smallest piece of carcass was ever wasted. The sinews would be used for bowstrings, the paunches for water carriers and the bones as hammers, clubs or toys for the children.

In this kind of hunt, or carnage, the entire animal is used up, even to the bones; these are cracked and broken apart for soup. The marrow of the bones is the finest part of the whole animal and the most agreeable to the taste. The meat is cut into long strips and dried in the sun. When the chase is over, one horse easily carries the spoils of an entire bison.

C and R, p. 1376.

Father De Smet records asking seven Flatheads how many bison they had killed between them in their last hunt.

The number amounted to 189 – one alone had killed fifty-nine. One of the Flatheads told me of three remarkable coups that had distinguished him in that chase. He pursued a cow, armed merely with a stone, and killed her by striking her while running, between the horns; he afterward killed a second with his knife; and then finished his exploits by spearing and strangling a large bull. The young warriors frequently exercise themselves in this manner, to show their agility, dexterity and strength. He who spoke looked like a Hercules.

C and R, p. 1011.

Life for the Indians was one constant struggle for survival against nature. One day De Smet himself experienced what such survival involved.

He was called out to visit a sick woman. This journey involved a steep climb. The track was narrow. In fact, it was no wider than a deer track. He stopped – for two reasons. One, for breath; it had been an exhausting climb. Secondly, to admire the view. He watched the morning sun come blasting over the hills. From his pocket he withdrew a kerchief and dried the perspiration from his face.

He resumed the climb. Soon his thoughts were a million miles away: thinking of relatives back home in Termonde. There was a bend in the track ahead. As he got nearer he put out his arm to brush aside some sagebrush that had grown wild across the path; a branch had already whipped his face. As he did so he stopped dead in his tracks, rigid in a kind of frantic immobility. His whole frame froze in panic and amazement. In front of him was a huge grizzly bear, with wide extended jaws. He held his breath. All thoughts of family and home vanished in a twinkling. There was one paramount thought – survival. And all he possessed was a walking stick; for once, not even a knife. He was staring into the glistening brown eyes of a huge silver-tip grizzly. It let out a roar. As it uttered its hoarse, choking snarl, baring its teeth, it rose up on its hind legs. What could a man do now? One of the two must surely die. The huge creature, at least 900 pounds of grey animal flesh, made for De Smet. With its right paw it swiped out at the black-robed priest. The Jesuit stepped back. The momentum of the bear's swipe carried it forward on to him; as it fell the priest kicked its right back leg from under it. The grizzly tumbled forward taking De Smet with it, digging its claws into his flesh. As the two fell to the ground De Smet grabbed the animal by the jugular. He twisted his head away from the huge angry jaws that snapped at his face. He squeezed and squeezed with the gigantic strength born of danger. The animal struggled to escape, bruising and bloodying De Smet as it did so. He could feel warm blood flowing over his body. His only hope was to cling on to the animal's neck and squeeze. The bear began spluttering, spitting saliva into his face. De Smet closed his eyes, and he prayed. Slowly he felt the brown muscular creature that was trying equally to squeeze the life out of him grow limp. But he continued pressing. The eyes of the animal closed; it fell away from him. He squeezed longer – to make sure there was no life left in the grizzly.

He got off the animal and rested on a boulder by the path. He gazed across to the dead bear. Strangely enough he felt quite sad at seeing the furry, almost cuddly, animal lying dead. He rested for several minutes. His black soutane was ripped; blood oozed from his arms, chest and face. He took off his soutane and tried to stem the blood as best he could with his kerchief.

He carried on up the track. Around another corner, which he approached with great circumspection, his eye caught grey smoke curling up into the lowering grey sky, the clouds swollen with impending rain. He stopped as he heard a noise. He listened carefully. It was the sound of human voices. That was a relief. He was in no mood or condition to wrestle with another grizzly. Seeing Father De Smet, an Indian stopped dead in his tracks, utter surprise and astonishment across his face. The young lad beside him looked even more puzzled. As the Indian came closer he recognised Father De Smet. He smiled but his greeting was mingled with concern.

'What happened?' he inquired, as he looked the Black Robe up and down. 'Are you all right?'

De Smet nodded.

The Indian looked closely at the claw marks on De Smet's arm and chest.

'A bear!' He knew straight away, from bitter experience. Some months ago one of the young men in his village had been killed by a grizzly. For weeks a grizzly had been attacking and killing their animals – cattle, horses, pigs, anything. A young brave had decided to end the menace. He tracked the bear to its haunt in the mountains. But while he was hunting the bear, the bear was tracking him. It waited for him. Before he could let off a shot the bear had removed half the man's face with a mighty swipe of its paw. In a matter of moments the young man was dead. A search party next day had found the badly mauled body, mutilated beyond recognition.

The bear was the terror of all Indians. They addressed prayers

49

and invocations to it; they offered it sacrifices of tobacco, belts and other prized objects.

'We must kill the bear,' the Indian said to his young companion. He unloaded the rifle off his shoulder. 'I presume it is down there,' he said, pointing in the direction from which Father De Smet had come.

'Don't bother,' Father De Smet said. 'The bear is dead.'

The words stopped the Indian from moving off. 'Dead?' he queried. 'But how can that be?' he asked, a frown over his face.

'I killed it,' De Smet replied.

That was too incredible to believe.

'You killed it?' he said in disbelief. 'But how? You have no weapon.'

'I killed it,' the priest replied, 'with these,' showing his blood-covered hands to the unbelieving Indian.

The two Indians were speechless. They couldn't believe that a man, unarmed, could have taken on a grizzly bear and lived to tell the tale.

'If you go back down that path a little distance you will see the dead bear,' De Smet said to his astonished listeners.

'No. We must get you to our camp first. You need rest; you need medicine.'

With his axe the younger man slashed off a bough to make a walking stick for the priest. The three made off towards the wigwams.

The headman of the village drew a bundle of fragrant brush from beneath a pile that filled a corner of his hut, seated De Smet on it and cleaned up the wounds.

Father De Smet was well known and well loved by the Flathead Indians. When they learned that he had fought and killed a grizzly with only his bare hands he was looked upon as some super being.

The next day the chief called a gathering of the tribe. After smoking the calumet Father De Smet was presented with a collar made out of the claws of the bear he had killed. Each claw was seven inches long. Such a bear claw collar, which is presented to any Indian who single-handedly kills a grizzly bear, is the highest decoration for gallantry any Indian can wear, prized even more than the scalp of an enemy.

For eight months Father De Smet shared in every way the

nomadic life of the Indians. In his *Voyages aux Montagnes-Rochenses* he wrote of this life:

I think you will not read without interest a short account of my stay among them and of my excursions in their company. Do not be surprised at my having led the wandering life of a savage from the month of April to December, living by hunting and on roots, without bread, sugar or coffee, my only bed a bison robe and a woollen blanket, passing my nights under the stars when the weather was good and braving the storms and tempests under a little tent. I have mentioned a fever that I had, which seemed determined not to leave me; well, by leading this hard life, I rid myself of it entirely; I have been in wonderful health since September.

C and R, p. 993.

Father De Smet also confirmed the high moral calibre of the tribe.

The Flatheads may be called a grave, modest and decent people. The gross vices so common among many other nations are unknown among them. Adultery is of the rarest occurrence and their honesty has been ever acknowledged by all travellers and strangers who have visited their country. Any object found is immediately restored to the owner, if known; if not, it is deposited with the chief or Black Robe.

A member of the celebrated exploration by Captain Lewis and Lieutenant Clark of the First United States Infantry in 1803 to explore the Missouri River to its source, in speaking of the moral degradation in which many of the tribes were sunk, stated:

To the honour of the Flatheads who live on the eastern slopes of the Rocky Mountains, they must be cited as an exception. This is the only tribe that has any idea of chastity.

Lavaille, p. 98.

Ross Cox, who in 1812–1814 traded furs with them, tells us that the Flatheads possessed nobler qualities than any of the other Western tribes. 'They are,' he said, 'honest, obedient to their chiefs, clean in their huts and personal habits, and hold lying in abhorrence. Polygamy is almost unknown among them. The women are excellent wives and mothers.' The Flatheads were a nation of heroes. They would never begin an attack, but woe to those who provoked them. Flatheads always retrieved their dead after a battle.

Winter would now soon be setting in. As this was only an exploratory visit to the Flathead country, Father De Smet decided to return to his base in St Louis where he could begin preparations for a more permanent mission.

Before dawn on 27 August, all the Flatheads assembled to bid farewell to him.

Father De Smet describes the farewell.

All the tribe assembled round my hut. No one spoke; but sorrow was expressed on every countenance. The only word that seemed to comfort them was my formal promise that in the spring I would return, and bring with me several other missionaries. I said morning prayers amidst the sobs and tears of these good Indians, whose grief drew from me, in spite of myself, the tears I wished to repress. I then pointed out to them the necessity of my departure; and I exhorted them to persevere and serve the Great Spirit fervently; and, to avoid all subjects of scandal, I reminded them of the principal truths of religion; and I appointed as their spiritual chief a very intelligent Indian, whom I had taken care to instruct myself, in a special manner. He was to take my place in my absence; to assemble them to prayers every night and morning, and on Sundays to exhort them to virtue; to baptise the dying, and even the children in case of necessity. There was but one voice to promise me that all I recommended should be observed. With tears in their eyes they wished me a happy journey. The old chief then rose, and said: 'Black Robe, may the Great Spirit accompany you in your long and perilous journey. We shall pray night and morning that you may arrive safely among your brethren at St Louis; and we shall continue our prayers till you return to your children in the mountains. When the snow disappears from the valley, after the winter, when the trees begin to bud forth, our hearts, now so sorrowful, will begin to rejoice. As the grass grows in height, our joy will increase; and when the flowers are in bloom, we will set off to meet you.'

C and R, p. 273.

The sky flared with true dawn, like damp paper suddenly catching fire, and before the sun was an hour high, Father De Smet had taken his leave.

Chapter 4

Into Enemy Territory – The Blackfeet

Father De Smet resolved to return to St Louis by a different route. He intended to follow the Yellowstone to its junction with the Missouri. On the way he hoped to visit the forts established for trade along the river, where he might possibly find a number of half-blood children waiting to be baptised. This involved travelling through the country of the Crows and the Blackfeet, the two tribes most hostile to the white man. Seventeen warriors of the Flatheads accompanied Father De Smet as escort. His devoted compatriot, the Fleming John de Velder, also accompanied him. Father De Smet relates the story.

> We had to cross plains that stretched out of sight, sterile and arid lands, cut up with deep ravines, where at every step one might come upon enemies lying in wait. Scouts were sent out in every direction to reconnoitre the country; all traces, whether of men or animals, were attentively examined. It is here that one cannot but admire the sagacity of the savage; he will tell you what day an Indian has passed by the spot where he sees tracks, he will calculate the number of men and of horses, he will make out whether it was a war or hunting party; he will even recognise, from the impression of their footgear, to what nation they belonged. Every evening we chose a favourable place to pitch our camp, and built in haste a little fort with trunks of dead trees, to shelter us from a sudden attack.
>
> *C and R, p. 235.*

The little cavalcade took up the route from the Three Forks very much along today's line of the Northern Pacific Railroad. For two days they ascended the east fork of the Gallatin (the south-eastern fork of the

Missouri), crossed a narrow pass – what is now the Bozeman Pass, thirty miles in length, between the valleys of the upper Missouri and the Yellowstone rivers. They reached the Yellowstone River, the second greatest tributary of the Missouri, at the Great Bend, where Livington now stands. The Yellowstone has a mouth 800 yards in width and at that point seemed as large as the main Missouri River. The Yellowstone is a region of great beauty and grandeur. The 1,200-foot rim of the Grand Canyon of Yellowstone was a sight that took the breath away. Wild lupins bloomed across the lush valley. The caravan soon came to a camp of the Crows, a tribe at the time on friendly terms with the Flatheads. This encampment of the Crows was in the Bighorn valley, some distance above the mouth of that river. Among all the tribes of the north-western portion of North America the Crows were considered the most warlike and most valiant. They roamed over the valley of the Yellowstone, in the region of the Black Hills and the Rocky Mountains. They got their name 'Crows' because they were the most indefatigable marauders of the plains, carrying to one side what they had stolen from the other. 'This race is one of the noblest in the desert; they are tall, robust and well formed, have a piercing eye, aquiline nose and teeth of ivory whiteness.' (*C and R, p. 1035.*)

In ancient times the Crows held the beaver in the highest veneration because they believed that they became beavers after death. This article of their creed entailed the loss of their scalp for many white trappers, for every Crow Indian considered himself bound to protect, defend and avenge, even with death, the spirits of his 'near relations', in their second state of existence.

Father De Smet and his party were received with great cordiality. All the chiefs and warriors wore their embroidered moccasins, leggings and buckskin shirts ornamented with beads and porcupine quills; white eagles' feathers crowned their heads. One of the Crows had hair eleven feet long. The tribe's larder was well provisioned and so the time was spent in feasting and rejoicing. In one afternoon Father De Smet assisted at twenty successive banquets.

Scarcely was I seated in one lodge before I was invited into another one. My digestion not being as accommodating as that of the Indians, I contented myself with only tasting their stews, and for a bit of tobacco, the *eaters*, whom I had had the foresight to take with me, emptied the dishes carefully in my stead.

C and R, p. 239.

The law of the feast was that each one must eat all that was given to him; however, one could get rid of his plate by giving it to another guest with a present of tobacco.

When Father De Smet lit his pipe with lucifer (phosphoric acid) matches, the Crows were amazed. They had never seen anything like that. He was at once considered the greatest medicine man that had ever visited the tribe. He was treated with even more respect. The chiefs and principal warriors were overjoyed when he gave them each some boxes of 'mysterious fire'.

From this camp they made their way to the Big Horn, the largest tributary of the Yellowstone. It was a fair, broad river with crystal clear water. It traversed extensive plains, well wooded on both banks, and offering excellent grazing grounds.

They continued their journey down the right bank of the Yellowstone. The danger of the hostile Blackfeet remained imminent.

Buffalo were scarce, for war parties had traversed the same plains a few days previously. All the country along this river is very gravelly and full of round and oblong boulders, shaped by the water; here and there little patches of woods were seen in the distance on the banks of rivers.

Below the mouth of Clark's Fork the Yellowstone is hemmed in by high cliffs. We climbed them by a narrow trail to gain the uplands, or rather a chain of rough hills, which we were six days crossing. In this march we suffered much from thirst. We found all the springs exhausted and the beds of the streams dry.

As we went on, we perceived frequent tracks of horses. On the 5 September we came to a place where numerous troops of horsemen had passed an hour before. Were they allies or enemies? Right here I will remark that in these solitudes, though the howling of wolves, the hissing of venomous serpents and the roaring of the tiger (mountain lion) and grizzly bear are capable of freezing one with terror, this fear is nothing in comparison with that which fresh tracks of men and horses can arouse in the soul of the traveller, or the columns of smoke that he sees rising round him. In an instant the escort came together to deliberate; every one examined his firearm, whetted his knife and the points of his arrow and made all preparations for a resistance to the death; for to surrender in such an encounter would be to expose one's self to perish in the most frightful torments. We resolved to follow the trail, determined to know who were ahead of us; it led us to a heap of stones piled up on a little eminence. Here more signs were manifest; these stones were coloured with freshly shed blood. The head chief presently said to me, 'Father, I think I can explain to you what we see before us. The Crows are not far away; we shall see them in two hours. If I am not mistaken, we are upon one of their battlefields; their nation will have met with some great loss here. This heap of stones has been raised to the memory of the warriors who have fallen under the blows of their enemies. Here the mothers, wives, sisters, daughters of the dead (you see their traces) have come to weep over their graves. It is their custom to tear their faces, cut their arms and legs and shed their blood upon these stones, rending the air at the same time with their cries and lamentations.' He was not mistaken; presently we perceived a considerable troop of Indians some three miles off. They were in fact Crows returning to their camp, after having paid the tribute of blood to forty of their warriors, massacred two years before by the Blackfeet. Since they are just at present allies of the Flatheads, they received us with the greatest transports of joy. Soon we met groups of women covered with dried blood, and so disfigured that they aroused at once compassion and horror. They repeat this scene of mourning for several years, whenever they pass near the tombs of their relations and so long as the slightest spot of blood remains on their bodies they may not wash themselves.

C and R, pp. 236–7.

After several more days in surmounting the difficulties of travel, across endless sterile and broken hills, they reached the American Fur Company's trading fort for the Crows, Fort Alexander, on the left bank of the Yellowstone, opposite the mouth of the Rosebud River.

Father De Smet was now at the entrance to Blackfoot country. Now began the most difficult and perilous part of the journey. He had to pass through a country overrun by war parties – of Blackfeet, Assiniboins, Grosventres, Aricaras and Sioux. All these nations were hostile towards the Flatheads.

Fearing to expose the faithful Flatheads who had accompanied him so far, Father De Smet dispensed with their services and sent them back to their home.

He was now alone, with only his Flemish friend, John de

Velder, to make the rest of the journey through wandering bands
of Indians that thirsted for the blood of white men. They set out
with courage upon a solitary and dangerous trip of several hundred
miles through the most dangerous country any explorer had visited,
across an unknown desert in which there was no trail, nor any
other guide than the compass or star. For a long time they followed
the course of the Yellowstone, except in some places where chains
of rocks intercepted their march and obliged them to make long
detours, crossing rough hills four or five hundred feet high. They
dipped down through cliff-sided ravines and climbed from wooded
canyons where black trees tangled so densely in confusion that
even at midday dusk reigned save where a random shaft of light
penetrated a gap in the foliage; here an ambush could be awaiting
them. Down the length of one such canyon ran a creek that in rainy
months was a frothing torrent of wild white water, sweeping tree
trunks and boulders along with its current. Today it lay serene,
with thickets of redbud along its banks, their darkly handsome
branches clustered with magenta blossoms.

Having spent many moons in Indian territory they both knew the
simple rules of survival. They knew that a ride silhouetted against
the skyline of a ridge was your last ride. They knew that to sleep
by a campfire meant you saw no dawn. You kept the wind blowing
on your cheeks – or the Indians would scent you. They learnt to
fade into the barest cover at a minute's notice.

They always held well to the side of valleys, working their way
along the bottom, keeping close to trees or under them. By riding
at the bottom of creeks or under trees they could go unseen. They
frequented the shadows where they remained concealed. They
always stopped against a background against which their shapes
offered no outline. Their lives now depended on the quickness of
their eyes, and on the vigilance of their ears. Their noses must
scent any danger in the wind. They would cross no rivulet without
attentively considering the quantity, speed and colour of its waters.
They would leave the sandy wash at separate points so that the
indentations left by their horses' hooves would confuse the trail.

They were able to recognise one set of pony tracks from another;
they could tell the size and height of the animal by the shape and
depth of its print; whether an unshod pony had been travelling fast
or slow. They could tell a trail over which squaws and old men had
passed, the hooves of their ponies muffled to cut out any noise.

They knew unseen foes could be watching from the dark coverts.

They kept looking back with salutary watchfulness against attack from the rear, from a foe following in their footsteps. De Smet was sure he was being followed; yet on several occasions when he had drawn up in the thick timbers to study his back trail, he saw nobody.

Methodically their eyes searched the slopes and valleys, their eyes sweeping from side to side, taking in every clump of brush or aspen, every outcropping of rock, each colour change in the grass. They suffered no sign, friendly or hostile, to escape them. They noted rods planted in the earth but inclined in such a manner as to indicate a route. They observed the movements of birds and animals as indications of danger. Their vigilant eyes were quick to observe the tracks and droppings of deer. They looked for telltale signs at every waterhole. On moist alluvium they picked out the print of moccasins – but from which tribe they knew not. Here and there the bark of trees had been nibbled by unshod horses.

Every hour they came across signs of the possible near presence of the dreaded Blackfeet. The tracks of fresh hooves that had never been shod pointed to Indians. The absence of *travois* trails meant the Indians had no families with them. It must be a war party. The Indians used *travois* drawn by dogs or ponies, with their rolled *tipis* trailing behind, for following the game with their families. The squaw would ride behind her lord and master, with a papoose strapped across her back.

In a letter to his brother Francis, Father De Smet later wrote:

Such a solitude, with all its horrors and dangers, has notwithstanding one very real advantage; it is a place where one is constantly looking death in the face, and where it presents itself incessantly to the imagination in the most hideous forms. There one feels in a very special manner that he is wholly in God's hands ... That was, in fact, the best 'retreat' that I have ever made in my life.

C and R, p. 241.

He went on to record some of the further perils of the journey.

On the second day of the journey, I espied, upon waking very early in the morning, the smoke of a great fire a quarter of a mile away; only a rocky point separated us from a savage war-party. Without losing time, we saddled our horses and started at full gallop; at last we gained the hill, and crossing the ravines and the dry bed of a torrent, we reached the top without being perceived. That day we made forty to fifty miles without a halt, and did not camp until two hours after sunset, for fear of the savages coming upon our trail and following us. The same fear prevented our lighting a fire, and so we had to do without supper. I rolled myself in my blanket and stretched myself on the sod, commending myself to the good God. My grenadier, braver than I, was soon snoring like a steam engine in full swing; running through all the notes of the chromatic scale he closed each movement of his prelude with a deep sigh, by way of modulation. As for me, I turned and rolled, but spent a sleepless night; what they call a *nuit blanche*. At dawn next morning we were already under way; we had to use the greatest precautions, because the country we had to traverse was most dangerous. Towards noon, a fresh cause for alarm; buffalo had been killed, not more than two hours before, in a spot by which we had to pass; his tongue, marrowbones and some other delicate morsels had been taken. We trembled at this sight, thinking the enemy was not far away; but we ought rather to have thanked the Lord, who had thus prepared food for our evening meal. We turned in the opposite direction to the tracks of the savages, and that night we camped among rocks that are the resort of bears and panthers and wolves. There I had a good sleep. This time the music of my companion's snoring did not trouble me.

We always took the road early in the morning; but it was to confront fresh dangers each time, to meet here and there recent footprints of men and horses. Towards ten o'clock we came to an abandoned camp of forty lodges; the fires were not yet out; but luckily we saw no one.

C and R, p. 242.

Despite the ever-present danger of attack, Father De Smet still had an eye for the scenery and the surroundings.

The Yellowstone country abounds in game; I do not believe that there is in all America a region better adapted to the chase. I was for seven days among innumerable herds of buffalo. Every moment I perceived bands of majestic elk leaping through this animated solitude, while clouds of antelopes took flight before us with the swiftness of arrows. The *ashata* or bighorn alone seemed not to be disturbed by our presence; these animals rested in flocks or frolicked upon the projecting crags, out of gunshot. Deer were abundant, especially the black-tailed deer, which is hardly found elsewhere than in mountainous country. All the rivers and streams that we crossed in our course, gave evident signs that the industrious beaver, the otter and the muskrat were still in peaceable possession of their solitary waters. There was no lack of ducks, geese and swans. This country abounds in coal and in iron-mines. The Yellowstone appeared to me to be full of currents; it is not navigable, unless in the middle of summer, when the water from the melting snows rushes down in torrents from the mountains.

C and R, p. 243.

The Yellowstone and its upper forks had also their wonders. In a volcanic region, huge jets of stem, geysers, issue from the soil like the exhaust of steamboats. There are also mounds thrown up by volcanic forces. Indians passed these places in profound silence and with superstitious dread. They regarded them as 'the abode of underground spirits, always at war with one another, and continually at the anvil forging their weapons'. They never passed that region without leaving some offering.

In the same region, in the side of a steep cliff, was a wide and high opening believed to be very steep. To Indians it was 'the place of coming-out and going-in of underground spirits', and to render them propitious, at each visit an Indian would throw in one or more arrows with his hand. At the foot of the rock a heap of arrows or offerings that had missed the opening could be seen. No Indian, however much he might be in need of them, would have dared to touch one of these objects, much less to take them away; they were sacred.

At last the two travellers reached the Missouri, but at a point where 100 lodges of Assiniboins had crossed just an hour before. Soon they were in Fort Union.

Fort Union is the vastest and finest of the forts that the Fur Company has upon the Missouri; it is situated 2,000 miles from St Louis. The gentlemen residing there overwhelmed us with civilities; they could not get over their astonishment at the dangerous journey which we had just concluded so fortunately. During our stay among them, they supplied all our wants most liberally, and at our departure for the village of the Mandans they loaded us with all sorts of provisions. I shall be most thankful to them all my life.

C and R, p. 244.

The two stayed several days at Fort Union. After having regenerated sundry half-blood children in the holy waters of baptism, Father De Smet left the fort on 23 September for the village of the Mandans.

We met on our way a war party of fifteen Assiniboins, returning from a fruitless expedition against the Grosventres of the Missouri. It is chiefly on such occasions as this that it is dangerous to meet the savages. To come home without horses, prisoners, scalps, is for them the climax of dishonour and shame; accordingly they showed us much displeasure, and their looks were nothing if not sinister. These Indians are, however, cowards, and this particular band were poorly armed. I was accompanied by three men from the fort, who were going to the Aricaras with a herd of horses, and though we were only five, each of us laid his hand upon his weapon, assuming an air of determination, and we had a little talk with them and continued our route without being molested. The next day we passed through a forest on the banks of the Missouri which had been in 1835 the winter quarters of the Grosventres, Aricaras and Mandans; it was there that these unfortunate nations had been attacked by the epidemic, which, in the course of a year, made such ravages among the Indian tribes; several thousand of the savages died of smallpox. We observed in passing that the corpses, wrapped in buffalo hides, had remained bound to the branches of the largest trees. Two days later we came to the miserable remnants of these three unfortunate tribes. The Mandans, who today scarce number ten families, have united with the Grosventres, who themselves had joined the Aricaras; altogether there were about 3,000 of them. Some of the young men having perceived us afar off, gave notice to the chiefs of the approach of strangers. At once they rushed out by hundreds to meet us; but the three men from Fort Union made themselves known, and presented me to their chiefs as a Black Robe of the Frenchmen. They received us with the greatest signs of friendliness and forced us to pass the afternoon and night in their camp.

The kettles were soon filled in all the lodges, and the roasting pieces were set to the fire to celebrate our arrival. Here again, as among the Crows, it was a succession of invitations to feasts that we had to undergo to midnight. To refuse would have been the height of rudeness, and besides they believe us as capable as themselves of eating hugely and at any hour of the day or night.

These Indians helped us next day to cross the Missouri in their bull-boats. These are shaped like a round basket, made of willows as thick as one's thumb interwoven and covered with a buffalo skin. Our horses, that had followed us swimming, became mired to the neck on the opposite bank; it took a half-day's work to get them out of the mud.

C and R, p. 246.

At last they came to the large village of the Aricaras, consisting of about 100 earthen wigwams, only ten miles distant from that of the Mandans. The Fur Company had a fort here also – Fort Clark, named after William Clark of the Lewis and Clark expedition of 1803.

These Aricaras commonly wear no other garment than a loin-cloth. On feast days, they put on a handsome tunic, leggings and moccasins of gazelle-skin embroidered with porcupine quills of lively colours, then they envelop themselves in a buffalo robe loaded with ornaments and colours, throw their quiver filled with arrows over the left shoulder, and cover their head with a bonnet of eagle feathers. He who killed an enemy on his own ground is distinguished by tails of animals, which he attaches to his legs. He who kills a grizzly bear wears the claws of that animal in the form of a collar, and it is the most glorious trophy of an Indian hunter. The warrior who returns from the enemy with one or several scalps, paints a red hand across his mouth, to show that he has drunk his enemies' blood.

C and R, p. 247.

They stopped a short time at Fort Clark. Then, in the company of a Canadian *voyageur* travelling in the same direction, set off down the right bank of the river for Fort Pierre, on the Little Missouri, a further ten days' journey.

We had no guide, but full of confidence in the protection of God, we sought our way in a country where there is no trodden path, guided through these desert expanses like a mariner upon a fast ocean.

The fifth day found us in the neighbourhood of the Sioux Blackfeet, an offshoot of the Blackfeet of the mountains. Their very name struck terror into our hearts. We crept through ravines to be out of range of the piercing eye of the Indian that ever searches the plain.

Toward noon a nearby spring invited us to rest and make our midday repast. We were congratulating ourselves upon having escaped the dreaded enemy, when suddenly a war cry, accompanied by deafening noises, sounded from the direction overlooking our hiding-place. A band of Blackfeet that had been following our tracks for several hours, armed with guns, bows and arrows, half-naked, weirdly daubed with colour, descended upon us at full gallop.

I immediately rose and extended my hand to the one who appeared to be chief of the band. 'Why are you hiding in a ravine?' he said, 'Are you afraid of us?' 'We were hungry,' I replied, 'and the spring tempted us to take a few moments rest.' Then addressing the Canadian, who spoke a little Sioux, he said: 'Never before in my life have I seen this kind of man. Who is he, and where does he come from?' Given such an opportunity, the Canadian was not backward in according titles. 'This man,' he replied, 'converses with the Great Spirit. He is the French Black Robe and is come here to visit the different Indian tribes.'

At these words the savage softened, commanded his warriors to lay down their arms, and each one gave me his hand. I made them a present of a large package of tobacco, and immediately the warriors seated themselves in a circle to smoke the pipe of peace and friendship.

Twelve warriors and their chief, in full costume, shortly afterward presented themselves before my lodge and spread a large and fine buffalo robe. The head chief took me by the arm and leading me to the skin made me a sign to be seated. I had no idea of the meaning of this ceremony, but I sat down, thinking that it was an invitation to smoke the calumet with them. Judge my surprise when I beheld the twelve warriors seize this kind of carpet by the ends, lift me from the ground and, preceded by their chief, carry me in triumph to the village, where everybody was instantly afoot to see the Black Robe.

I was given the place of honour in the chief's tent, who,

surrounded by forty of his braves, addressed me in the following words: 'Black Robe, this is the happiest day of our lives, for today, for the first time, we see in our midst a man who is near to the Great Spirit. These are the principal warriors of my tribe. I have invited them to the feast I have prepared for you, that they may never forget the great day.'

C and R, p. 251–2.

During the repast the great chief showered attentions on his guest, even to giving him a mouthful of his own food to chew, a refined usage among the tribe. At night, after Father De Smet had retired and was about to fall asleep, he saw the chief who had received him with so much honour enter his tent. Brandishing a knife that gleamed in the light of the torch, he said: 'Black Robe, are you afraid?' The Black Robe, taking the chief's hand, placed it on his breast and replied: 'See if my heart beats more rapidly than usual! Why should I be afraid? You have fed me with your own hands, and I am as safe in your tent as I would be in my father's house.' Flattered by this reply, the Blackfoot renewed his profession of friendship; he had wished only to test the confidence of his guest.

The next day Father De Smet continued his journey. The great chief gave him three Indians to accompany him to Fort Pierre; among them was his own son, whom he begged the priest to instruct. 'I want to know,' he said, 'the words the Great Spirit has communicated to us through you.'

The country between the upper Missouri and the Yellowstone was ranged by Assiniboins, Crows, Blackfeet, Sioux, Flatheads, Pend d'Oreilles, Kootenais, Nez Percés, Bannocks and Snakes, where all contended for the bison, and was the centre of countless skirmishes and battles.

On 17 October Father De Smet reached Fort Pierre. After several days at the fort he set out for Fort Vermilion, in company with two Canadian trappers. 'We met very few Indians on this journey of nineteen days; the plain was burnt up. We were often obliged to cook our victuals with dried herbs – not a stick was to be found.' They crossed the Medicine River, the Chapelle, James and Vermilion rivers. At Fort Vermilion a bitter sorrow awaited Father De Smet. The Sioux had violated the peace concluded the year before with his dear Potawatomies, at Council Bluffs, 300 miles away. A Santee war party was just back from the Potawatomies bearing a scalp. Father De Smet at once called a council of the tribe, and reproached the chiefs for breaking their word, menacing them with terrible reprisals if they did not at once repair the injury done. Thoroughly frightened, the Sioux entreated him to be once more their interpreter, and to assure the Potawatomies that they were resolved to forever bury the hatchet.

Happy to be the bearer of a message of peace to his neophytes, Father De Smet wished to start at once. His horse was exhausted, so with a half-blood Iroquois he started in a canoe. It was then the middle of November. Green and angry waters lashed the shore. If, in descending, a point of rock or a loose boulder was touched, the shock would be fatal to the craft, crushing the hull despite the strongest framing. The Missouri was filled with floating ice, which continually jammed the frail skiff against snags.

> Five times we were on the point of perishing by being over-turned among the numerous snags, upon which the ice floes dragged us despite all our efforts. We passed ten days in this dangerous and disquieting navigation, sleeping on sandbars at night and taking only two meals, evening and morning; besides, we had nothing in the way of food but frozen potatoes and a little fresh meat. The very night of our arrival 24 November, among our Fathers at Council Bluffs, the river froze over. It would be in vain for me to attempt to tell what I felt at finding myself once more amidst our brothers, Fathers Verreydt and Hoecken, after having travelled 2,000 Flemish leagues, in the midst of the greatest dangers and across the territories of the most barbarous nations.
>
> *C and R, pp. 257–8.*

In the name of the Sioux he renewed peace with his beloved Potawatomies. On 14 December he left Council Bluffs for Westport. Since the river was frozen he travelled by horseback to Independence and thence to St Louis by stage, where he arrived on New Year's Eve. His journey had lasted nine months.

Chapter Five

Back to the Flatheads

Father De Smet had promised the Flatheads that he would return to the Rocky Mountains and bring with him new missionaries. But this required funds. He approached his Superior. In a letter dated 1 May 1841, however, he writes:

> My heart sank within me on learning from him that the funds at his disposal for missionary purposes would not enable him to afford me scarcely half of what was necessary for the outfit and other expenses of an expedition. The thought that the undertaking would have to be given up, that I would not be able to redeem my promise to the poor Indians, pierced my very heart and filled me with the deepest sorrow.
>
> *C and R, p. 38.*

He would have to find his own funds. So he went to New Orleans on a begging expedition. In the course of a few months he succeeded in raising the necessary amount from that city and other cities such as Philadelphia, Cincinnati and Kentucky.

When the snow of winter melted and the green of spring reappeared, Father De Smet set off from St Louis on the steamer *Oceana* on 24 April 1841. He was accompanied by two priests, Father Nicholas Point and Father Gregory Mengarini, and three brothers. Father Mengarini, recently from Rome, was specially selected by the Father General himself for this mission. He was famous for his skill in medicine and in music. Father Nicholas Point, a young Englishman, was an accomplished draughtsman. The brothers were also skilled: one as a blacksmith, one as a carpenter, and the third a tinner and a sort of general factotum.

Seven days later, on 30 April, they arrived at the frontier town of Westport (Kansas). The 400-mile journey took this length of time because, though the ice had melted, the water was still low, the sandbanks close together and the snags so numerous that the boats could not make great headway. They landed on the right bank of the Missouri.

They took refuge in an abandoned little cabin, made of bull-rushes, where a poor Indian woman had died a few days before. They stayed there until 13 May. At Westport they joined a party of sixty travellers heading for the California gold rush. Several days were spent in loading the wagons and mules before the caravan could start.

> I hope that the journey will end well; it has begun badly. One of our wagons was burned on the steamboat; a horse ran away and was never found; a second fell ill, which I was obliged to exchange for another at a loss. Some of the mules took fright and ran off, leaving their wagons; others, with the wagons have been stalled in the mud. We have faced perilous situations in crossing deep declivities, deep ravines, marshes, and rivers.
>
> *C and R, p. 279.*

After five days' march they reached the banks of the Kansas River. Here they met those of their companions who had travelled by water. Two relatives of a grand Kansa chief had come twenty miles to meet them. One of them helped their horses to cross the river by swimming in front of them. The other announced their arrival to the principal men of the tribe who were waiting for them on the opposite bank.

> Our baggage, wagons and men crossed in a pirogue, or hollowed tree trunk, which, at a distance, looked like one of those gondolas that glide through the streets of Venice. As soon as the Kansas understood that we were going to encamp on the banks of the Soldier's River, which is only six miles from the village, they galloped rapidly away from our caravan, disappearing in a cloud of dust, so that we had scarcely pitched our tents when the great chief presented himself with six of his bravest warriors, to bid us welcome. After having made me sit down on a mat spread on the ground, he, with much solemnity, took from his pocket a portfolio containing the honourable titles, bestowed by the American Congress, that gave him a right to our friendship, and

placed them in my hands. I read them, and having, with the tact
of a man accustomed to the etiquette of savage life, furnished
him the means of smoking the calumet, he made us accept for
our guard the two braves who had come to meet us. Both were
armed like warriors, one carrying a lance and a buckler, and the
other a bow and arrows, with a naked sword and a collar made
of the claws of four bears which he had killed with his own
hand. These two braves remained faithful at their post during the
three days and three nights that we had to wait the coming up of
the stragglers of the caravan. A small present which we made
them at our departure secured us their friendship.

On the 19th we continued our journey to the number of
seventy souls.

C and R, p. 280.

Father De Smet and Father Point deviated from the route to visit a
village of the Kansas. The women alone seemed to be doing any
work. They had placed their papooses tightly swathed and fastened
to a board to prevent them being injured. The men spent their time
lolling in their wigwams, seemingly beautifying themselves. No
menial tasks for warriors. They bore the quiet vacant composure
that distinguished an Indian warrior when his faculties were not
required for any of the greater purposes of his existence. Or the
men would spend their time gambling on the 'game of the hand'.
One of the players would enclose a gravel stone in the cup of his
hands by placing the palms together. After several revolutions he
would suddenly part his palms. If his opponent guessed in which
palm the stone was he won. Large amounts were often wagered on
this play – arrows, bows, robes, even one's scalp. Unlike most
other tribes where the men let the hair on their heads grow long,
these men had their heads shaven, except for a well curled tuft on
the crown, destined to be wreathed with a warrior's plume of eagle
feathers.

Do you wish to have an idea of a Kansa satisfied with himself in
the highest degree? Picture him to yourself with rings of vermilion encircling his eyes, with white, black or red streaks running
down his face, a fantastic necklace, adorned in the centre with a
large medal of silver or copper, dangling on his breast; bracelets
of tin, copper or brass; a cincture of white around his waist, a
cutlass and scabbard, embroidered shoes or moccasins on his

feet; and, to crown it all, a mantle, it matters not for the colour, thrown over the shoulders and falling around the body in such folds or drapery as the wants or caprice of the wearer may direct, and the individual stands before you as he exhibited himself to us.

C and R, p. 283.

On 3 July they reached Independence Rock, one day before Independence Day. In a letter to his Provincial, headed 'Sweetwater River, July 4, 1841', Father De Smet wrote:

We find only barren mounds on all sides, filled with cliffs formed by the falling of the waters and serving as dens to an infinite number of rattlesnakes and other venomous reptiles.

C and R, p. 1350.

As in the preceding year, the missionaries followed the Platte River until reaching the first spurs of the Rocky Mountains. The immensity of that river and its verdant, graceful banks was in cheerful contrast to the lugubrious desert. But every now and then a destructive cyclone would devastate these enchanted shores. In a letter to Father Verhagen dated 14 July 1841, Father De Smet gives a marvellous description of a cyclonic summer storm so dreaded in the central prairies.

Fine weather is common in this temperate climate. However, it happens sometimes, though but seldom, that the clouds floating with great rapidity open currents of air so violent as suddenly to chill the atmosphere and produce the most destructive hail storms. I have seen some hailstones of the size of a turkey's egg. It is dangerous to be abroad during these storms. A Cheyenne Indian was lately struck by a hailstone and remained senseless for an hour. Once as the storm was raging near us, we witnessed a sublime sight. A spiral abyss seemed to be suddenly formed in the air. The clouds followed each other into it with such velocity that they attracted all objects around them, whilst such clouds as were too large and too far distant to feel its influence turned in the opposite direction. The noise we heard in the air was like that of a tempest. On beholding the conflict we fancied that all the winds had been let loose from the four points of the compass. It is very probable that if it had approached much nearer, the whole caravan would have made an ascension into the clouds; but the Power that confines the sea to its boundaries and has said: 'Hitherto shalt thou come,' etc., watched over our preservation. The spiral column moved majestically toward the north, and alighted on the surface of the Platte. Then another scene was exhibited to our view. The waters, agitated by its powerful action, began to spin round with a frightful noise, all the river boiled, and, more quickly than a rainstorm falls from the clouds, it rose toward the whirl in the form of an immense cornucopia whose undulant movements were like the action of a serpent endeavouring to raise itself to the sky. The column appeared to measure a mile in height; and such was the violence of the winds which came down in a perpendicular direction that in the twinkling of an eye the trees were torn and uprooted and their boughs scattered in every direction. But what is violent does not last. After a few minutes the frightful visitation ceased. The column, not being able to sustain the weight at its base, was dissolved almost as quickly as it had been formed. Soon after the sun reappeared; all was calm and we pursued our journey.

C and R, p. 1352.

In a letter from Hell Gate, dated 21 September 1841, to his Provincial and to his sister Rosalie in Termonde, Father De Smet recalls the danger and hazards in crossing rivers.

The first which we found it very hard to cross was the South Fork of the Platte.

The crossing of a river, with a retinue such as ours, was no small affair. Commending ourselves to God, we ordered the drivers to whip up the mules; the animals tugged and strained valiantly and gained the other bank.

The second difficult passage was over the North Fork, which is less wide, but deeper and more rapid than the Southern. We had crossed the latter in carts. Having mustered a little more courage, we determined to cross the North Fork on horseback. We were induced to do so, on seeing our hunter drive before him a horse on which his wife was mounted, whilst at the same time he was pulling a colt that carried a little girl but one year old. To hold back under such circumstances would have been a disgrace for the missionaries. We therefore resolved to go forward. It is said that we were observed to grow pale, and I am inclined to believe we did; yet, after our horses had for some time battled against the current, we reached the opposite shore in safety, though our clothes were dripping wet. Here we witnessed a scene which, had it been less serious, might have excited laughter. The largest wagon was carried off by the force of the current, in spite of all the efforts, shouts and cries of the men, who did all they could to keep themselves from being drowned. Another wagon was literally turned over. One of the mules showed only his four feet on the surface of the water, and the others went adrift entangled in the gears. Here, a horse reached the shore without a rider; further on, two riders appeared on the same horse; finally the good Brother Joseph dancing up and down with his horse, and Father Mengarini clinging to the neck of his, and looking as if he formed an indivisible part of the animal. After all our difficulties, we found that only one of the mules was drowned.

C and R, p. 308.

In mid July, two months after they had set out, they came within sight of the Rocky Mountains, towering into the clouds. Beyond those summits lay the tribes they were hoping to evangelise. The whole plain that they traversed for 1,500 miles after leaving Westport was a veritable Prairie Ocean.

The route followed was practically the same as that of 1840 as far as South Pass (7 July). From South Pass they followed the route of the Oregon Trail to Bear River, Soda Springs (13 August), across the dividing ridge, then down the Portneuf River to Fort Hall, on the banks of the Snake. From Sweetwater River they headed for the heights of the Far West. They reached a summit from which Oregon Territory lay before them. They then ascended towards the Pacific, crossing first the Little and Big Sandy rivers. The caravan then got lost for three days, till they finally reached Green River. After resting for two days on the shores of the Green River, the caravan started again in the direction of Fort Hall, situated on Snake River and north of Salt Lake.

It was not only crossing rivers that proved hazardous and difficult.

Our train of wagons then worked its way through a labyrinth of valleys and mountains. opening, as we went, a trail in the depth of a ravine, or through dense brush on the slope of a steep rock.

72

At this juncture the mules were taken out and hitched abreast, then every man's shoulder went to the wheels, and every inch of rope was requisitioned to steady the convoy on the edge of the chasm, to keep it from a too rapid descent! Yet all these precautions did not save us from many tumbles. Our Brothers, forced by circumstances to take the reins, would often find themselves, one on a mule's neck, another on his hind quarters, and a third under the fore feet of the animal, not knowing how they got there, and each time thanking God for a miraculous escape.

Those on horseback were accorded the same divine protection. During the journey Father Mengarini was six times thrown from his horse, Father Point almost as often, and once at full gallop I was pitched over my horse's head; yet none of us had so much as a scratch.

C and R, pp. 300-1.

After ten days of such travel they reached Bear River, which flowed through a beautiful valley. For eight more days they followed the horseshoe of the river before it fell into the Great Salt Lake. They finally reached Soda Springs. Father De Smet continues his narration.

On the evening previous to the departure of the camp from Soda Springs, I directed my course toward the fort (Fort Hall) to make a few necessary arrangements. The young Francis Xavier was my only companion. We were soon involved in a labyrinth of mountains, and about midnight we were on the summit of the highest chain. My poor guide, being able to see nothing by the weak light of the moon but frightful precipices, was so pitifully embarrassed that after veering about for a while, like a weathercock, he confessed himself lost. That was not a place, nor was it a time, to wander at random; I therefore took what I considered the only alternative, that of waiting for the morning sun to extricate us from our embarrassment.

Wrapped up in my blanket and with my saddle for a pillow, I stretched myself upon the rock, and immediately fell into a sound sleep. Early the next morning we descended by a small cleft in the rocks, which the obscurity of the night had concealed, and arrived on a plain watered by the Portneuf, one of the tributaries of Snake River. We trotted or galloped over 50 miles in the course of the day. The whole way presented evident remains of volcanic eruptions; piles and veins of lava were visible in all directions, and the rocks bore marks of having been in a state of fusion. The river, in its whole length, exhibits a succession of beaver ponds, emptying into each other by a narrow opening in each dyke, thus forming a fall of between three and six feet. All these dykes are of stone, evidently the work of the water (the trappers call them the work of the beaver) and of the same character and substance as the stalactites found in some caverns.

We arrived late in the evening, within half a mile of the Fort (Hall), but being unable to see our way in the darkness, and not knowing where we were, we encamped for the night among the bushes, near the margin of a small brook and amid a cloud of mosquitoes.

C and R, pp. 303–4.

Mosquitoes were the bane of Father De Smet's life.

And what shall I say of mosquitoes? I have suffered so much from them, that I cannot leave them unnoticed ... There is no defence against their darts but to hide under a buffalo skin, or wrap one's self up in some stuff which they cannot pierce, and run the risk of being smothered. When green or rotten wood can be procured, they may be driven away by the smoke, but in such case the traveller himself is smoked, and in spite of all he can do his eyes are filled with tears.

C and R, p. 1392.

They arrived at Fort Hall on the feast of the Assumption, 15 August. At Fort Hall they met the advance guard of the Flatheads, who had come over 300 miles to meet the Black Robes. Among them was Young Ignace, Father De Smet's guide of the previous year. Ignace had been running for four days without food or drink in order to be the first to welcome the missionaries.

Three days after their arrival at Fort Hall the missionaries left the caravan and headed north to the main Flathead encampment in Bitter Root Valley. From there they ascended Snake River as far as the mouth of Henry's Fork. In crossing the Snake River a huge disaster was only just prevented.

I mentioned before that great danger awaited us on Snake River.

74

This stream being much less deep and wide than the other two, and having such limpid waters that the bottom can everywhere be seen, could only be dangerous to incautious persons. It sufficed to keep our eyes open, for any obstacle could easily be distinguished and avoided. But whether it was owing to want of thought or attention, or to the stubborn disposition of the team, Brother Charles Huet found himself all at once on the border of a deep precipice, too far advanced to return. Down went the mules, driver and vehicle, and so deep was the place that there scarcely appeared any chance to save them. Our hunter, at the risk of his life, threw himself into the river to dive after the poor brother, whom he had to pull out of the carriage. All the Flatheads who were with us tried to save the vehicle, the mules and the baggage. The baggage, with the exception of a few articles, was saved; the carriage was raised by the united effort of all the Indians, and set afloat but we lost what we considered the most safe, the team of the carriage. The gears had been cut to enable the mules to reach the shore, but it is said that these animals always perish when once they have had their ears under water. Thus we lost our three finest mules. This loss was to us very considerable.

C and R, p. 309.

From the mouth of Henry's Fork they steered their course toward the mountains, clouds of light vapour rising in spiral wreaths from their summits like smoke from hidden lodges, over a sandy plain furrowed by deep ravines, and covered with blocks of granite.

They continued across the most barren of all the mountain deserts. It abounded in wormwood, cactus and all such plants and herbs as are found on arid lands. With dismal monotony and startling variety the weird and uncanny shapes of cacti lifted their twisted trunks and green stumpy hands to block the way. The strange plant, which appeared to live without rain or soil, tempted the parched traveller with its lush greenness. What looked like open paths merely lured the trespasser into blind, impassable spine-defended areas from which retreat was often difficult. To be lost in the prickly pear flats was to die the death of the thief on the cross, pierced by nails and hemmed in with grotesque shapes of fiends. They circled, twisted and finally traced their way out of the bewildering trail. They had to resort to fishing for the support of life and the animals were compelled to fast and pine, for scarcely a mouth-

75

ful of grass could be found during the eight days it took them to cross the wilderness. They spent a day and a night without water. In the distance soared the colossal summits of the Rocky Mountains. The Three Tetons were about fifty miles to their right, with the Three Buttes thirty miles to their left.

On 30 August, four months after their departure from St Louis, they entered the Beaver Head Valley, where the Flatheads were encamped.

> As we approached the camp we saw one courier after another advancing. A gigantic Indian then appeared, coming toward us at full gallop. Cries of 'Paul! Paul!' were heard, and it was in fact Paul (Big Face), so named in baptism the year before. They thought him absent from the camp, but he had just returned, wishing himself to present us to his people. Toward nightfall an affecting scene took place. The neophytes – men, women, young men, and children in arms – struggled with one another to be the first to shake hands with us; our hearts were too full for utterance. It was a great day.
>
> *C and R, p. 305.*

On his first visit to the Flatheads De Smet had urged them to look about for a fertile tract of land where the tribe could settle. Instead of their encampments continually following in the wake of the roaming bison, they could have a base to retire to after the hunting season, complement with farming what they did not get from hunting, and experience the softening influence of home life. They would be drawn from idleness, learn economy, and unconsciously acquire the habits of civilisation. The suggestion was enthusiastically received. The Flatheads chose a suitable site twenty-eight miles up Bitter Root Valley.

The missionaries set off to inspect the site. They re-crossed the Divide to the valley of Deer Lodge Creek. They visited the well-known hot springs in the vicinity, and even boiled meat in one of them. They descended Deer Lodge Creek and Hellgate River to its junction with Bitter Root where the present town of Missoula now stands between Stevensville and Fort Owen.

They ascended about thirty miles up the Bitter Root Valley. The Bitter Root River, which further on becomes the Clark, watered this extraordinarily fertile region. The richness of the soil, the beauty of the situation, and the proximity of other tribes influenced the missionaries when they decided to make this place the seat of their mission. This became the location of St Mary's Mission, the first Catholic Indian Mission in the Pacific North West. It was to be modelled on the Paraguay 'reductions' (missions), established in South America in 1610.

They commenced work on it on 25 September 1841. In a letter to the Father Provincial, De Smet wrote:

Bitter Root, the Place selected for the first Reduction.
October 18th, 1841.

After a journey of four months and a half on horseback through the desert, and in spite of our actual want of bread, wine, sugar, fruit and all such things as we called the conveniences of life, we found our strength and courage increased.

C and R, p. 315.

Chapter 6

Missions of Rescue

One month after his arrival at St Mary's Mission, Father De Smet was obliged to leave his fellow-missionaries to go to Fort Colville on the Columbia River, about 300 miles north-west of the mission. The journey was undertaken with two objects in view.

First, the needs of the mission, which was in dire poverty. Brother Specht was clothed in a garment made of animal skins, a battered, wide, straw hat on his head, and one of the Fathers had been obliged to transform an Indian blanket into a cassock. Moreover, provisions for the winter, seeds for the spring crops, tools, agricultural implements, beeves, cows, in a word all that was needed for the establishment of a 'reduction', had to be purchased.

The second object of his journey was to visit the Kalispels (a tribe allied to the Pend d'Oreilles) who camped in the autumn on the borders of the Clark River.

On the eve of Father De Smet's departure he informed the Flatheads of his intentions. He requested them to procure some horses, and a small escort, in case he should meet with any of their enemies, the Blackfeet. They brought him seventeen horses; and ten young and brave warriors, who had already been often pierced with shot and arrows in different skirmishes, presented themselves to accompany him on his journey.

On the afternoon of 28 October 1841, escorted by the ten warriors, Father De Smet left St Mary's Mission and commenced the march. In his *Voyages aux Montagnes-Rochenses* he recounts the journey.

We made about forty miles down the valley of the Bitter Root. That day we met no one but a solitary hunter, who was carrying a buck, the half of which he offered us with great eagerness.

This furnished us with an excellent supper, and a good breakfast for the next morning. The 29th, snow fell in large flakes, notwithstanding which we continued our march. We crossed, in the course of the day, a fine stream, without a name – the same one which the famous travellers Lewis and Clark ascended in 1805 on their way to the section of country occupied by the tribe of the Nez Percés. I will call it the river of St Francis Borgia. Six miles further south we crossed the beautiful river of St Ignatius (Hell Gate). It enters the plain of the Bitter Root – which we shall henceforward call St Mary's – by a beautiful defile, commonly called, by the mountaineers or Canadian hunters, the Hell Gate; for what reason, however, I know not. These gentlemen have frequently on their lips the words devil and hell; and it is perhaps on this account that we heard so often these appellations. Be not then alarmed when I tell you that I examined the Devil's pass, went through the Devil's gate, rowed on Satan's stream, and jumped from the Devil's horns. The 'rake', one of the passes, the horns, and the stream, really deserve names that express something horrible – all three are exceedingly dangerous. The first and second, on the Missouri, on account of the innumerable snags which fill their beds, as there are entire forests swallowed up by the river. The third pass of which I spoke, adds to the difficulties of the others a current still stronger. A canoe launched into this torrent flies over it with the speed of an arrow, and the most experienced pilot trembles in spite of himself. Twice did the brave Iroquois, who conducted our light canoe, exclaim: 'Father, we are lost'; but a loud cry of 'Courage – take courage John, confide in God, keep steady to the oar', saved us in that dangerous stream, drew us out from between the horns and threatening teeth of this awful 'rake'.

We spread our skins on the borders of a little river at the foot of a high mountain, which we were to cross the next day, having traversed St Mary's valley, a distance of about forty miles. This valley is from four to seven miles wide and above 200 long. It has but one fine defile, which serves as the entrance to, and issue from, the valley. The mountains which terminate it on both sides appear to be inaccessible; they are piles of jagged rocks, while the Norwegian pine grows on those that are covered with earth, giving them a very sombre appearance, particularly in the autumn, in which season the snows begin to fall. They abound in bucks, buffalo and sheep, whose wool is as white as snow and as fine as silk; also in all kinds of bears, wolves, panthers and carcajoux (an animal with short paws, some four feet long and remarkably powerful; when he has killed his prey, deer, antelope or bighorn, he tears off a piece of skin big enough to stick his head through after a fashion of a hood, and thus drags it off to his den). There are also found tiger cats, wild cats, and whistlers, a species of mountain rat. The moose is found here, but seldom caught, on account of its extraordinary vigilance, for on the slightest rustling of a branch it leaves off eating, and will not return to its food for a long time afterward.

Amongst the most remarkable birds were distinguished the Nun's eagle (so called by travellers on account of the colour of its head, which is white, whilst the other parts of the body are black), the black eagle, buzzard, waterfowl, heron, crane, pheasant and quail.

The 30th, three horses were found to have strayed off while grazing freely during the night (a liberty that they rarely abuse) and we could not start until eleven o'clock in the morning. We then ascended a gap in the mountain. The two sides were very lofty and studded with large pines, all the branches of which were covered with a black and very fine moss, that hung in festoons, or in the shape of mourning garlands, and added to the already funereal appearance of this pass. We here filed off by a little path, scarce worthy, however, of the name, for a distance of six miles. The road was filled with large blocks of stone and trunks of trees, placed as if on purpose to render the pass difficult and impracticable. The summit once attained, we proceeded to cross a smiling little plain, called the Camas Prairies, where the Flatheads come every spring to dig up that nourishing root, which, together with the game they are able to procure, forms their chief nourishment. We very soon descended the mountain in a zigzag direction and reached a beautiful plain, which is watered by two rivers, the St Aloysius and St Stanislaus. They unite in this plain, whence they go to join the forks at Clark's otherwise called the Flathead River. This valley extends about ten miles. While the tents were being set up I perceived one of those formidable Blackfoot Indians in the act of hiding himself. I did not speak of it to my young companions, fearing that I might not be able to prevent a bloody struggle between them. I, however, took the precaution of having a good watch kept over our horses.

The next day was Sunday, a day of rest. I celebrated the holy sacrifice of the Mass, and baptised three little children of the Pointed Hearts' tribe, whose parents had joined us on the road.

The 1st of November – All Saints' Day – after having celebrated the holy sacrifice under a large poplar tree, we proceeded on our journey through a defile of about six miles. At the fort of Clark's Fork, we met two encampments of the Kalispel tribe, who, having heard of our approach, had come thither to see us. Men, women and children ran to meet us, and pressed our hands with every demonstration of sincere joy. The chief of the first camp was called Chalax. As we had a barren country ahead of us, he procured six bales of buffalo meat for us. I baptised twenty-four children in his little village, and one young woman, a Kootenai, who was dying. The chief of the second camp was named Hoytelpo; his band occupied thirty huts. I spent the night amongst them; and, although they had never seen me before, they knew all the prayers that I had taught the Flatheads on my first journey.

C and R, pp. 343–5.

The mystery was soon solved. Having heard the previous year of the arrival of a Black Robe in the mountains, the Kalispels sent an intelligent young Indian, possessing an excellent memory, to visit the Flatheads. In their camp he learned the prayers, the hymns, and the great truths of religion, and upon his return was made the apostle of the tribe. His instructions were handed on from one lodge to the other, and before the winter was over, more than half the tribe was Christian.

Overjoyed at the admirable attitude of these people, Father De Smet at once baptised the children and the sick of the tribe, and when taking leave of the Kalispels he promised to send a priest who would remain with them.

That morning we crossed a mountain and entered the great Camas plain. Wolves are very numerous and very ferocious here; last spring they carried off and devoured more than 40 of the Kalispels' horses. There is a boiling spring a short distance to the north-east. A mountainous defile ten miles long led us thence to the lovely Horse Prairie.

On the 3rd of November, we continued our march. We were on the borders of Clark's Fork, to which we were obliged to keep close during eight days, whilst we descended the country bordering the stream. Our path during a great part of the day was on the declivity of a lofty, rocky mountain; we were here obliged to climb a steep rough pass from 400 to 600 feet high. My courage failed at the first sight; it was impossible to remain on horseback, and on foot my weight of 211 pounds was no trifle. This, therefore, was the expedient to which I resorted: my mule Lizette was sufficiently docile and kind to allow me to grasp her tail, to which I held on firmly: crying at one moment aloud, and at other times making use of the whip to excite her courage, until the good beast conducted me safely to the very top of the mountain. Here I breathed freely for a while, and contemplated the magnificent prospect that presented itself to my sight. The windings of the river with the scenery on its banks were before me; on one side hung over our heads rocks piled on rocks in the most precipitous manner, and on the other stood lofty peaks crowned with snow and pine trees: mountains of every shape and feature reared their towering forms before us. It really was a fine view and one that was well worth the effort we made. On descending from this elevation I had to take new precautions. I preceded the mule, holding her by the bridle, while she moved cautiously down to the foot of the 'Bad Rock' (as it is called by the Indians), as though she feared stumbling and rolling with her master into the river which flowed beneath us.

At this place Clark's Fork runs through a narrow defile of rocky mountains. Wherever it is narrowed or intercepted by rocks it forms rapids, with falls and cascades, the noise of which, like that caused by a storm in the forest, is heard at a great distance.

We crossed a high mountain by a wild winding path. Several times whilst ascending the mountain I found myself on parapets of rocks, whence, thanks to my safe-footed mule, I retired in safety. Once I thought my career at an end. I had wandered from my companions, and following the path, I all at once came to a rocky projection which terminated in a point about two feet wide; before me was a perpendicular descent of three feet; on my left stood a rock as straight as a wall, and on my right yawned a precipice of about a thousand feet. You can conceive that my situation was anything but pleasant. The slightest false step would have plunged the mule and her rider into the abyss beneath. To descend was impossible, as on one side I was closed in by the rock, and suspended over a dreadful chasm on the other. My mule had stopped at the commencement of the descent, and not having any time to lose, I recommended myself to God, and as a last expedient sank my spurs deeply into the sides of my poor beast; she made one bold leap and safely landed me on another parapet much larger than that I had left.

On the 4th we entered a cedar and pine forest so dense that in its whole length we could scarcely see beyond the distance of twenty yards. Our beasts of burden suffered a great deal in it from the want of grass. We scarcely got through it after three days' march. It was a real labyrinth: from morning till night we did nothing but wind about to avoid thousands of trees, fallen from either fire, storms or age. This forest is a marvel of its kind. It would be difficult to find elsewhere, such gigantic trees. The cedar towers majestically in a wilderness of birch, alder, and beech. I measured one forty-two feet in circumference; another fallen cedar lay 200 feet along the ground. The branches of these colossi, interlaced above the birch and beech trees, form a canopy so dense that the sun's rays never reach the moss and lichen-covered earth.

C and R, pp. 346–50.

Upon emerging from the forest they caught a glimpse of Kalispel (Pend d'Oreille) Lake, with its islands and pine trees, its sloping shores, lined with wild ducks, its horizon of hills, one above the other, reaching up to summits of eternal snow. The lake was about thirty miles long and from four to seven miles wide. From Lake Kalispel, they spent eight hours in crossing a lofty mountain to Mill Creek, which runs into the Coliha River, and descended its valley to Fort Colville, on the Columbia, where they arrived on 15 November.

Father De Smet put on record some of his thoughts and feelings regarding his travels.

Certainly the life of a missionary has its trials and dangers; yet, however great these may be, he guards the serenity of his soul by centring his mind upon God. The desert is immense and the journey across it monotonous. The howling of the wolves, the grunting of the bear, and the screams of the wildcat and panther are heard, but only in the distance, for these beasts flee at the sight of man. Providence has provided admirably for the needs of those who inhabit the wilderness; buffalo, deer, gazelle, roebuck, bighorn, and elk roam here in thousands. Yet a fast of a day or two – I speak from experience – gives zest to appetite. Should a storm keep one awake, one sleeps better the following night. The sight of the enemy lying in wait to take one's life teaches more confidence in God; teaches one to pray well, and to keep his account with God in order.

Lavaille, p. 140.

After three days spent in repairing saddles and procuring provisions and tools and seeds for planting in the spring, Father De Smet left Fort Colville on 18 November. He returned to the Bitter Root by practically the same route.

On the 1st December, I found myself again in Horse Prairie, among the Kalispels, who had repaired thither from different parts of the mountains to see me as I returned. I stayed with them three days, instructing and exhorting them from morning till evening. My ten young Flatheads all assumed the functions of catechists, and went about it with a zeal which could be equalled only by the assiduity, attention and eagerness to learn of the savages who listened to them. On the 3rd, the feast of St Francis Xavier, I baptised sixty persons in this place, of whom thirteen were adults. The night preceding had been very stormy, as if hell had been unchained against us. A terrible gust of wind carried my tent away and cast it into the branches of a great pine. As I could not replace it, I found myself exposed for the rest of the night to hail, snow and rain; but there is a remedy for every evil; I found one under a thick buffalo robe, where I passed the time that was left me for sleep agreeably enough.

C and R, p. 358.

Father De Smet arrived at St Mary's Mission on 8 December, 'amid shooting and shouting from our good Indians running to meet us'. He brought back from Fort Colville several bushels of oats, wheat and potatoes for planting. Meanwhile construction work on building a permanent mission had been put well in hand. In a short time the Flatheads cut 2,000 to 3,000 stakes, and the three brothers, with no other tools than an axe, saw and auger, constructed a school and a church with pediment, colonnade and gallery, balustrade, choir, seats, etc. By St Martin's Day it had been decorated with mats and straw to cover the floor and ceiling and to hang around the walls. An organ too was installed. All this in the middle of a desert where, until recently, the name of God was unknown.

The church and the school were the centre of the Mission. The houses, workshops, stores and other buildings of common utility were grouped around the central points. The Indians were taught reading, writing and basic arithmetic, crafts to improve their standard of living and how to cultivate the land better. The only implements they had to turn the earth with were instruments of the most primitive construction, a few mattocks and poor spades, made from the shoulder blades of bison. A pointed stick of very hard wood is all they had used from time immemorial to dig up the *camas* root (like a white, insipid onion), the bitter root, the *wappatoo* (sagittafolia), the *caious* or biscuit root and other like vegetables. Agriculture afforded them an entirely new experience. Brother Claessens had already ploughed an enclosed piece of land adjoining the Mission, and in the spring he sowed the seeds and planted the potatoes that Father De Smet had brought.

The Indians, filled with wonder at this proceeding, thought it folly to plough and destroy grass that fed their horses and to bury seeds that were good to eat. In vain Brother Claessens assured them the seeds would rot in the ground and produce a hundredfold. No one believed him. When things began to sprout in the spring, the Flatheads remained whole days at a time perched upon a fence to see if what was told them would come true. Shouts of joy greeted the first blades that appeared above the ground. Before long the ears formed upon the tender stalks, and when summer came the enclosure resembled a huge basket overflowing with golden harvest. The crops were divided among the Indians, who now could appreciate the advantage derived from tilling the soil. The missionaries seized this occasion to explain to them the mystery of the resurrection of the body. Within a few months the new Mission was a centre of flourishing Christianity. The whole Flathead nation was converted.

Father De Smet and Father Mangarini were kept busy translating the catechism into the Flathead tongue. They spent many hours regularising the many unions that had already taken place where there was no concept of the unity and indissolubility of Christian marriage. This involved some heroic sacrifices on the part of the Indians. A mass baptism had been arranged. But nature, in the

85

form of a hurricane, intervened the day before, and the church windows were broken, large trees uprooted and three huts torn down. Even so, the ceremony went ahead, with 202 adults being baptised.

On Christmas Eve of that year (1841), Father De Smet reports that the Virgin Mary appeared to an orphan boy named Paul. In a letter to a colleague, headed 'Madison Forks, August 15, 1842', he writes:

> On Christmas Eve, a few hours before the midnight Mass, the village of St Mary was deemed worthy of a special mark of heaven's favour. The Blessed Virgin appeared to a little orphan boy named Paul, in the hut of an aged and truly pious woman. The youth, piety and sincerity of this child, joined to the nature of the fact which he related, forbade us to doubt the truth of his statement. The following is what he recounted to me with his own innocent lips: 'Upon entering John's hut, whither I had gone to learn my prayers, which I did not know, I saw some one who was very beautiful – her feet did not touch the earth, her garments were as white as snow; she had a star over her head, a serpent under her feet; and near the serpent was a fruit which I did not recognise. I could see her heart, from which rays of light burst forth and shone upon me. When I first beheld all this I was frightened, but afterwards my fear left me; my heart was warmed, my mind clear, and I do not know how it happened, but all at once I knew my prayers.' (To be brief I omit several circumstances.) He ended his account by saying that several times the same person had appeared to him whilst he was sleeping; and that once she had told him she was pleased that the first village of the Flatheads should be called 'St Mary'. The child had never seen or heard before anything of the kind; he did not even know if the person was a man or woman, because the appearance of the dress that she wore was entirely unknown to him. Several persons having interrogated the child on this subject, have found him unvarying in his answers. He continues by his conduct to be the angel of his tribe.
>
> *C and R, p. 359.*

In the spring of 1842 provisions and clothing again ran short. Unable this time to obtain them from Fort Colville, Father De Smet journeyed to Fort Vancouver near the mouth of the Columbia and about 1,000 miles west of St Mary's Mission. He set out on 13 April 1842. He went by Flathead Lake and the route of the previous year most of the way to Fort Colville, where he arrived at the beginning of May. Near the head of Flathead Lake he met a Kootenai band.

Crossing the beautiful plain near the Clark or Flathead River, called the Horse Prairie, I heard that there were 30 lodges of the Skalzi or Kootenai tribe at about two days' journey from us. I determined whilst awaiting the descent of the skiff, which could only start six days later, to pay them a visit, for they had never seen a priest in their lands before. Two half-breeds served as my guides and escorts on this occasion. We galloped and trotted all the day, travelling a distance of sixty miles. We spent a quiet night in a deep defile, stretched near a good fire, but in the open air.

The next day (April 14th), after having traversed several mountains and valleys, where our horses were up to their knees in snow, we arrived about three o'clock in sight of the Kootenai camp. They assembled immediately on my approach; when I was about twenty yards from them the warriors presented their arms, which they had hidden until then under their buffalo robes. They fired a general salute, which frightened my mule and made her rear and prance, to the great amusement of the savages. They then filed before me, giving their hands in token of friendship and congratulation. I observed that each one lifted his hand to his forehead after having presented it to me. I soon convoked the council in order to inform them of the object of my visit. They unanimously declared themselves in favour of my religion, and adopted the beautiful custom of their neighbours, the Flatheads, to meet night and morning for prayers in common. I assembled them that very evening for this object and gave them a long instruction on the principal dogmas of our faith. The next day I baptised all their little children and nine of their adults, previously instructed, amongst whom was the wife of an Iroquois, who had resided for thirty years with this tribe.

My visit could not be long; I left the Kootenai village about twelve o'clock, accompanied by twelve of these warriors and some half-blood Crees, whom I had baptised in 1840. They wished to escort me to the entrance of the large Flathead Lake, with the desire of giving me a farewell feast. The warriors had gone on ahead and dispersed in every direction, some to hunt and others to fish. The latter only succeeded in catching a single trout. The warriors returned in the evening with a bear, goose and six swan's eggs. The fish and goose were roasted before a good fire, and the whole mess was soon presented to me. Most of my companions preferring to fast, I expressed my regret at it, consoling them, however, by telling them that God would certainly reward their kindness to me. A moment after we heard the last hunter returning, who we thought had gone back to the camp. Hope shone on every countenance. The warrior soon appeared laden with a large elk, and hunger that night was banished from the camp. Each one began to occupy himself; some cut up the animal, others heaped fuel on the fire and prepared sticks and spits to roast the meat. The feast that had commenced under such poor auspices continued a great part of the night. The whole animal, excepting a small piece that was reserved for my breakfast, had disappeared before they retired to sleep. This is a sample of savage life. The Indian when he has nothing to eat does not complain, but in the midst of abundance he knows no moderation. The stomach of the Indians has always been a riddle to me.

The plain that commands a view of the lake is one of the most fertile in the mountainous regions. The Flathead River runs through it and extends more than 200 miles to the north-east. It is wide and deep, abounding with fish and lined with wood, principally with the cottonwood, aspen, pine and birch. There are beautiful sites for villages, but the vicinity of the Blackfeet must delay for a long while the good work, as they are only at two days' march from the great district occupied by these brigands, from whence they often issue to pay their neighbours predatory visits.

C and R, pp. 371–2.

At the Bay of the Kalispels Father De Smet was invited by the Coeur d'Alènes to visit their country. Accordingly, he made a detour. After crossing the Bitter Root Mountains he came to Coeur d'Alène Lake, where the tribe were encamped. It was a fertile, lovely valley stretching westward for hundreds of miles. Clusters of dark pines and cedars emerged from the green plain, in the centre of which lay the lake, well stocked with fish.

He was invited to the lodge of the chief, where he smoked the calumet and was given refreshments – 'scraps of dried meat, a black cake cooked of moss that tasted like soap and a glass of river water, all of which was as nectar and ambrosia to a man who had not tasted food since sunrise'.

He spent three days instructing them. He would have remained longer but the Indians were without provisions. There was scarcely enough for one person in the whole village. And he was still four days from Fort Colville.

Two days later he visited the Spokanes.

The Spokane River rises in the lake, and crosses the whole plain of the Coeur d'Alènes.

The river is wide, swift and deep in the spring, and contains, like all the rivers of Oregon, many rapid falls and cascades. The navigation of the waters of this immense territory is generally dangerous, and few risk themselves on them without being accompanied by experienced pilots. In descending Clark's River, we passed by some truly perilous and remarkable places, where the pilots have full opportunity to exhibit their dexterity and prudence. The rapids are numerous and the roar of the waters incessant, the current sweeping on at the rate of ten or twelve miles an hour; the rugged banks and projecting rocks creating waves resembling those of the troubled sea. The skilful pilot mounts the waves, which seem ready to engulf us, the canoe speeds over the agitated waters, and with the aid of the paddle, skilfully plied, bears us unharmed through numberless dangers.

The most remarkable spot on this river is called the *Cabinets*; it consists of four apartments, which you have hardly time to examine, as you are scarcely half a minute passing by them. Represent to yourself chasms between two rocky mountains of stupendous height, the river pent in between them in a bed of thirty or forty feet, precipitating itself down its rocky channel with irresistible fury, roaring against its jagged sides, and whitening with foam all around it. In a short space it winds in four different directions, resembling very much forked lightning. It requires very great skill, activity and presence of mind to extricate yourself from this difficult pass.

C and R, pp. 378–9.

He travelled to the sources of Mill Creek, which he then descended all the way to Fort Colville.

Toward evening we were on the borders of a deep impetuous torrent, having no other bridge than a tree which was rather slight and in constant motion from the rushing of the waters. We were fortunate enough to cross the trembling bridge without accident.

C and R, p. 382.

From time to time they perceived an Indian burial-ground, remarkable only for the posts erected on the graves, and hung with kettles, wooden plates, guns, bows and arrows, left there by the nearest relatives of the deceased – humble tokens of their grief and friendship. Pursuing the journey for three days over mountains and through dense forests, they arrived safely at Fort Colville.

The melting of the snows had caused complete flooding all around. It was not possible to travel overland to Fort Vancouver. They would have to use the Columbia River, one of the most dangerous, its course frequently impeded by rapids. De Smet waited while a barge was constructed. On 30 May he embarked on one of the barges of the Hudson Bay Company for Fort Vancouver. Numerous rapids and submerged rocks made navigation extremely dangerous.

I will not detain you with a description of the rapids, falls and cascades, which I saw on this celebrated river; for from its source in the mountains to the cascades it is but a succession of dangers. I will endeavour, however, to give you some idea of one of its largest rapids, called by the Canadian *voyageurs* the Great Dalles. A *dalle* is a place where the current is confined to a channel between two steep rocks, forming a prolonged narrow torrent, but of extraordinary force and swiftness.

C and R, p. 384.

On the second day, when near the Okinagan Dalles, he was told by the boatman that the pass was a bad one. Father De Smet chose to go ashore.

I had gone ashore and was walking along the bank, scarcely thinking what might happen; for my breviary, papers, bed, in a word, my little all, had been left in the barge. I had proceeded about a quarter of a mile, when seeing the barge-men push off from the bank and glide down the stream with an easy, careless air, I began to repent having preferred a path along the river's side, so strewn with fragments of rocks that I was compelled at every instant to turn aside or clamber over them. I still held on my course, when all at once the barge is so abruptly stopped that the rowers can hardly keep their seats. Regaining, however, their equilibrium, they ply the oars with redoubled vigour, but without any effect upon the barge. They are already within the power of the angry vortex; the waters are crested with foam; a deep sound is heard which I distinguish as the voice of the pilot encouraging his men to hold their oars – to row bravely. The danger increases every minute, and in a moment more all hope of safety has vanished. The barge, the sport of the vortex, spins like a top upon the whirling waters – the oars are useless – the bow rises – the stern descends, and the next instant all have disappeared. A death-like chill shot through my frame – a dimness came over my sight, as the cry 'we are lost!' rang in my ears, and told but too plainly that my companions were buried beneath the waves. Overwhelmed with grief and utterly unable to afford them the slightest assistance, I stood a motionless specta- tor of this tragic scene. All were gone, and yet upon the river's breast there was not the faintest trace of their melancholy fate. Soon after the whirlpool threw up, in various directions the oars, the capsized barge, and every lighter article it had contained. Here and there I beheld the unhappy barge-men vainly struggling in the midst of the vortex. Five of them sank never to rise again. My interpreter had twice touched bottom and after a short prayer was thrown upon the bank. An Iroquois saved himself by means of my bed; and a third was so fortunate as to seize the handle of an empty trunk, which helped him to sustain himself above water until he reached land.

C and R, pp. 386–7.

Father De Smet stopped at Fort Okinagan. He visited Fort Walla Walla and the Protestant mission at the Dalles. He passed the Dalles by boat but portaged around the cascades. He finally arrived safely at Fort Vancouver on the morning of 8 June. Fort Vancouver was the Hudson Bay Fur Company's principal fort west of the Rocky Mountains. The company had been founded in 1670 and had the monopoly of all trade. It collected furs from the inte- rior of the country and furnished the supplies for the various posts. The fort consisted of an enclosure 750 by 500 feet, surrounded by a pallisade over twenty feet in height, within which were some forty buildings, including a Catholic chapel. There was a village of sixty houses adjacent to it and a farm some nine square miles in extent, 1,500 acres or over being in cultivation.

He ascended the Williamette Valley to the Williamette Falls and travelled from there to the mission of St Paul where he met two Canadian missionaries, Father Blanchett and Father Demers, who had come to Oregon from Canada in 1838.

The territory of Oregon at the time comprised the whole region lying between the Rocky Mountains and the Pacific Ocean. Until the beginning of the nineteenth century, Oregon, to the white man, was an unexplored land. The Hudson Bay Company was the first to discover and exploit its richness.

But what were two priests in the vast work of converting a population of 200,000 souls, scattered over an area aggregating 900 miles in length and 600 miles in width? Plans for Christianising the country were discussed. Father De Smet realised the necessity of establishing a large mission in Western Oregon, where civilisation was rapidly advancing, and from where Catholicism would penetrate into the mountains. But alas! men and money were wanting. The Fathers from St Louis hardly sufficed for the needs of the new converts, and, moreover, that immense territory required not one but many missionaries. Sisters were also needed to undertake the Christian education of the children.

Father De Smet decided to go himself to his Superior to plead the cause of the Oregon Mission and resolved that, failing to obtain help in St Louis, he would seek it in Europe. A few days later the missionaries separated, as Father De Smet was eager to return to St Mary's with the provisions, tools and clothes he had purchased at Vancouver for the mission.

The wind being favourable, the sails of the barge were unfurled, and the sailors, plying their oars at the same time, took him up the Columbia as far as Fort Walla Walla, where he landed on 11 July.

Accompanied only by my interpreter we continued our land route to the 19th, through woods and immense plains. The 20th, I continued my journey over terrific mountains, steep rocks, and through apparently impenetrable forests. I could scarcely believe that any human being had ever preceded us over such a road. Thence northerly across the Nez Percé and Spokane deserts to the Couer d'Alène Lake. Thence via St Joseph River and over the mountains to Missoula River. At the end of four days' journey, replete with fatigue and difficulties, we reached the borders of the Bitter Root River. On the evening of July 27th I had the happiness of arriving safely at St Mary's, and of finding my dear brethren in good health.

C and R, p. 390.

Father Point was away. He had accompanied the Flatheads on their summer hunting expedition. Father Mengarini had remained in the camp with the old people and children left behind.

Father De Smet had been strongly advised by Father Blanchett, by the Governor of the Hudson Bay Company, Dr John McLoughlin, and others to return to St Louis for personnel and material succour for the missions. He arranged for the commencement of two new missions: one with Father Mengarini, among the Kalispels of the Bay, and another among the Couer d'Alènes with Father Point on his return from the hunting expedition, along with Brother Huet.

On 29 July Father De Smet set off, for the fourth time, to cross the dangerous American desert, through a region infested by thousands of hostile Indians, to return to St Louis in search of recruits for the new missions. He set out first to join Father Point and the Flathead hunters. Accompanied by ten Indians to serve as guides and hunters, he ascended the Bitter Root River, to its source.

On 1 August, having clambered up a high mountain, they planted a cross on its very summit, near a beautiful spring, one of the sources of the Missouri. The next day, after a forced march, they joined the camp of the hunters where they had such news to share, so many interesting facts to communicate to each other, that they sat up a greater part of the night. They spent 2–15 August in the plain of the Three Forks with the Flatheads.

On 15th August, the Feast of the Assumption, I offered up the sacrifice of the Mass in a noble plain, watered by one (the Madison) of the three streams that form the headwaters of the Missouri, to thank God for all the blessings he had bestowed on us during this last year. I had the consolation of seeing 50 Flatheads approach the holy table in so humble, modest and devout manner, that to my perhaps partial eye, they resembled angels more than men.

On 16 August Father De Smet set off for St Louis, following much the same route as he did in 1840. Leaving Father Point and the Flathead camp on the Madison River, with twelve Flatheads he travelled in three days a distance of 150 miles, crossing two mountain chains in a section frequently visited by the Blackfeet warriors, without however, encountering one of them. After a few days' rest with a friendly tribe they set out for the Crows. He was escorted to the Crow country by the twelve Flatheads and had as travelling companions an Iroquois by the name of Ignatius, and a Cree half-blood by the name of Gabriel.

The Crows spied us from afar, and when they recognised us cried out 'the Black Robe! the Black Robe!' Men, women, and children to the number of about 3,000 poured out of their huts like bees out of a hive. My entry into the village occasioned a wild scene, of which I found myself, *ex abrupto*, the principal actor. The chiefs and highest braves, numbering about fifty in all, in gala attire, suddenly pressed around me, impeding my passage, one pulling me to the right, another to the left; a third held my cassock, and an athlete wished to carry me, all talking at once and appearing to be quarrelling.

Not understanding the language, I wondered if I should laugh or be serious. Happily, the interpreter relieved my embarrassment, telling me that this tumult was but an expression of politeness and high regard for my person. All solicited the honour of feeding and lodging the Black Robe. Acting upon the interpreter's advice, I chose my host. The others immediately fell back as I followed the chief into his lodge. The social calumet, symbol of Indian unity and brotherhood, was kept lighted and passed around to the entire assembly.

One of the chiefs testified a special friendship for me. 'It is to thee, Black-gown,' said he to me, 'that I owe all my glory in the victories I have gained over my enemies.' His language astonished me greatly, and I begged him to explain. Without delay he took from his neck his Wah-kon, or medicine-bag, wrapped in a bit of kid. He unrolled it, and displayed to my wondering view the remnant of the matches I had given him in 1840! 'I use them,' said he, 'every time I go to battle. If the mysterious fire appears at the first rubbing, I dart upon my enemies, sure of obtaining victory.' I had considerable difficulty in disabusing their minds of this singular superstition.

C and R, pp. 396, 1036.

Father De Smet continues:

These Indians (Crows) have one thing in their favour upon which I base great hopes. So far they have resisted the efforts of American merchants to introduce intoxicating liquors into their tribe. 'What is your fire-water good for?' said the chief. 'It only does evil. It burns the throat and stomach and makes a bear of a man: he bites, growls, yells, and finally falls down like a dead body. Take this liquor to our enemies; they will kill each other, leaving their wives and children in a pitiable condition. We do not want whisky. We are crazy enough without it.'

I was in the village of the Crows when the news was brought that two of their most distinguished warriors had fallen victim to the rage and cruelty of the Blackfeet. The heralds or orators went round the camp, proclaiming in a loud voice the circumstances of the combat and the tragic end of the two brave men. A gloomy silence prevailed everywhere, only interrupted by a band of mourners, whose appearance alone was enough to make the most insensible heart bleed, and rouse to vengeance the entire nation. This band was composed of the mothers of the two unfortunate warriors who had fallen, their wives carrying their new-born infants in their arms, their sisters, and all their little children. The unhappy creatures had their heads shaven and cut in every direction; they were gashed with numerous wounds whence the blood constantly trickled. In this pitiable state they rent the air with their lamentations and cries, imploring the warriors of their nation to have compassion on them – to have compassion on their desolate children – to grant them one last favour, the only cure for their affliction, and that was, to go at once and inflict signal vengeance on the murderers. They led by the bridle all the horses that belonged to the deceased. A Crow chief mounting immediately the best of these steeds, brandished his tomahawk in the air, proclaiming that he was ready to avenge the deed. Several young men rallied about him. They sang together the war-song, and started the same day, declaring that they would not return empty-handed (viz: without scalps).

On the 25th I bade adieu to my faithful companions, the Flatheads, and the Crows. Accompanied by the Iroquois Ignatius, a Cree half-breed named Gabriel, and by two brave Americans, who, although Protestants, wished to serve as guides to a Catholic missionary, I once more plunged into the arid plains of the Yellowstone, infested with wild tribes. This desert is undoubtedly dangerous, and has been the scene of more tragic deeds, combats, stratagems and savage cruelties, than any other region. It is the battleground where the Crows, the Blackfeet, Sioux, Cheyenne, Assiniboins, Aricaras, and Minnetarees, fight out their interminable quarrels, avenging and revenging, without respite, their mutual wrongs.

After six days' march, we found ourselves upon the very spot where a combat had recently taken place. The bloody remains of ten Assiniboins who had been slain three days before, were scattered here and there – almost all the flesh eaten off by the wolves and carnivorous birds At the sight of these mangled limbs – of the vultures that soared above their heads, and the region round me, which had so lately resounded with the savage cries of more savage men, engaged in mutual carnage – I own that the little courage I thought I possessed seemed to fail me entirely, and give place to a secret terror, which I sought in vain to stifle or conceal from my companions. We observed in several places the fresh tracks of men and horses, leaving no doubt in our minds as to the proximity of hostile parties; our guide even assured me that he thought we were already discovered, but by continuing our precautions he hoped we might perhaps elude their craftiness and malicious designs, for the savages very seldom make their attacks in open day.

The following is the description of our regular march until the 10th September. At daybreak we saddled our horses and pursued our journey; at 10 o'clock we breakfasted in a suitable place, that would offer some advantage in case of an attack. After an hour and a half or two hours' rest, we resumed our march a second time, always trotting our horses, until sunset, when we unsaddled them to dine and sup; we then lighted a good fire, hastily raised a little cabin of branches, to induce our ever watchful foes, in case they pursued us, to suppose that we had encamped for the night; for as soon as the inimical videttes discover anything of the kind, they make it known by a signal to the whole party. They then immediately assemble and concert the plan of attack. In the meantime, favoured by the darkness, we pursued our journey quietly until ten or twelve o'clock at night, and then, without fire or even shelter, each one disposed himself as well as he might, for sleep as best he could. We were in a country where you waste no time in taking off your shoes;

you wrap your buffalo robe around you, the saddle serves as a pillow, and thanks to the fatigues of a long journey of about 40 miles under a burning sun, you have scarcely laid your head upon it before you are asleep.

About 10 September they reached Fort Union at the Missouri mouth of the Yellowstone.

The American gentlemen who carry on the Assiniboin fur trade at Fort Union, at the mouth of the Yellowstone, received me with great politeness and kindness. I rested there during three days. A journey so long and continuous, through regions where the drought had been so great that every sign of vegetation had disappeared, had very much exhausted our poor horses. The 1,800 miles that we had yet to travel were not to be undertaken lightly. After having well considered everything, I resolved to leave my horses at the fort, and to trust myself to the impetuous waters of the Missouri in a skiff, accompanied by Ignatius and Gabriel. The result was most fortunate, for on the third day of our descent, to our great surprise and joy, we heard the puffing of a steamboat. It was a real God-send to us; accordingly, our first thought was to thank God, in all the sincerity of our hearts. We soon beheld her majestically ascending the stream. It was the first boat that had ever attempted to ascend the river in that season of the year, laden with merchandise for the Fur Company. Four gentlemen from New York, proprietors of the boat, invited me to enter and remain on board. I accepted with unfeigned gratitude their kind offer of hospitality; the more so, as they assured me that several war-parties were lying in ambush along the river. On entering the boat I was an object of great curiosity – my black gown, my missionary cross, my long hair, attracted attention. I had thousands of questions to answer and many long stories to relate about my journey.

I have but a few words to add. I baptised some fifty little ones, principally in the forts. The waters were low, the sandbanks and snags everywhere numerous, the boat consequently encountered many obstacles in her passage. We were frequently in great danger of perishing. Her keel was pierced by pointed rocks, her sides rent by the snags. Twenty times the paddle wheels had been broken to pieces. The pilot's house had been carried away in the tempest; the whole cabin would have followed if it had not been made fast by a large cable. Our boat appeared to be little more than a mere wreck, and in this wreck, after forty-six days' navigation from the Yellowstone, we arrived safely at St Louis.

On the last Sunday of October, at twelve o'clock, I was kneeling at the foot of St Mary's Altar, in the Cathedral, offering up my thanksgiving to God for the signal protection he had extended to his poor, unworthy servant. From the beginning of April I had travelled 5,000 miles. I had descended and ascended the dangerous Columbia River. I had seen five of my companions perish in one of those life-destroying whirlpools, so justly dreaded by those who navigate that stream. I had traversed the Williamette, crossed the Rocky Mountains, passed through the country of the Blackfeet, the desert of the Yellowstone, and descended the entire length of the Missouri to St Louis, and in all these journeys I had not received the slightest injury.

C and R, pp. 401–2.

Chapter 7

The Oregon Missions

The harvest in Oregon was rich, but there were not enough men; money was needed and this the St Louis Fathers could not provide. 'We are up to our eyes in debt,' wrote Father Van de Velde, 'and God alone knows how we shall be able to extricate ourselves. The assistance formerly received from Belgium and Holland has decreased, and our expenses increase in the measure our resources diminish.' (*Letter dated 10 January 1843.*)

Father De Smet again set about raising funds, and after publishing an account of his journeys, started a begging tour. Early in the year 1843 he went as far south as New Orleans and as far east as Boston soliciting funds for his work. He also visited Louisville, Cincinnati, Pittsburgh, Cumberland, Baltimore, Washington, Philadelphia and New York. By the end of the winter he had collected 5,000 dollars, a sum sufficient to defray the expenses of the journey of new missionaries and to purchase the necessities for the development of a mission. He had three recruits – Father Peter de Vos, Father Adrian Hocken, and Brother J B McGean. Father De Smet accompanied the little party on their way as far as Westport, going by the steamer *John Auld*.

Immediately after his return to St Louis in June 1843, Father De Smet made a second voyage to Europe on the disagreeable task of begging funds and personnel for the new missions just being started in the Rocky Mountains. He embarked at New York, on his fourth voyage cross the Atlantic. After a voyage of twenty-one days he landed in Ireland. He visited Cork and Dublin. Here he heard the great Irish nationalist and champion of freedom, Daniel O'Connell, speak.

From Ireland he crossed to Liverpool and London. From there he travelled through the principal cities of France, Italy, Holland

and Belgium. From Marseilles he passed to Genoa, the city of palaces, then to Leghorn and Civita Vecchia and Rome. He was in Rome for the first time. Father Roothaan, Father General of the Jesuits, kindly presented him to Pope Gregory XVI – 'who lent a paternal attention to my little narrative of the missions.' Father De Smet went on to tell the Pope that he had told Victor, chief of the Flatheads, about how Christ promised to St Peter and his successors that the gates of hell shall never prevail against his church. Attempts to overthrow the Church and its supreme pastors had lasted for over 1,800 years and the Church had survived all her enemies. At this point, Father De Smet went on:

> Victor hastily rose, full of animation, and said: 'Should our Great Father, the Great Chief of the Black Robes, be in danger, – you speak on paper (write) – send him a message in our name and invite him to our mountains. We will raise his lodge in our midst; we will hunt for him and keep his lodge provided, and will guard him against the approach of his enemies.'
>
> *C and R, p. 1340.*

Father De Smet comments that the Pope smiled at Victor's generosity and invitation. 'But then he said, with a seriousness of tone that has always lingered in my mind, "Truly, the time is at hand when we shall be forced to quit Rome."'

In 1848, the Pope (Pius IX) did, indeed, have to leave the Vatican and take refuge in Gaeta.

Five years later, in 1853, Victor was still going strong and still as attached to his faith as ever. In that year a Captain Mullan was undertaking a survey of the region. In a report to Washington on 14 September 1853 he wrote:

> When the guide and myself had reached the Flathead camp, three or four men met us at the entrance, and invited us to enter the lodge of the chief, Victor. They very kindly took care of our horses, unsaddling and watering them. As soon as the camp had heard of the arrival of a white man among them, the principal men of the tribe congregated in the lodge of the chief. When they had all assembled by a signal from their chief they offered up a prayer. This astonished me; it was something for which I had not been prepared. Every one was upon his knees and in the most

solemn and reverential manner offered up a prayer to God. For a moment I asked myself, was I among Indians? I could scarcely realise it. To think that these men should be thus imbued and so deeply too with the principles of religion, was to me overwhelming.

C and R, p. 1338.

A great tribute to Father De Smet and his colleagues.

Even later, in 1869, a Report of the Commissioners of Indian Affairs, wrote:

The missionary labours of the Reverend Fathers have not been in vain, for many of them are exemplary Christians. I may here remark that the labours of the Reverend Fathers have been very arduous and difficult. Poor and unaided, they have established their mission, built their church and school, and maintained themselves solely by their own exertion. Not only this, but they have been, at the same time, priest, physician and benefactor to these tribes. ... Still more, in conjunction with the noble Sisters of Charity they educate, clothe and feed the orphans of these tribes without fee or reward. Without their aid and influence, the wrongs inflicted upon these people would long since have driven them to war.

C and R, p. 1227.

While in Rome Father De Smet became much alarmed on hearing that plans were afoot to make him a bishop. With the aid of Father General he managed to have this honour bestowed on Father Blanchett, of the Oregon missions, who was his senior both in years and as a missionary in the Rocky Mountains.

In his fund-raising efforts Father De Smet pointed out the enormity of the task before the missionaries.

Pray that the Lord of such a rich harvest may send us numerous fellow labourers; for in so extensive a field we are but five, and beset with so many dangers, that at the dawn of day we have often reason to doubt whether we will live to see the sun go down.

In our wilds, a man takes his life in his hands, not because the climate is unhealthy – far from it; if men died only of sickness, they would live to an advanced age; but because of rivers, forest, and prairie, of fires, and the guns and shafts of savages. Of every hundred men who journey through our country, not ten escape them.

C and R, p. 389.

Father De Smet was successful in collecting almost 30,000 dollars in cash, together with a large amount of supplies for the missions, and most importantly, labourers for the rich harvest that awaited in the vineyard.

On 12 December 1843 Father De Smet sailed from Antwerp on the two-masted brig *Infatigable* to return to the Columbia River via Cape Horn at the tip of South America. He was accompanied by four priests, a brother and six Sisters of Notré Dame de Namur. They descended the Schelde down to Flushing, where they were detained for twenty-eight days by contrary winds. On 8 January an east wind sprang up to take them out to the North Sea. They waited for a Flushing pilot to steer the vessel between the many sandbars and numerous surrounding craft. Eventually the pilot appeared the next day, not in a very fit state to do any steering. They captain was not pleased. From the deck they watched other vessels, their sailors all singing, get away before them. There was a further delay as one of the boats, taking emigrants to Texas, collided with them. In the afternoon the vessel put to sea and swiftly passed Rammekens' Roads. In the evening the pilot handed over the vessel to the brig's pilot, and soon the vessel's sails caught the wind on the North Sea. The motion of the sea soon had most of the ship, including Father De Smet, laid low with seasickness. They passed Calais Light. On 12 January they passed the Isle of Wight, then Plymouth and finally the lighthouse off the Lizard, to brave the mountainous waves of the Atlantic. On 20 January they passed the island of Madeira. The next day the sea was calm and flat as a mirror, bringing some respite from seasickness. On 1 February they passed the island of San Antonio, of the Cape Verde group. Clouds of flying fish provided amusement, several even landing on deck. On 15 February they crossed the Line, duly celebrated with traditional ceremonies to Neptune. The thermometer showed a pleasing 88°F. The constellations of the Northern Hemisphere yielded to the brighter ones of the Southern Hemisphere, notably the Southern Cross. On 16 February they passed the Falkland Islands. They rounded Cape Horn without seeing it. In the night of 20 February two icebergs, 100 feet high, came dangerously near to the ship. An albatross wheeled constantly over them. The stormy petrel, too, kept them company.

Soon after passing the Horn they encountered a succession of terrific storms. Several of the sails were torn to shreds and the brig was the plaything of the winds and waves. It was a terrible time, but the danger was met with consummate skill by the crew and with calm resignation by the passengers.

In his *Letters and Sketches*, Father De Smet describes the scene.

A tempest is truly a sublime spectacle, but the description is infinitely more agreeable than the reality. If there had been less of the frightful about it, probably I should have enjoyed it more. Such was the roaring of the winds and waves that the captain's voice, even through the trumpet, could hardly be distinguished. The waves rose in pyramids around us, and masses of water, torn off by the fury of the winds, were hurled upon us in floods that filled the deck with foam. Never in any of my voyages had I seen such evidence of the might of wind and water, nor of the admirable manner in which a vessel resists the fury of the elements.

C and R, p. 46.

The hurricane drove the ship almost upon the coast of Patagonia, but veered south in time to prevent a wreck. The ship was driven south to the 66° south latitude among the icebergs.

A favourable wind brought the ship back to the coast of Chile in sight of the Cape of Tres Monthes on 8 April. They had been at sea for three months and were anxious to get ashore. On 12 April they entered the beautiful bay of Valparaiso, the second city of Chile. Father De Smet went ashore to find suitable lodgings for them. The Sisters were invited to stay with a party of French nuns; Father De Smet and his companions lodged with some Jesuits from Buenos Aires. On 16 April the Fathers and Sisters set off in horse-drawn carriages for Santiago, the capital of Chile, an important centre for the Jesuits in South America, until their influence was curtailed during the suppression. 'The skill and swiftness with which these postilions take you along are really admirable.' The winding road took them up bare hills covered only with brush and enormous cactuses, with pretty, bright red flowers. At the foot of the Mapocho Mountains, in a beautiful fertile valley, lay the city of Santiago. Surrounding them were the snowy summits, rising 22,000 feet above sea level, of the Great Andes. It was 25 April.

After a short stay they returned to Valparaiso to re-embark on the *Infatigable* on 2 May. They made for Callas, the port of Lima, 500 leagues away. They reached the capital of Peru on 11 May. There was much to see of the civilisation built by the Jesuits and other Spanish missionaries over the past 300 years. While in Lima they felt three sharp earthquakes. In an earthquake in 1828, 1,000 lives had been lost. They were struck by the poverty of the people, amidst the gold and silver and other mineral mines. 'In Peru they walk on gold and silver and lack for bread.'

On 27 May they left the port of Lima. The south-east trade winds filled their sails and took them comfortably towards the Tropic of Cancer. Occasionally they were hit by squalls from every direction. On other occasions they were becalmed for days. Father De Smet refers to these miserable experiences. In a letter to his Provincial, headed 'Lima, May 26, 1844', he writes:

> Then an expression of discouragement and melancholy appears on the captain's face and on those of all the crew. It seems as if one were condemned to perish here. A blackened sea all around, a sombre sky above, and clouds on the horizon, like impenetrable obstacles, changing form every instant and calling to mind all kinds of phantoms; while the ship, like a weak toy upon the sea in torment, swelling and sinking unceasingly, rocks and rocks until the head and stomach both turn.
>
> *C and R, p. 435.*

In June they re-crossed the Equator. They bade farewell to the Magellanic Clouds and other constellations of the Southern Hemisphere. By July their provisions were running low. They were finally reduced to rice boiled in water and salt meat. However, their privation was relieved by joy when on 28 July they sighted the coast of Oregon. But scarcely had the first outburst of joy passed when the ominous sight of rolling breakers at the mouth of the Columbia River changed all to gloomy foreboding. This was the one enormous obstacle that stood in their path before the journey was ended – crossing the mouth of the 'great river of the west', where the most dangerous bar in all America blocked the entrance. The captain had no charts; he was totally unacquainted with the rocks and breakers that made the passage impracticable and dangerous. Cape Disappointment came into view.

The morning of 29 July was dark and gloomy, as were their

spirits. At about 10 o'clock the sky cleared and, surrounded by enormous breakers, they approached the mouth of the Columbia slowly, and with great care. The lead sounders reported seven fathoms, soon six, then five, four and a half, presently four.

At the shout of 'three', the vessel's minimum draft, all countenances were visibly discomposed ... At the cry of two and one half fathoms I felt annihilated ... Heaven was for us – the next cast of the lead showed four fathoms and the depth increased at every plunge until we heard 'no bottom'. We were safe. Without a chart or any knowledge of the Columbia we traversed, as if borne on angels' wings, this formidable river.

C and R, p. 440.

It was the end of July 1844 when the *Infatigable* finally anchored off Astoria, at the mouth of the Columbia River. On 2 August Father De Smet set off in a Chinook canoe, manned by nine Indians, for Fort Vancouver, to report his arrival to Dr John McLoughlin, Governor of the Hudson Bay Company, and Father Blanchett, who, meanwhile, had been made Bishop and Vicar General of the Oregon missions. Favoured by a good wind catching the two sheets spread for sails the canoe reached its destination the following evening.

Father De Smet met Dr McLoughlin, but Father, now Bishop, Blanchett was away at the mission of St Paul on the Williamette, a tributary of the Columbia. A messenger was at once despatched to him. But he never received the message. It was eight days before Reverend Father Blanchett arrived. On 14 August they all set off for St Pauls: Father De Smet, along with his four priests, one brother and six nuns. The squadron consisted of four canoes, manned by Indians from St Pauls. They sailed up the Columbia and soon entered Williamette. At night they camped on the shore. But there was no sleep for anybody: the swarms of mosquitoes made sure of that. Finally they reached the mission on 17 August.

The search began for a site for a new mission – that of St Francis Xavier. A suitable site was found not too far away. Soon the task of cutting the trees and clearing the underbrush began. Construction of the first residences began. But not for long. A strange malady (body flux) hit the region. Father De Smet, too, succumbed and was confined to bed, and a rigorous diet, for fifteen days. On 9 September the Sisters began their teaching of women and children, aged from sixteen to sixty. These all came from a distance, bringing with them their own provisions for several days and sleeping in the woods, exposed to all the inclemencies of the weather.

Father De Smet longed to get back to his Indians (the Flatheads) in the mountains whom he had not seen for two years. On 3 October, though not fully recovered, he left the regular mission of St Pauls and the new mission of St Francis Xavier, and set off on horseback for Fort Vancouver. He reached Vancouver on 5 October, just in time to catch a barge, manned by eight men, that was heading for Walla Walla. They travelled along the foot of Mount Hood, the most elevated mountain (16,000 feet) on this stupendous chain, covered in snow. On 7 October they had to carry their goods overland to avoid the Dalles Rapids at the Cascade. They crossed the Des Chutes (Elk) River and the John Day River. Father De Smet reached Walla Walla on 20 October. He stayed there for several days, preparing for the rest of his journey. He still had twenty horses to buy and as many saddles and bridles to have made.

He set off on 28 October, with an Iroquois Indian and a Canadian, from Colville, to act as guides. The first night they camped on the Walla Walla River. The next day they crossed the Lewis or Nez Percé River, one of the longest tributaries of the Columbia. On 2 November they reached the Spokane River. They crossed the Spokane Desert. His two guides left him at the foot of the great mountain of the Kalispels, to go on their way to Colville. Father De Smet continued on his way alone. On 6 November he reached St Ignatius, the mission of the Kalispels of the Bay, where he was greeted joyously by Father Hoeken. (The Bay was a great bend in Clark's Fork of the Columbia River, some forty miles above its mouth.) He was conducted to the village amid volleys of musketry and every demonstration of rejoicing. The season was already advanced and he still had to get back to his own Flathead mission of St Mary's before winter. He was busy making preparations for his departure when on the evening of 8 November a deputation arrived from the Coeur d'Alène tribe, who wanted a visit from the Black Robe. He couldn't disappoint them so he set off with the three deputies and two Kalispels.

In his *The Oregon Missions* Father De Smet writes:

On 10 November the sun rose majestically and everything promised a fine day. But all these fair appearances disappeared in threatening reddish clouds, and soon after the first snow began to fall in great flakes and the rain that followed soaked us to the skin. We crossed the Spokane River at the foot of the great rapids and kept to the road until sunset.

It continued to rain and snow all day on the 11th. But we set out however, hoping to be able to reach the mission. But the trail had become so slippery, along the sides of the high hills that we had to cross that we barely made twenty miles. A large part of this desert is more prairie than forest, dotted with red pines, 100 to 200 yards apart, and here and there with fine little bunches of spruce.

We struck camp early on the 12th in a blizzard of snow. We reached the summit of a high mountain. Our horses slid and stumbled at every step on the narrow, winding path. At two in the afternoon we found ourselves on the banks of the St Joseph's River, the southern fork that feeds the Coeur d'Alène Lake and an hour later I was in the mission of the Sacred Heart, with Father Point and a Brother; and surrounded by some 500 Coeur d'Alènes, who ran up in crowds to shake hands and welcome me among them.

C and R, p. 463.

On 19 November Father De Smet left the mission on his way to St Mary's on the other side of the Bitter Root Mountains. He was accompanied by four Indians to serve as guides and hunters. For several days they wound through thick woods and along the side of cliffs, among the most prodigious cedars. 'The silence of these places is unearthly.'

Presently they were met by two Nez Percés, who had just come down from the mountains. They gave a frightening description of the trail. In view, therefore, of the unremitting snowfall, and the force of the torrents, ever increasing in volume, which were rushing down from the mountains, and which made the passage impracticable and impossible, they decided to turn back – fast.

We were confronted by a new deluge; the little brooks of the day before were now swollen torrents, rushing uproariously down. They delayed us continually, to make bridges or throw trees across, and unload and load again our pack animals. After endless miseries, tumbles and headers, we at last came again to the St Ignatius River, which had risen over ten feet, and was carrying down great masses of tree-trunks. It was not crossed without the greatest danger. Once I found myself under water, and under my mule; but I held fast to my beast, which dragged me to the farther shore. We camped for the night near the large cross planted on the territory of the chief Paulin. The river was still several feet below the top of the bank, and we all lay down to sleep without the least uneasiness; but toward midnight one of my men was surprised and amazed to find both his legs in the water. He put his head out of the tent, and lost no time in giving the alarm to his companions. It was, in fact, high tide; we found ourselves surrounded by water, as by an immense lake. The plain was flooded throughout its entire extent of some seventy miles. I had barely got on my shoes and cassock and tied up my baggage and provisions, when I found myself in water up to the knees. But here, as in a hundred other places, Providence had furnished us a means of escape; there were two infirm little canoes of bark at the precise spot where we had encamped, and by their means we were enabled to take refuge, with arms and baggage, though all soaked, upon an eminence two miles away. Our horses and mules had made their way to the mountainside during the night, where there was still abundant grass. We elected one of the Coeur d'Alènes to go to the mission with the news of our distress, and two days later, five canoes, under two of the chiefs, came to our rescue and carried us back to the village. The Indians seemed to rejoice in the mishaps that had brought me to them again, and manifested the same cordiality and gladness with which they had received me the first time.

C and R, p. 465.

On 4 December Father De Smet set off again to try to reach the Flatheads by way of Clark's Fork. On 8 December, with four Kalispels and two canoes, he travelled up the river unhindered for four days.

When we reached the great lake, the ice began to impede our progress. We were constantly having to land, to re-gum the thin bark of which our canoes were composed. Thus I found myself stopped for the second time. All navigation had ceased a month before – my pilot declared that to advance was to expose ourselves to imminent danger.

C and R, p. 466.

There was no option but to turn back and pass the winter months with the Kalispels of the Bay.

On 24 December 1844 Midnight Mass was celebrated at the mission, encircled by ranges of lofty, snow-clad peaks. Twelve young Indians, taught by Father Mengarini, performed with accuracy several pieces of music by the best German and Italian composers. One played a flute made from an eagle's wing bone.

After the second Mass, all the adults (124 of them), with the chiefs at their head, presented themselves in the church to receive baptism. An old man and woman whom Father De Smet had baptised two years earlier acted as sponsors for all.

Father De Smet reflects on the great joy and happiness a missionary experienced on such occasions.

> The trifling things of the world he abandons are nothing to be compared with the blessings he finds in the wilderness. 'Ye shall receive a hundred fold.'
>
> *C and R, p. 469.*

At 3 o'clock in the afternoon the solemn benediction of the Blessed Sacrament was given, after which upward of fifty couples, many of whom were eighty years old, came forward to renew their marriage promises.

> I could not help shedding tears of joy at witnessing this truly primitive simplicity, and the love and affection with which they pledged again their faith to each other.
>
> *C and R, p. 470.*

Early in February 1845, while five feet of snow lay on the ground, Father De Smet set off before the snow began to melt, to visit the various settlements and stations and to establish new ones among the tribes of the mountains. At Easter time he was among his dear Flatheads and Pend d'Oreilles of the mountains, at St Mary's mission. Three hundred Pend d'Oreilles from the station of St Francis Borgia presented themselves for baptism. Among them were some of the great warriors of the Rocky Mountains – Chief Stiet tiedloodsho, Chieftain of the Braves, Chief Selpisto and Chief Chelax (White Robe). Chief Chelax was the same chief who on Father De Smet's first visit to the mountains, had, aided by only sixty men, sustained over five days a battle against 200 lodges of

Blackfeet, killing eighty of them for the loss of one Flathead wounded. Father De Smet writes: 'to the name of Chelax I affixed that of the prince of the apostles ... How consoling it is to pour the regenerating waters of baptism on the furrowed and scarified brows of these desert warriors.'

The Kalispels of the Bay were awaiting his return. He got into a fragile, bark canoe, guided by two Indians. The Indians wielded their paddles with sinews that never tired. With measured and regular strokes that grew longer and longer the little bark sprang forward and covered a distance of 250 miles down Clark's Fork, from the Bay of Pend d'Oreilles to the Horse Plain. You get some idea of the swiftness of the river when you realise that whereas it took him sixteen days to ascend the river, the descent took only four.

With Father Hoeken and the chiefs they examined a possible site for a new mission, to be called St Ignatius. Father De Smet felled the first tree. When he revisited the site in July 1845, they had already put up fourteen log houses, besides a large barn, had the timber prepared for a church, and had upward of 300 acres in grain, enclosed by a substantial fence. The whole village, men, women and children, had worked most cheerfully. He counted thirty head of horned cattle – the squaws had learned to milk the cows and to churn; they had a few hogs and some domestic fowls. The number of Christians had doubled since Christmas 1844.

Father De Smet now set off for Walla Walla. He embarked on a small boat and descended the Columbia as far as Fort Vancouver. On the way they passed the place where

a few months previously, four travellers from the United States had miserably perished, victims of their own temerity and presumption. When advised to provide themselves with a guide, they answered they had no need of any; and when warned that the river was dangerous and deceptive, the pilot, with a scoffing boast, replied, 'I am capable of guiding my barge, were it even across the infernal gulf.' The monitor wished them a fortunate voyage, but at the same time trembled for their fate, saying: 'This pilot is not a native Indian, he is not an Iroquois, nor even a Canadian.' The turbulent stream soon engulfed its presumptuous and daring victims. They steered out into the midst of the river, and in an instant the canoe was borne along with the rapidity of lightning, leaving in its train a thick foam, caused by the violent plying of oars. Approaching the rapids, they fearlessly hurried onward. Alas, their fate was soon to be decided. Drawn by the eddy into the centre of a whirlpool, vainly they struggled to extricate themselves – they beheld the dread abyss yawning to receive its prey! Yet an instant the ill-fated barge twirled upon the surface, and then sank amidst the despairing shrieks of the helpless crew, which the roaring waves rendered the more appalling, whilst the dismal sounds, re-echoing from shore to shore, proclaimed a new disaster of the Columbia. Soon the waters resumed their wonted course, and left no trace of the sad catastrophe. This fatal spot might appropriately be designated Presumptive's Rapids; doubtless it will be a lesson to future boasters not to venture, without pilot or guide, upon this formidable tributary of the western ocean.

C and R, p. 474.

A five-day journey brought Father De Smet to Fort Vancouver. There was cheering news for him. At Williamette the Convent of the Sisters of Notre Dame was making good progress, with already fifty boarders. The residence at St Francis Xavier was completed and would serve as a novitiate and seminary to prepare young men for the missions.

Father De Smet set off by land from St Francis Xavier mission for Walla Walla, taking with him eleven horses laden with ploughs, spades, pickaxes, scythes and carpenters' implements. They met with huge problems, particularly in the region of the Cascade Mountains, where, because of the vast amount of water, they were surrounded by angry torrents that crashed with irresistible fury on the rocks over which they had to cross. They passed the foot of Mount Hood. The journey took twenty days from the Williamette to Walla Walla, across desert and undulating lands, abounding in absinthium or wormwood, sagebrush and cactus. In the sandy regions the salamanders abounded and even the armadillos would show their snouts. Fort Walla Walla, surrounded by sand, was like a little Arabia. Around about were the delightful pastures, where it never snowed, of the Nez Percés and Cayuses, the most prosperous tribes in Oregon.

On 15 July 1845 they arrived at the Bay of Kalispels (St Ignatius) with all the effects for the new mission. Father De Smet established St Paul's mission at Kettle Falls, the beautiful falls on the Columbia River, in the vicinity of Fort Colville, two day's journey from St Ignatius. There were Indians on every projecting rock, piercing fish with their wooden spears for their winter store. The spears glinted downward swift as a shaft of sunlight through the leaves. The quivering whitefish were tossed on to the bank. Others collected salmon in baskets.

On the feast of St Ignatius Father De Smet baptised more than one hundred children and eleven old men, borne on bison skins, including an Okinagan, one hundred years old and blind. Father De Smet recollected that on the same Feast one year earlier he had been crossing the dangerous bar on the mouth of the Columbia River. On 4 August Father De Smet left Kettle Falls, accompanied by several Crees, to examine a site they had selected for another mission. He established another station, St Francis Regis, at Lake Boey. On 6 August he traversed the high mountains of the Kalispels. In the evening he was back at St Ignatius mission.

On 9 August 1845 Father De Smet set off for the Blackfeet country of the Arcs-à-plats (Flatbows) via the Upper Columbia. The roads were still inundated by the great freshet. So he ascended the Clark River in a bark canoe. He sent his horses across the forests that bordered the river to await him at the great lake of the Kalispels – Lake Pend d'Oreille. The route from the great Kalispel Lake to the Flatbow country was across dense forests, to the Kootenia River, which he called the Flatbow or McGillivray River. They entered the sombre forests. Axe in hand, they were forced to cut their way and wind about to avoid hosts of trees that had been levelled by the autumnal blasts and storms. Some of these forests were so dense that at the distance of twelve feet, he could not distinguish his guide. The most certain way of extricating one's self from these labyrinths was to trust the horse, which, if left unguided, would follow the track of other animals. This expedient had saved him many times.

In a letter to his bishop (2 September 1845), Father De Smet confesses to his fears and forebodings.

I cannot refrain from communicating to your lordship the gloomy and harrowing thoughts which imagination conjures up in these dismal regions. The most fearful apprehensions dismay the bravest heart and cause an involuntary shudder, as some dire apparition of a bear or panther stalks in fancy before the mind, whilst groping our way amidst these dark and frightful haunts, from which there is no egress.

C and R, p. 492.

Out of the forests there were further dangers of a different kind –
precipices, cataracts and whirlpools.

At a place called the Portage the river crossed a defile of precipitous and frightful rocks where they were compelled for a distance
of several miles to risk life at every step and brave obstacles that
at first sight appeared insuperable. He wrote movingly of this *ne
plus ultra* of the wilderness.

> Whatever can be imagined appalling seems here combined to
> terrify the heart – livid gashes of ravines and precipices, giant
> peaks and ridges of varied hue, inaccessible pinnacles, fearful and
> unfathomable chasms filled with the sound of ever-precipitating
> waters – the ear is stunned by the confused sounds of murmuring
> rills, rushing streams, impetuous falls and roaring torrents.
>
> The path winds in the neighbourhood of a stream, which follows
> in one place a mountain gorge, or rather a precipice of appalling
> height. Amid such obstacles one must travel for a distance of eight
> miles, scaling, by the aid of a pickaxe, steep declivities, awe-inspir-
> ing heights, and long and narrow sloping banks, which must be
> alternately ascended. Many times have I been obliged to take the
> attitude of a quadruped and walk upon my hands. At each step the
> danger is so evident that the blood freezes in one's veins and a cold
> sweat breaks out. After each crossing I thanked God as though I had
> just escaped death and its agonies.
>
> *C and R, p. 492.*

Father De Smet headed for the Kootenais and the Flatbows, who
lived on the borders of the Clark River. After a few days' journey
he arrived at the Prairie du Tabac, the usual abode of the
Kootenais. (Flatbows and Kootenais were now united into one
tribe.) They hailed him with a long and boisterous discharge of
musketry. Several showed him their journal, consisting of a square
stick on which they had notched the number of days and weeks
since he had last lived with them near the great Flathead Lake.
They had computed forty-one months and some days.

The dogs of the Kootenais were the bane of his life. At every
village they would rush out in packs, yapping furiously. Father De
Smet makes special mention of these.

> If the traveller has only one tent, he must be careful before he
> retires to barricade the entrance wall, and surround it with

brush; he must stop every crack and cranny and carefully hang out of reach not only all his provisions, but anything made of leather, or that has once been connected with flesh, otherwise he will find on waking that himself and his cattle are deprived of provender. The Indian dogs are as bad as their masters are good. Their masters abhor theft, but these dogs make it their business, and subsist entirely by pilfering.

C and R, p. 914.

On another occasion Father De Smet had occasion to touch on the honesty and moral uprightness of the Kootenais.

My mission-house was of necessity often left alone, but nothing was ever missed. My friends, the Kootenais, had a trading post on their lands provided with goods for their use. The trader (Mr Berton) was sometimes absent for weeks or months. The Indians went in and served themselves according to their wants; replaced in furs and skins for the goods taken out; and upon the testimony of the trader (I use his words), 'his confidence in their honesty was never abused.' Their moral conduct was admirable and commendable. Every attempt at seduction, either by young men or by adults, was punished with a severe flogging. During my several years' intercourse and experience with these mountain Indians, I never heard of an adulterer.

C and R, p. 1225.

The Flathead mission of St Mary's was often attacked by the Blackfeet. The annual bison hunt gave rise to arguments between the two tribes. The Blackfeet claimed the exclusive right to hunt upon the eastern slopes of the mountains. The Flatheads maintained that their ancestors had always enjoyed this privilege, and furthermore, that so long as a brave of their tribe could bear arms they would defend their rights. Hence sanguinary encounters ensued, in which the Flatheads, inferior in numbers, were defeated. In a country covered with thick underbrush, it was possible for the Blackfeet to remain hidden for days, waiting to attack. Like beasts of prey they waited till the gathering darkness of night would render their blows more fatally certain. The unfortunate victims were killed and scalped and the assassins escaped unseen. It was dangerous to venture beyond the mission stockade, and night and day a sentinel stood guard, firing from time to time to intimidate the enemy.

Father De Smet decided to visit the Blackfeet with a view to inducing them to bury the war-hatchet and conclude a truce with the warring tribes. The undertaking was perilous in the extreme, for he would be unarmed and without any escort. Moreover, the whites were the bitter enemies of the Blackfeet, who would murder them without any scruple to satisfy their hate and superstitions.

The Blackfeet lived on the other side of the Rockies upon the Upper Missouri. It would have been much easier to reach the Blackfeet by going directly east from the Flatheads to the Missouri River. But he preferred to take the Canadian route, north and across the mountains near the source of the Saskatchewan, in the hope of discovering new tribes to whom he might preach the Gospel.

On 30 August 1845 Father De Smet bade farewell to his Indians and set out north across the mountains in search of the Blackfeet. Two young men of the tribe offered to conduct him to the country of the Blackfeet, and a third Indian, an expert hunter and a good interpreter, completed the number of his little escort. They crossed magnificent dark forests where the sound of the axe had never resounded.

On 4 September they reached the source of the Columbia. The vast canopy of woods spread itself to the margin of the river, over-hanging the river and shadowing its dark current with a darker hue, just as the tall trees had tottered on the brows of precipices here and there. He was glad to emerge from the half-light and gloom of the black and savage wilderness.

Father De Smet was spellbound at the grandeur of the spectacle that lay before him. Two small lakes, from four to five miles in length, formed by a number of springs and streams, were the reservoirs of the first waters of a stream, dashing and foaming down the mountainside which becomes, in its capricious turns and windings, the most dangerous river on the western side of the American hemisphere. The lakes were covered with swarms of aquatic birds – coots, ducks, waterfowl, cormorants, bustards, cranes and swans. The two lakes were tombs for the masses of salmon that die from exhaustion in them.

In the absence of man, the grey grizzly, black and brown bear, the wolf, the eagle and the vulture assemble in crowds at this season of the year. They fish their prey on the banks of the river and at the entrance of the lakes – claws, teeth and bills serving them instead of hooks and darts. From thence, when the snow begins to fall, the bears, plump and fat, resume the road back to their dens in the thick of the forests and hollows of rocks, there to pass the four sad wintry months in complete indolence, with no other pastime or occupation than that of sucking their four paws.

If we may credit the Indians, each paw occupies the bear for one moon (a month) and the task accomplished, he turns on the other side and begins to suck the second, and so on with the rest.

C and R, p. 496.

They crossed over to the Columbia, then descended it past a number of lakes near the source. On 9 September they quit these upper lakes by a narrow valley on a small footpath by the bank of a great torrent between two lofty chains of mountains which soon led to a narrow mountain defile, where the light of day hardly penetrated, amidst huge, bold barriers of colossal rocks. They watched the cliffs stretch their red shadows across the valley.

After a day's journey they reached the banks of the Arc-à-plats. The route lay through dense forests, raging torrents and beside appalling precipices. In front of them mountains, snow-crested, rose like holy towers where man might commune with the sky. Trees of various species clung to the mountain's rugged flanks: the poplar rustled in the autumn north wind, the slender birch waved its golden plumes, and the blue turpentine and the juniper-tree, heavy with its crimson berries, filled the valley with their perfume. When De Smet came across plants not indigenous to Belgian soil, he got off his horse and filled his pockets with seeds for the friends and benefactors of the mission back in Europe.

After much fatigue and labour, they set off on 15 September to re-cross the dividing range to the Kootenai near the mouth of the Vermilion River. They ascended this tributary to its source in the Continental Divide, traversed the high lands separating the waters of the Columbia from those of the south fork of the Saskatchewan. On the summit De Smet planted a large cross, 'the Cross of Peace'. They began the descent of the eastern side of the mountain. They travelled to the headwaters of the south branch of the Saskatchewan. They travelled through dense forests and rugged mountainous country to the Rocky Mountain House, a Hudson Bay trading post on the north fork of that stream. In the midst of the wilderness he came across a Canadian family, called Morigeau,

116

'sole occupants of this empire of rugged grandeur'. Father De Smet baptised Mrs Morigeau, who was dressed in a white deerskin dress, trimmed with elk teeth, her children and six little Indians.

On 18 September they reached the Bow or Askow River in the evening. Here De Smet pitched his tent. They came upon the traces of a band of Indians: could these be the feared Blackfeet?

> I was now on the very confines of these barbarous people, from which, possibly, I should never return! It not infrequently happens that in their unbridled fury when they hear some relative has been killed, the Blackfeet dispatch the first stranger they meet, scalp him – and then abandon to the wolves and dogs the palpitating limbs of the unfortunate victim of their vengeance, hatred and superstition. I declare to you, I was beset by a thousand disquietudes concerning the fate that awaited me. Poor nature! this timid and fragile *meus homo* is sometimes terrified.
>
> *C and R, p. 508.*

Fear also seized his escort, and in the hope of turning the missionary's mind, they related their dreams of evil portent. But Father De Smet realised the salvation of souls was at stake. The incursions of the Blackfeet on the Flatheads at the mission of St Mary's were too frequent. He would have to face them and plead for peace. On 19 and 20 September they followed tracks, which became ever more distinct. Father De Smet despatched two guides to reconnoitre. With the caution of natives they ascended every hillock, descended every gully, to reconnoitre, indicating by gestures what they found. One of them returned the same evening with the news that he had found a small camp of Assiniboins of the Forest; that they had been well received; that a disease raged in the camp, of which two had lately died, and that they expressed a great desire to see the Black Robe. The following morning Father De Smet joined them and remained several days with them.

In a letter to his Provincial headed, 'Camp of the Assiniboins, September 26, 1845', Father De Smet wrote:

> This tribe, numbering not more than fifty families, live in the woods and the mountains. Agriculture is unknown to them, and they feed on animal flesh, especially porcupines, which abound in this region. When short of food they eat roots, seeds, and the inner bark of the cypress. The chief of the tribe told me that last

winter a man in the extremity of hunger had eaten his wife and four children.

In default of horses, the Assiniboins possess a large number of dogs, and more voracious animals could scarcely be imagined. One night I neglected to put stakes around my tent, and in consequence found myself in the morning shoeless, my cassock minus a collar, and my breeches short of a leg.

The Assiniboins are filthy beyond description, and devoured by vermin which they themselves eat. 'Are you not ashamed,' I asked an Indian, 'to eat these insects?' 'They eat me first,' he replied, 'and I have the right to retaliate.' Wishing to be particularly amiable, one day I assisted at a porcupine feast, a scene that would have turned the strongest stomach. Failing a tablecloth and dishes, several of the company took off their leather shirts shining with grease and laid them on the ground. Upon this covering the meat was cut and served; to dry their hands they wiped them on their hair. An old woman whose face was smeared with blood – a sign of mourning – presented me with a wooden bowl of soup. The horn spoon reeked with grease, which she kindly licked before putting it in my unsavoury broth.

Then to the famous Rocky Mountain hash. But hashed with the teeth. If a bit of dried meat, or any other provision is in need of being cleansed, the dainty cook fills her mouth with water and spurts it with her whole force upon the fated object. Then half a dozen old women chew and chew again, mouthful after mouthful, the meat is then put into the kettle for boiling. This was followed by dessert of cakes made of crushed ants, grasshoppers and locusts dried in the sun.

C and R, p. 510.

When it came to dealing with their traditional enemy, the Blackfeet, they were cruelty personified, even to old men, women and children. Victims of their revenge were speedily immolated. One warrior spoke of how they:

tore from the arms of their mothers and took with them a great number of little children, and that on their way, amid their songs and scalp-dances, they amused themselves with flaying them alive and running pointed sticks through their bodies, in order to roast them alive before the fire. The piercing shrieks of these little creatures fell upon the ear of these barbarians, amid their inhuman orgies, like the sweetest and most delightful melody. All that a pitiless and savage heart could invent of torture was put into practice on this occasion. The Assiniboins declare that they satiated themselves with cruelty, to satisfy the manes of their deceased parents and kindred, and their implacable and long wished-for vengeance against the greatest of their enemies, the Blackfeet.

C and R, p. 1128.

The Assiniboins never buried their dead. They believed that the souls of the dead migrated toward the south, where the climate was mild, the game abundant and the rivers well stocked with fish. Their hell was the reverse of this picture; its unfortunate inmates dwelling in perpetual snow and ice, and in the complete deprivation of all things. They bound the bodies with thongs of rawhide between branches of large trees, and more frequently placed them on scaffolds, to protect them from wolves and other wild animals. There they were left to decay. The ceremony was concluded by tears, wailings, howlings and macerations of all those present. They tore their hair, gashed their legs, till finally the calumet was lit, the culmination of every rite.

During his stay with the Assiniboins Father De Smet learned much about their beliefs. In common with other Indian tribes each Assiniboin who considered himself a chief or warrior possessed what he called his *Wah-kon* (medicine), in which he placed his confidence. This consisted of a stuffed bird, a weasel's skin, or some little bone or tooth of an animal. These charms or talismen accompanied them on all their expeditions for war or hunting. In every difficulty or peril they invoked the protection of the *Wah-kon*.

The 'little medicine-wolf' (coyote) was held in great veneration among the Assiniboins. When it approached the camp at night the Assiniboins counted the number of its yelps, whether the bark was strong or feeble, and from which part of the camp it came. This information was passed on to the medicine men, who interpreted it for their prognostications.

Next to the sun, thunder was their great *Wah-kon*. Thunder was the voice of the Great Spirit speaking from the clouds. Every spring, at the first peal of thunder, the Assiniboins offered it sacrifices – tobacco, or the most exquisite pieces of bison meat. Others fasted and even made incisions in the fleshy parts of their bodies or cut off the first joints of their fingers, to offer in sacrifice. After a storm they saw the effects of lightning on trees, on their horses and on men; hence it was an object of dread which they tried to appease by sacrifice.

Theft, among the Assiniboins, was only considered disgraceful when it was discovered; then shame and infamy were attached to the thief.

Adultery was punished with death in almost every case. The seducer seldom escaped if the husband and his family had the power and the courage to execute this law. Hence this crime was rather uncommon. The woman was sometimes killed, but always severely punished. The husband caused her head to be closely shaved, and her person painted over with a heavy coat of vermilion mixed with bear's grease; she was then mounted on a horse, the mane and tail of which had been cut off, and the whole body also daubed with vermilon; an old man conducted her all around the camp and proclaimed aloud her infidelity; at last he committed her to the hands of her own relatives, who received the culprit with a good beating.

On 27 September Father De Smet took his leave of the Assiniboins. He set off with three guides on a long expedition to the south in search of the main Blackfeet band. The interlaced branches of the cypress forest which they traversed, tore and scraped their hands, faces, and clothes, as the travellers pushed their way through. Nor did De Smet escape without an adventure. In a letter to his Provincial headed 'Rocky Mountain House, Octobers 5, 1845', Father De Smet mentions some of his adventures.

I had to pass under a tree that hung over the path; one of its branches, broken off at the end, presented a dangerous hook. I bent down on my horse's neck, but this was a useless manoeuvre, for it seized me by the collar of my coat and lifted me up, my horse passing on from under me. There I hung like a fish on a hook. My battered hat, black eye, and torn cheek in a civilised land would have laid me open to suspicion as being a highwayman from the Black Forest, rather than a missionary in search of souls.

To render a bad forest superlatively so, a great fall of snow is necessary. This special favour was lavished upon us in this last passage. Woe to the first pedestrians! The branches groan under the burden of their wintry shroud, and seem to present the motto: *'si tangas, frangas!'* and assuredly, at each rubbing of the hat, the least touching of the arm or leg, a deluge of snow showers down upon the shivering cavalier and horse.

C and R, p. 514.

After pushing their way for several weeks through the mountains the caravan descended into the vast plain of prairies that lies between the Saskatchewan and Upper Missouri. The grasses of the great buff plains had ceased to grow for another year. Here, besides the Blackfeet, lived the Crows, Aricaras, Crees, and Assiniboins of the Forest, the Cheyenne, the Sioux, and others.

After three weeks of intense suffering he returned to the Rocky Mountain Post belonging to the Hudson Bay Company. But he had not accomplished the object of his travels, which was to locate the Blackfeet. The heavy snowfalls had destroyed their trail.

A detachment of Blackfeet was due at the Fort. The commander of the Post promised to bring about a friendly meeting. Father De Smet then discharged his escort.

On 25 October a band of thirteen Blackfeet arrived at the fort.

Upon learning the object of my journey, the old chief embraced me. His accoutrements distinguished him from his companions, for he was covered from head to foot with eagle feathers and wore upon his chest a medallion consisting of a large breast plate decorated with blue flowers. Every mark of friendship was shown me, and each time I visited him he seated me beside him.

C and R, p. 523.

Father De Smet was determined to find the Blackfeet. But he needed a good interpreter. The only one at the Post was a suspicious, dangerous character, of whom everyone spoke evil. Father De Smet had no option but to take him. He arranged with the thirteen Blackfeet that they should precede him among their people and prepare their minds to receive him. On 31 October Father De Smet set off, accompanied by the interpreter and a young half-blood Cree to care for the horses.

The interpreter became sullen and peevish, always choosing to halt in those places where the poor beasts of burden could find nothing to eat after their long day's journey. The farther we penetrated into the desert, the more and more sulky he became. It was impossible to draw from him a single pleasant word, and his incoherent mutterings and allusions became subjects of serious apprehension. Thus passed ten sorrowful days; my last two nights had been nights of anxiety and watching; when fortunately I encountered a Canadian, with his Indian family, on whom I prevailed to remain with me some time. The following day my interpreter disappeared. Although my situation was extremely precarious in this dangerous desert, without interpreter, without guide, yet I could not but feel relieved of a heavy burden by the departure of this sullen and gloomy fellow. Had it not been for my opportune meeting with the Canadian, it is probable I should not have escaped his deep-laid scheme against me.

C and R, pp. 526–7.

Father De Smet then set about to find another interpreter, as he was determined not to turn back. He was told that further on he would find one who was also en route to the Blackfeet. For eight days he searched for him through a labyrinth of narrow valleys, but all in vain. Nor did he come upon any Indians. The Crees, who were on the warpath, had overrun the country in every direction, everyone fleeing before them. For four days it snowed heavily. The horses were exhausted. His rations were at a low ebb. Nothing more remained except to try to reach one of the Fur Company's posts and winter there, putting off his visit to the Blackfeet until spring. So Father De Smet retraced his steps back to the plain, where the snow was not so deep, arriving at Fort Augustus (Edmonton) on the Saskatchewan on the last day of the year 1845.

Chapter 8

To the Rocky Mountain Tribes

Father De Smet stayed two months at Fort Augustus, the great emporium of the Hudson Bay Fur Company, in the region of the Upper Saskatchewan and Athabasca (Elk) Rivers. As soon as the approach of spring held out a prospect of travel he determined to get back to his Flatheads at the mission of St Ignatius, beyond the mountains. It had been the opinion of the people at Fort Augustus that Father De Smet's weight was too great to permit him to make the journey, much of which would have to be upon snowshoes. But with quick resolution he set out to reduce his weight by a rigorous fast of thirty days and was measurably successful.

On 12 March 1846 he set off for Fort Assiniboin, on the Athabasca River, accompanied by an escort of three half-bloods. His plan was to approach the mountains through the Athabasca Valley and from there to descend the Columbia to Fort Colville.

As the whole country lay buried in snow, they travelled by sledge, drawn by dogs. The provisions and baggage were placed on two sledges; the third, drawn by four dogs, was reserved for the Black Robe. After six days, on 18 March, they reached Fort Assiniboin, built in a meadow on the river Athabasca. Ascending the river on its ice for 300 miles they finally reached Fort Jasper. They remained there for fifteen days. At Fort Jasper De Smet met an Iroquois who had not seen a priest since he left his country forty years before. The old Indian's joy knew no bounds, for now his children could be baptised. Father De Smet remained several days to instruct this interesting family, thirty-six in number. He celebrated Mass at Easter, and afterwards administered baptism and married seven couples.

On 25 April he resumed his journey. The parting was impressive. In a letter to his brother Francis (6 May 1846) he wrote:

The new Christians wished to honour me in a way that would leave a lasting impression on their children and keep before them ever the name of him who had placed them in 'the way of life'. The assembled family gave three rousing hurrahs, at the same time firing their guns in the direction of the mountain to which they gave my name. The men escorted me ten miles on my journey, each one shaking my hand effusively at parting. We exchanged good wishes and mingled our tears, and when they departed we found ourselves alone in one of those wild ravines enclosed by mountains rising like insurmountable barriers.

C and R, p. 188.

The Upper Athabasca is, unquestionably, the most elevated part of North America. All its mountains are prodigious, the snow-capped summits losing themselves in the clouds. Father De Smet reached the top of the highest peaks in the Rocky Mountains and beheld Mount Brown lifting its snow-clad summit over 10,000 feet in the empyrean. Crossing these mountains is difficult at all seasons, but it was especially difficult now, for the melting snow caused frequent avalanches, carrying with them enormous rocks that bounded down the mountainside with deafening noise, felling trees, crushing herds and flocks, and filling up the valleys.

He ascended the Athabasca to a tributary, Trou or Hole River, and followed this nearly to its source in the pass over the divide at the foot of the Great Glacier. On 1 May he encamped at the foot of the Great Glacier to await the arrival of the annual brigade of the Hudson Bay Company from the Columbia.

Father De Smet describes some of his experiences.

I have spread my bearskin and my buffalo robe, which formed my bed, and passed many nights in profound slumber, after the fatigues of a long day's travel, now at the sources of the Athabasca, Saskatchewan or Missouri, now those of the Columbia. In that elevated region the atmosphere is of almost remarkable purity; by night, in the blue-black firmament, the moon and stars shine with wonderful brilliancy.

C and R, p. 1366.

Exhausted by the seemingly fruitless journey of several months Father De Smet appears to have lost heart temporarily.

My health is nor longer what it was. Every time I climb a mountain now, my strength seems to leave me. The rigours of the climate, fasts, sleepless nights, with ever-increasing anxieties, and the dangers and agonising moments I pass through, are sapping my constitution. Only lately did I miraculously escape the hands of a vile assassin.

This was an incident that had occurred a few weeks previously. While residing at one of the mountain missions, an overbearing sullen Indian, who was feared on account of his gigantic strength, swore to kill the missionary, and do away with the religion he preached. He was possibly one of the medicine men, who under their incantations hid their ignorance and impotency, which they foisted on the gullible people, and Father De Smet had exposed their charlatanry.

One day Father De Smet started off on horseback to visit a neighbouring post armed only with his Breviary and his riding-whip. There was a sudden, distant pounding of hooves. This was followed by a bloodcurdling war cry, the yell of a demon. Father De Smet turned his horse round. Out of the cloud of dust emerged the figure of a horseman, galloping at full speed, his tomahawk waving menacingly. As the horseman closed De Smet saw it was a horseman of giant stature and frightening mien. It was, in fact, the chief who had vowed to kill him. The shrieking yell and his evil demeanour confirmed he meant to do just that. As his horse swept past like a whirlwind he lashed out with his tomahawk. De Smet managed to avert the blow that would have torn his scalp off his head. The chief's horse pawed the dust cloud as its rider brought it to a halt. He turned the horse round and made a second furious charge. Father De Smet made a defensive whirl on his own horse. Crouched low in the saddle, his face painted with black and vermilion, the Indian came in on a dead run. With tomahawk raised he lashed out at the priest as he closed in. Father De Smet threw a right hand punch that caught the Indian full in the face. The blow threw the Indian toppling head-long from the bare back of his mount. He rolled over twice in the dust, losing his tomahawk as he did so. He got up and darted to reclaim the gleaming hatchet. Meanwhile Father De Smet had dismounted. Crouching low like a panther the Indian crawled in on the priest, his right hand raised menacingly. The two men circled each other. It was now hand-to-hand combat to the kill. The Indian suddenly pounced on De Smet.

The latter grabbed the raised knife-hand. They struggled chest to chest, eyeball to eyeball. The two combatants exerted all the power of their muscles as they grappled with each other for mastery. The naked body of the Indian afforded De Smet no means of holding him as he squirmed his way out of his grasp. Finally the huge weight of the Indian forced De Smet to the ground. The Indian got the priest on his back. With one knee on his chest he pressed De Smet down with all the weight of a giant. He raised the hatchet for its final act. De Smet grabbed his arm before the tomahawk could descend. Slowly the weapon descended closer to its target. Suddenly De Smet threw his legs up and clamped a head-scissors lock on his adversary, bending him far back, with both of his ankles under the Indian's chin. The Indian cried out some obscenity as his back was bent farther back. Like a cornered rattlesnake the Indian lashed out desperately in all directions. Bracing himself with his left hand De Smet sat up part way, closed his fingers into a big fist and threw his punch. The hard fist collided with the Indian's nose, almost pulping it. The hold on the tomahawk loosened. De Smet swung his fist against the Indian's solar plexus. The Indian tried to double up. Another fist crashed again to his midriff. Father De Smet threw the warrior off him and struggled to his feet. The Indian, all his wind knocked out of him, was slow in getting up. De Smet grabbed the hatchet that had fallen loose from the Indian's hand. Father De Smet was trembling as never before – and angry. He gave the Indian a 'good cow-hiding', to use his own words. He gasped for breath, exhausted by his tremendous effort. His face was white; the muscles in his legs trembled. Blind with shame and fury the Indian struggled to his feet, scowling and groaning, wiping away the blood that streamed from his nose. Whimpering, brought to heel like a hunting dog, he begged for mercy, swearing to treat the Black Robe henceforth with the greatest respect. Father De Smet promised him his liberty upon condition that he would himself tell the whole tribe that he had been beaten by the Black Robe. The proud warrior had little option but to agree. He pleaded for his tomahawk. It would be a great disgrace for him to return to his tribe, not only with a bloody nose and bruised face, but without his tomahawk. But Father De Smet kept the hatchet, saying that if he wished to get it back he must come himself in a few days to the mission to fetch it.

The Indian was not yet converted, but the way was prepared. A week later he approached the mission and asked to speak to Father

De Smet. The latter received him kindly, ordered refreshments to be served, and encouraged him to talk about his victories and the number of scalps he had taken from the enemy. Gradually the Indian's face brightened. Then the conversation was changed to the subject of religion. The missionary exposed the absurdity of superstitious practices, and revealed the great truths of the Christian faith. The Indian acknowledged he had been vanquished a second time, and asked to become a neophyte. The new catechumen finally received baptism, and became one of the best Christians of the tribe.

In early May Father De Smet set off to continue his journey across the main chain of the Rocky Mountains to link up with the Columbia and sail down it to his mission in Oregon. He now had seventy miles to travel on snowshoes (for the first time) to reach the Boat Encampment, where the Canoe River entered the Columbia. He had hoped to do this in two and a half days. He was soon assured that because of his corpulency that would be impossible. Indeed, they tried to dissuade him from attempting it at all. They set off in single file, over snow sixteen feet deep.

In a letter to his Provincial, dated 10 May 1846, Father De Smet describes the journey.

Alternately ascending and descending – sometimes across plains piled up with avalanches – sometimes over lakes and rapids buried deeply under the snow – now on the side of a deep mountain – then across a forest of cypress trees, of which we could only see the tops. I cannot tell you the number of my somersaults. I continually found myself embarrassed by my snowshoes, or entangled in some branch of a tree. When falling, I spread my arms before me, as one naturally would do, to break the violence of the fall; and upon deep snow the danger is not great – though I was often half-buried, when I required the assistance of my companions, which was always tendered with great kindness and good humour.

We made thirty miles the first day, and then made preparations to encamp. Some pine trees were cut down and stripped of their branches, and these being laid on the snow furnished us with a bed, whilst a fire was lighted on a floor of green logs.

C and R, pp. 543–4.

Wrapped up in bison robes, Indian fashion, they extended themselves and slept under the starry heavens, blinking like so many fireflies. In the dead stillness not even the mourning of the wolf came over the frozen wilderness.

The next morning they began the descent of what is called the Great Western Slope. This took five hours. At the foot of the mountain a new obstacle presented itself. The snows had considerably swollen the Great Portage River. In their march down the river valley, for a day and a half, they were forced to cross the river not less than forty times,

> with water frequently up to our shoulders. So great is its impetuosity that we were obliged mutually to support ourselves to prevent being swept away by the current. The rest of the journey was made in dripping garments. The cold, together with extreme fatigue, caused my legs to swell; my toenails came off and the blood coagulated in my boots. Four times I felt my strength failing, and I should certainly have perished in this grim wilderness if the courage and strength of my Indian companions had not sustained me in my distress.
>
> We left the Portage valley and entered a thick and mountainous forest, where the ground was encumbered with thousands of trees felled by the tempests. Then followed marshes through which we crossed in mud and water up to our knees. Finally on the 10th we came to the Boat Encampment on the Columbia, at the mouth of the Portage River. Those who have crossed the Rocky Mountains (3,600 feet above sea level) at 53° of north latitude when the snow is melting know what it means to be a good traveller. It had required all my strength to accomplish this crossing, and I confess I would not dare to undertake it again.
>
> *C and R, pp. 545–7.*

After a few hours' rest, Father De Smet and his guides embarked upon the Columbia, swollen many feet above its normal level. After the horrors of the dark mountain passes, they were cheered by the smiling aspect of spring. The river islands were a mass of blossom and the mantle of snow was thinning on the mountainsides; a thousand little rivulets leaped singing from rock to rock.

His skilful guides urged the light vessel through the crooked and intricate channels – they shot the chutes of the falls and the falls themselves. They would dip a paddle deep and shoot the canoe off into space, hitting the water again with a smack. Another dip of the paddle and they were out of the churning whirlpools. Dodging the rocks, they descended as swift as an arrow.

But in the Dalles, some miles above Colville, their barge faced great danger. Father De Smet continues:

I had left it, to go on foot, to avoid the dangerous passage. The young boatmen, notwithstanding my remonstrances thought they could pass in safety. A whirlpool suddenly arrested their course and threatened to bury them beneath its angry waters. Their redoubled efforts proved ineffectual; I saw them borne on with an irresistible force to the engulfing centre – the bow of the boat descended already into the abyss and filled! I was on my knees upon the rock which overhung this frightful spectacle, surrounded by several Indians – we implored the aid of heaven in favour of our poor comrades – they seemed to be evidently lost – when the whirlpool filled, and threw them to safety from its bosom, as if reluctantly yielding up the prey which it had so tenaciously held. We all gave heartfelt thanks to Almighty God for having delivered them from a danger so imminent.

After some hours of descent we came to Martin's Rapid where a Canadian so called, together with his son, found a watery grave. Its roar is deafening, and the agitation of the water resembles that of a raging sea-storm. The whole bed of the river is here strewed with immense fragments of rocks. Guided by an expert Iroquois pilot, and aided with ten oars, the boat darted over the Great Rapids of the Columbia, dancing and leaping from wave to wave, with the rapidity of lightning.

At sunset we were at the Dalles of the Dead. Here, in 1838, twelve unfortunate *voyageurs* were swallowed up in the river. For about two miles the waters are compressed between a range of perpendicular rocks, presenting innumerable crags, fissures and cliffs, through which the Columbia leaps with irresistible impetuosity, forming as it dashes along frightful whirlpools, where every passing object is swallowed and disappears. By means of two long ropes we dropped down our boat through the Dalles, and encamped for the night at its outlet. On the 11th we continued our route at early dawn – the mountain scenery was hidden from our view, wrapped up in dense mist and fog, which were seen ascending in dense pillars, adding to the forming clouds above till the whole sky was overcast.

C and R, p. 550.

Towards the end of May 1846 De Smet arrived at Fort Colville. Here he met other priests who also had been working among the Indian tribes of the Far West, 'often with no food other than dog or wolf meat and for months a sort of moss mixed with insipid roots'.

The commander at Fort Colville kindly offered Father De Smet passage with a Hudson Bay party on a boat going to Fort Vancouver. Father De Smet first visited the missions in the Williamette Valley. It was obvious the missions needed additional assistance. It was decided that Father De Smet should go to the American cities and even Europe to procure help. He set off again from Fort Vancouver at the beginning of July, laden with supplies for the missions across the mountains. He would then go on to seek assistance in America. He had hardly left Vancouver when a powder horn exploded accidentally near him, scorching him severely and completely stripping the skin from his nose, cheek and lips. But he continued his journey. He procured an Indian canoe, well manned, and was soon, during a thunderstorm, in the great gap of the Cascade Mountains, through which the Columbia winds its way. On both sides of the stream perpendicular walls of rock rose sheer in majestic boldness. A favourable wind enabled them to unfurl two blankets by way of sails. On the third day they arrived at the Great Dalles. From the Great Dalles to the upper sources of the Columbia much care and attention were required in its navigation, for it presents a constant succession of rapids, falls, cascades and dalles. Men of great experience were here employed as pilots, and notwithstanding their skill and precaution no river probably on the globe, frequented as little, could tell of more disastrous accidents.

In a letter to Father Provincial, dated 26 July 1846, Father De Smet wrote:

The eighth day after my departure from Fort Vancouver, I landed safely at Walla Walla, with the goods destined for the different missions. In a few days all was ready, and having thanked the good and kind-hearted Mr McBride, the superintendent of the fort, who had rendered me every assistance in his power, we soon found ourselves on the way to the mountains leading a band of pack mules and horses over a sandy dry plain, covered with bunch grass and wormwood. We made about sixteen miles without wood or water, and encamped for the night in a beautiful little meadow, watered by the Walla Walla River, where we found abundance of grass for our animals – these were soon unloaded and left free to graze at leisure; we next made a fire, put on the camp-kettle, stretched out the bed, consisting of a buffalo-robe, and smoked together the friendly Indian pipe, whilst supper was preparing. The evening was clear and beautiful – not a cloud – our sleep, sound and refreshing, prepared us for an early start at dawn of day. We had a hot day's march, with pack animals, again without wood or water, over an undulating plain, before we could reach the crossing of the Nez Percés or Lewis Fork, whose source is in the angle of the Rocky and Snowy Mountains.

C and R, p. 560.

For the second time Father De Smet crossed the immense country of the Spokanes and Nez Percés. In passing he visited St Francis Regis Mission, where seventy half-bloods were leading Christian lives. At the Mission of the Sacred Heart he was received with great cordiality by Fathers Joset and Point and Brothers Magri and Lyons. All the Coeur d'Alène community came to welcome him. On 5 August he left the Mission of the Sacred Heart accompanied by Father Point. He arrived at his Flathead mission of St Mary's at Bitter Root about 10 August. He had been absent from his mission for eighteen months, visiting various tribes in the Rockies. Father Mengarini proudly pointed out the great changes and improvements that had been made: a bigger church, a mill, etc.

In a letter in 1845, Father Point recorded the remarkable change that had taken place: 'A church rose in the centre, and around it clustered the Indian cabins; and the peace, industry, and piety that reigned in the little colony recalled the golden age of Paraguay.'

Three years earlier, recognising the immensity of the task they had before them in converting the Flatheads, he had written:

Their intelligence was so narrow that although they adored all the animals they knew of they had no idea either of the existence of God or of their souls, and still less of any future state of existence. They were a race so degraded that they retained only two or three very obscure notions of even the natural law, and these they did not practically observe.

(P De Smet – *Voyages aux Montagnes Rocheuses.*)

131

Father De Smet left there on 16 August 1847. As his mission of the previous winter had miscarried, so far as making peace with the Blackfeet was concerned, he resolved to try to accomplish that desirable object on his way home.

Meanwhile the Blackfeet and Crows had continued harassing the Flatheads and neighbouring tribes. The Flatheads and Pend d'Oreilles formed an alliance. In 1840 a handful of them, scarcely numbering sixty, defeated a formidable band of 800 Blackfeet warriors. In the summer of 1845 a small band of Flatheads and Pend d'Oreilles defeated a band of Blackfeet four times their number. In 1846 the Crows began their attacks, on a united camp of Flatheads, some Nez Percés and a few Blackfeet. They, too, were heavily defeated.

The valiant conduct of the Flatheads made a deep impression upon the Blackfeet and paved the way for the desired peace between the two tribes. Shortly after his arrival at the Flathead camp, the Blackfeet, who had suffered badly in their recent defeat by the Crows, came in a body to Father De Smet to express in a manner truly eloquent, their admiration of the Flatheads, with whom in future they desired to live on terms of the closest friendship. The head chief of the Blackfeet was a warrior named Apistotoko or 'Father of a Large Family'. His countenance was almost square, with something of the lion in it. His head was surmounted with a sort of turban adorned with plumes. He was armed with a shield and a short sabre. They determined to hear the words of Great Manitou of the whites. They presented eighty of their children for baptism. The next day they had a celebration to mark their joy. The Black Robes were invited to see the special dance.

In a letter to his Provincial, headed 'Flathead Camp, on the Yellowstone River, September 6, 1846', Father De Smet describes the dances.

I need not tell you it was not the polka, the waltz or anything resembling the dances of modern civilised life. The women alone figured in it, old and young, from the youngest child capable of walking to the oldest matron present. The whole figure is surmounted by a casket of plumes, which the regular movements of the individual is made to harmonise with the song, and seems to add much gracefulness to the whole scene . . . The dance itself consists of a little jump, more or less lively, according to the beat of the drum. This is beaten only by the men, and all unite in the song. The women take the treble the men the bass.

C and R, p. 580.

After the dance followed the presentation of the calumet, to indicate that the best fruit of the victory they celebrate is the peace that follows.

The expenses for the support of all the mission establishments had been great and it was deemed necessary to send a Father to the United States (St Louis) to provide for them. The Fathers unanimously expressed their desire that Father De Smet should again undertake this long and hazardous voyage.

Father De Smet left St Mary's on 16 August, by a mountain gap called the 'Devil's Gate' – so named because it formed the principal entrance of the marauding parties of the Blackfeet. He crossed the mountains in the vicinity of Arrowstone Fork and descended a tributary of the Jefferson (Big Hole River). The 23 August found him encamped on the immense plain through which the forks of the Missouri diverged.

This region is infested by grizzly bears. We killed four in an hour. We met also at every step buffalo, deer, sheep and wild goats. But it is the especial haunt of marauders, assassins and robbers from the various tribes. In travelling through these wilds, great care is to be had in order to avoid the sudden attack of some of those straggling war-parties that infest this neighbourhood purposely to search for scalps, plunder and the fame of some daring exploit. We halted every evening for a few hours, to take a bite, as the trapper would say, and to give some food and rest to our animals. When it was quite dark, we would kindle a brisk fire as if to last until morning; then under cover of the night, proceed on our journey for about ten miles, to some unsuspected place, thus eluding our enemies, should any have followed in our track or be lurking in the neighbourhood, awaiting the midnight hour to execute their murderous designs.

C and R, p. 582.

He travelled by way of the Three Forks and the Bozeman Pass to the dangerous Yellowstone Valley. He descended the Yellowstone to the mouth of the Big Horn about 7 September. Four days later he was met by a few Flatheads who had come after him. They told him how the Crows had made a treacherous attack on the Flatheads. One morning the Flatheads saw a cloud of dust on the horizon; it was the enemy. Chanting death cries and firing their bows and arrows the Crows rushed on. Words gave place to silence as the warriors, seizing their arms, awaited the feared assault. When the Crows came within range of their rifles a volley was poured upon them. Disconcerted by this resistance the Crows changed their plan of attack. They circled and wheeled to fire again. But this series of revolutions merely wore out their horseflesh. Ranged around their council lodge the Flatheads fought with the fury of despair. The rush of blows passed with the fury of a whirlwind and the swiftness of lightning. Each man singled out an opponent from the opposing band. Axes cleaved the air; tomahawks swung with violence. A tomahawk would hit a forehead and check for a moment the onward rush. When he had brained his first Indian he would turn, like a hungry lion, to seek the next victim. The ground was quickly strewn with the enemy, some scalped, some the recipients of a keen and trembling axe, some the thrusts of a fatal knife. The victors stripped the dead of the bloody trophies of victory. The Flatheads brought in the torn emblems of victory from the unresisting heads of the slain.

Father De Smet travelled all through the night and arrived next day at the allied camp of the Flatheads. He found everything ready to repel a second attack. The camp breathed nothing but war. War, vengeance, was the 'breath of their nostrils'. The war-whoop reverberated round the camp. Bonfires were lit; groups were formed for invocations to their *manitou*. Each warrior examined his arms, tested the strength of new strings fitted to bows, and the whole scene changed into a vast workshop. The soldiers sharpened the double-edged knives and daggers, filed anew the lances and arrows, whetted the blades of their scalping knives against a flat, fine-grained stone, vermilioned the battleaxes and the tomahawks, bridled and saddled the horses, while the women mended and prepared the moccasins, the leggings and the sacks of provisions necessary for the journey. As though it was a grand gala occasion, everyone daubed his face with vermilion according to his fancy. Taking their medicine bags of doeskin, heavily ornamented with porcupine quills, they would begin the painting. First streaks of blue-black, ringing their faces in a broad circle. Then red and yellow smeared thick within the circle, covering the cheekbones, chin and upper lips. They would then comb out their long braids, oil them with sassafras oil and coil them tight about their heads. Taking little round trade mirrors from their pouches they would then eye their handiwork. Then they would array themselves in their finest garments.

A bright bonfire of pinewood blazed upon the green. A leader led his men twice and thrice in a circle round the fire with a measured step and solemn chant. Then suddenly halting the war-whoop, a shrill, plaintive howl was raised, the piercing shrieks of the women and children taking up the echo, and the war dance immediately began. Old men sitting at the head of the circle beat time upon the drum while women shook their *sheesheegwums* (sischiquoin) gourds filled with pebbles. A warrior, garbed only in a breech cloth, with a feathered bonnet and bison horn headgear, his body painted black, the ribs white, his face vermilion, brandished a coup stick, a stone-headed club hung with scalps, as he executed the scalp dance.

Father De Smet immediately sent an envoy to the Crows, to announce his arrival at the Flathead camp and at the same time to convey to them his great desire to meet them, especially for the purpose of effecting a reconciliation between the contending parties. But it seems the Crows, thoroughly mortified by their mauling by the Flatheads, had dispersed.

Father De Smet continued his search for the main Blackfeet camp to conclude peace with them. He set out with some Flatheads. They left the Yellowstone. Near the mouth of the Big Horn he turned north-west. They crossed an arid and mountainous country, destitute of any water fit to drink – stagnant pools of brackish water being the only kind found here to satiate the thirst. 'We were all sick for several days from this cause.'

On 12 September 1846 a guide mounted a high hill to survey the country. Fingers pointed at the horseman. He was standing on his horse, holding the stock of his gun high in the air. This was a signal to announce the presence of bison. That night they dined on beefsteaks, 'garnished with a wreath of tongues, humps and kidneys'.

The next day they met a party of Piegans, waiting on a hill. One of the men went off to meet them. The two parties trotted towards each other. At an agreed signal, the discharge of all the guns, everyone dismounted. The chief Tail Bearer came forward to meet Black Robe. He bore his name by reason of the enormous *toque* he wore on his forehead. The *toque* among the Blackfeet is a tail, seven or eight feet long, made of horse and bison hair, interwoven with their own. But instead of floating behind in the ordinary way this *toque* was located on the chief's forehead, reaching out spirally like a rhinoceros horn. Such a tail among the Blackfeet is a mark of great distinction and bravery; the longer the tail, the greater courage must the bearer display upon occasion. Greetings were exchanged; the calumet was smoked. After this symbol of peace, brotherhood and good harmony had gone around a few times, passing from mouth to mouth, tongues were loosened as if by magic and everyone began telling their news. Father De Smet spoke to them of his mission and purpose among the tribes of the Rockies.

At last, on 14 September, on the shores of the Judith River, a tributary of the Missouri, he came upon the principal camp of the Blackfeet.

It was the Feast of the Exaltation of the Holy Cross. What a joy it was to see united under the Cross the Blackfeet and Flathead warriors, whose scars told of many bloody battles with each other; these warriors who had never met save in mortal hatred.

The next day, 15 September, Nez Percés, Piegans, Bloods, Grosventres and Blackfeet of different tribes, to the number of more than 2,000, surrounded the humble altar that had been raised in the desert to the living God.

On 24 September they set off for Fort Lewis, later named Fort Benton. Fort Lewis was the highest post of the St Louis Fur Company, 3,000 miles above the mouth of the Missouri. On the way the Piegan Little Chief drew up alongside Father De Smet and asked him to dismount, as he did so himself. He invited the Black Robe to smoke the calumet; which is invariably the prelude to some serious matter.

In a letter to his Provincial, headed 'Fort Lewis, September 26, 1846', Father De Smet recounts the story.

'There is a quarrel,' he said, 'between me and a chief of the Bloods. I shall settle it at the fort. In a few minutes I shall see my mortal enemy, who for a long time has threatened to take my life. He is famous for his courage, but even more for the badness of his heart. He murdered by treachery a Nez Percé who was under my protection, while he was smoking my pipe, eating my food and resting under the sacred asylum of my tent. I would have been forever dishonoured if I had not taken prompt vengeance for this shameful and detestable act, and washed the stain from my tribe with blood. I shot the murderer at arm's length and in his own lodge. He did not die. His wound is healed now. He is waiting to kill me. I am not afraid, I am a chief too. Black Robe, I have heard your word, and I have new feelings in my heart. I would like to make peace with my enemy; but his heart is so sore that he will not hear of any arrangement. My brother has done all that he could, but he still keeps his resolution of shedding my blood. This is what I will do; I will offer him a horse to cover up his wound. If he is satisfied, it is good. If not I shall kill him.'

I suggested that everything ought to be tried before coming to the latter alternative. I even offered myself as mediator between them, and we made a vow to the Holy Virgin, that the affair might be settled amicably. For, as I had never witnessed the spilling of one drop of human blood, I felt assured that Almighty God would spare me the painful sight on this present occasion. We rode on. Little Chief and his companions prepared their arrows and loaded their guns. When we were within sight of the fort, two Blackfeet came out in haste to meet us; they tell Little Chief that if he or any of his men come nearer, their lives are in danger. They return at once to announce our arrival. Soon the great bell of the fort is heard. Paying no heed to the advice we had received, we started for the fort at a gallop. The gates were opened to us at once and all the whites saluted us with the greatest cordiality, despite the absence of the commandant, who came in a few minutes later to add still further to the civilities with which we were greeted.

After the first compliments, two horses were brought up to us, and we repaired to an island in the Missouri, upon which are a dozen lodges of the Blood Blackfeet, and in the midst of them, that of the murderer in question. The extreme cleanliness that prevailed in it showed that it had been prepared to receive us. We were introduced first; after us Little Chief the Piegan and his companions, Omakzikinne or Big Lake, Onisetêstamik or White Bull, Masteisttamok or Crow Bull, Minêpoassin or Chief's Word, Eketzo or Big Roller, Sata or the Wicked and Alaniaki or Bruised with Blows; next the Blood Blackfeet, and last of all the murderous chief, whose features sufficiently betrayed the vengeful feelings that were boiling in his heart.

I explained the motives of my visit and pleaded strongly in favour of reconciliation, at the same time declaring my determination not to leave the lodge until it was accomplished. The Blackfoot chief listened attentively, and then made a very apt reply; his last words were: 'All is forgotten. How could my heart be bad, after what the Black Robe has said!' These reassuring words gave rise to several short speeches from the assembly, which shows that there is eloquence everywhere when the heart speaks.

Little Chief's address closed with an act that moved me much; he went up to him who had been his most cruel enemy, and after embracing him tenderly gave him, beside the promised horse, a fair robe adorned with porcupine quills and pearls, which he threw over him on the spot. The pipe of peace was at once lighted to seal the agreement, went round the assembly several times, and all blew their smoke upward in a spirit of thanksgiving. Unnecessary to say that after the smoking all withdrew with their hearts full of a joy which it is easier to feel than to describe.

C and R, pp. 597–9.

The conversion of the Blackfeet presented difficulties that Father De Smet had not encountered among the Oregon Tribes. In a letter to a colleague from Fort Lewis, 27 September 1846, discussing a mission to this tribe he wrote:

It is assuredly a task full of difficulties and obstacles, requiring the zeal and courage of an apostle; one must be prepared for a life of crosses, privation and patience; they are savages in the full meaning of the word, accustomed to wreak vengeance on their enemies and wallow in blood and carnage. They are plunged in the grossest superstitions, which brutalise their souls; they worship the sun and moon, offer them sacrifices of propitiation and thanksgiving. They cut deep into their own flesh and even cut off joints of their fingers. 'I offer you my blood,' they say to their divinity, 'now give me success in arms and on my return I will offer you the homage of the scalps of my enemies.'

C and R, p. 947.

It was decided to leave Father Point with the Blackfeet, while Father De Smet should descend the river, 2,200 miles to St Louis and report on the state of the missions and the need for more missionaries. On 28 September 1846 Father De Smet embarked on the rapid current of the Missouri in a light canoe with only two guides to begin his long journey that was to last two months before he reached Westport. For the first seventeen miles of the Rocky Mountains, the Missouri races from cataract to cataract with a deafening roar. About 410 miles from its source the Missouri passes through the Gate of the Mountains, where it is compressed to a width of 150 yards. The floodwaters rush tumultuously and swiftly for a distance of six miles; the cliffs rise perpendicularly from the water's surface to a height of 1,200 feet. One hundred and ten miles further on come the Great Falls, the biggest cataract, in the midst of a desolate and sterile region. The Great Falls commence nine miles below the mouth of the Sun River, and reach for sixteen miles, in very rapid currents, falls and cascades, making a total descent of 380 feet. The last fall is the highest; the water drops a height of eighty-four feet. One half falls in a mass over a perpendicular rock, and the other half rolls its tumultuous cascades into the basin at the foot. The water, the rocks slightly covered with a veil of foam, the lofty cliffs which frame it all, that succession of rapid currents, the deafening noise of the fall and the cataract, spreading into the distance, the column of vapour rising and presenting to the sun all the vivid colours of the rainbow, make a scene very beautiful and very wild at the same time.

The departure was saluted by the discharge of the guns of the fort and a large number of small arms. It was noon when they lost sight of the fort. They soon passed Shonkin Creek and camped twenty-five miles further down, near Bird Island. On the morning of 1 October they were in a place called the Bad Lands. They shot a grizzly bear.

> He, however, tried to get even with us; after being shot twice he made a furious leap from a height of twenty-five feet, meaning to fall upon our skiff and rend us in return; luckily he missed the boat and found himself rolling in the river, but without renouncing his vengeance. As he came swimming after us, my two men reloaded their guns and shot him at arms' length, killing him this time. The grizzly is the king of animals here; all recognise his supremacy. The wolf and the panther dare not go near him, nor touch what belongs to him, not even the carcass of his prey, which he has buried with stones and earth. Still he always takes flight at the sight or smell of man; the eye of man has a magical power over him, as over all other animals; it is rare for him to

attack any one, unless he is wounded. When he has been struck by a ball, he rushes in rage toward the spot whence the shot came.

C and R, p. 602.

On 11 October Father De Smet reached Fort Union, near the mouth of the Yellowstone and 600 miles from Fort Lewis. So he had made about fifty miles a day. On 13 October he set out again with his two companions.

On 15 October the desire to proceed in spite of a violent wind was dashed all at once by

> a wave that filled our skiff and sent us to the bottom of the river. Fortunately the river was only five feet deep. We contented ourselves therefore with waiting for a more favourable wind and drying our garments, the only ones we possessed, and warming our stiffened limbs. After dinner the wind changed, and we came down gaily enough, and the next day we made up our lost time; with the aid of sails, we covered a distance of sixty to seventy miles. The buffalo continued to be very numerous; neither is there any lack of grizzly bears, which are all the time drawing the fire of my companions. We camped at about the middle of the first great bend of the Missouri.
>
> On the 18th a favourable wind encouraged us to hoist our sails again; we made about ten knots an hour and at dawn of the next day reached Fort Berthold, where we were politely received and treated by Mr Bruyère. The Grosventres have their main village here; the most of them were off on their winter hunt. Along the riverbanks bands of Indians would signal from the shore. To refuse to land would anger them and expose us to their thirst for vengeance, so through prudence we landed and rarely had cause to regret it. We accepted the calumet and filled it for them and exchanged news.

C and R, p. 606.

They camped for the night at the mouth of Knife River. Here they encountered real danger. Under cover of darkness a band of Aricaras, dreaded thieves and murderers, sworn enemies of the white man, armed to the teeth, approached their campfire without being seen. The campfire had betrayed their location. They crept forward, spears poised, tomahawks ready. Fortunately the Chief

140

Net-soo-taka or White Parfleche recognised Father De Smet by firelight. At the sight of the copper cross on his breast he flung away his tomahawk. Running to the Black Robe he embraced and hugged him saying, 'Ah! How near you were to starting for the spirit land. We took you for an enemy!' Then they all put their two hands over their mouths, a token expressive of their great astonishment. They exchanged all the marks of politeness and friendship and the evening was spent rejoicing. The calumet was presented, and after bison hump and tongues roasted on the spit, they honoured the missionary with a song and dance.

Next day they breakfasted at Fort Madison or Mandan.

They were much delayed in the five following days by adverse winds. On the morning of 26 October they came to the encampment of Mr Goulé, the American Fur Company's clerk in the neighbourhood of the *Butes au Grés* or Sandstone Buttes. There Father De Smet baptised several half-blood children.

Taking advantage of favourable weather, they went on four days and nights without stopping, and early in the morning of 30 October reached Fort Pierre, the main warehouse for furs and supplies of the America Company.

They were now in the midst of the Sioux tribe, perhaps the largest of all the North American tribes. Their territory stretched from St Peter's River on the Mississippi to the Missouri, and thence to the sources of the two great branches of the Platte. The Sioux numbered from 60,000 to 80,000. They were divided into several tribes, all speaking the same tongue with slight differences.

On 3 November they left Fort Pierre for St Louis, 1,500 miles away. But after a few miles they noted that their skiff was leaking. They had to stop for repairs. They dragged it up the bank, turned it upside down, checked it for leaks, and did the patching up. Two days later they were at Fort Bouis. By now the weather had cleared up, and taking advantage of a favourable wind, they covered the entire Great Bend of the Missouri.

On 6 November De Smet was at Fort Lookout. The principal chiefs of the Sioux were assembled there. Father De Smet told them of the conversion of the mountain tribes and of his recent visit to the Blackfeet.

And you, will you receive a Black Robe who wishes to live on your plains and dwell in the midst of you? Will you listen to his words and follow the path that Jesus Christ, Son of the Master of life, came on earth to show us, for in his path all nations must tread? The Flatheads, the Kalispels, the Stietshoi, the Skoyelpi, the nations of New Caledonia have all received the word of God; they are walking the trail that leads to heaven! They have thrown aside all that is bad; they have buried the hatchet; they have forsaken drink, which makes the Sioux mad and unhappy; they have renounced thievery and depredations. Speak, Sioux! I am listening and will carry your words to the great chief of the Black Robes; speak from your hearts.

C and R, p. 609.

After a few minutes' consultation and the usual ceremonies of the calumet the Great Orator rose, and having shaken hands with Father De Smet and with all his companions as well, he said:

Black Robe, I speak in the name of the chiefs and braves; the words that you announce from the Master of Life are fair; we love them; we hear them today for the first time. Black Robe, you are only passing through our country; tomorrow we will no longer hear your voice; we shall be as we have always been, children without a father to guide them, like ignorant beasts of the prairie. Black Robe, come and build your lodge in our midst; my heart tells me that you will be listened to. We are wicked, we have bad hearts, but those who carry the good word have never come to us. Come, Black Robe, the Sioux will listen to you and our children shall be instructed by you.

C and R, p. 610.

Later that day Father De Smet baptised four children of two Canadians married to Indian women, living nine miles from the fort. Unfortunately the winter was approaching; the river was already filling with ice, and Father De Smet could not delay an instant if he wished to reach his colleagues in St Louis, so it was with great regret that he had to put off the present evangelisation of this tribe.

On 10 November he passed the mouth of the river Niobrara, which rises in a little lake at the foot of the Black Hills. It was here, on the banks of this fair river two miles above its mouth and in the midst of the desert, that some hundred families belonging to the sect of Mormons had taken refuge, to find shelter from the unjust persecutions which other sectarians of the United States had made them suffer for several years past. Three times already their enemies had burned their homes and hunted them down like wild beasts.

On 13 November Father De Smet and his companions reached Fort Vermilion, 400 miles from Fort Pierre, where they were liberally supplied with provisions. Here Father De Smet baptised seven half-blood children. On 14 November he saw a Mormon on the shore; but he fled at their approach.

On 18 November 1846 De Smet was within sight of Council Bluffs, which he had visited in 1842. Not far from there, in the territory of the Omahas, he met Mr Brigham Young and his Mormons who were encamped on a vast and beautiful area, having been driven out from the city of Nauvoo on the Mississippi. There were more than 10,000 Mormons there. He became well acquainted with Brigham Young. In his letter to the Provincial (1 January 1847) Father De Smet wrote:

> I was introduced to their president, Mr Young, an affable and very polite gentleman. He pressed me very earnestly to remain a few days, an invitation that my limited time did not permit me to accept. The unheard-of persecutions and atrocious sufferings endured by these unhappy people will furnish a sad page to the history of the great valley of the West.
>
> *C and R, p. 611.*

Young asked Father De Smet, 'a thousand questions' about the regions he had explored. He was particularly pleased with the Father's account of the Great Salt Lake basin. It was this that persuaded the Mormons to finally settle in Salt Lake Valley.

That evening Father De Smet met several of his Potawatomi friends from Council Bluffs, including Chief Patakojee.

On 23 November Father De Smet reached the town of St Joseph, which hadn't existed when he passed through the region in 1842. Now it boasted 350 houses, two churches, a city hall and a jail. The population was comprised of Americans, French Creoles, Irish and Germans.

On 28 November he arrived at Westport. Already the ice had begun to run in the river and great quantities of snow fell. As he could not travel by river he took the stagecoach to St Louis, which he reached on 10 December, three years and six months after his departure in the opposite direction. Seven years had elapsed since

143

his first journey to the Rocky Mountains. Many, many times his life had been in danger.

It is worthwhile to consider here what Father De Smet had accomplished in those seven years. This is what the authors of his biography, Chittenden and Richardson, have to say:

His prodigious labours, travels, hardships and perils must be placed in the very first rank of similar exploits. In those seven years he had travelled, by the slow methods of the time, a distance equal to more than twice the circumference of the earth. He had travelled in almost every clime and by every sort of conveyance. From the burning summer of the Equator he had passed to the frozen winters of 54° 30′ north. He had travelled by sailing vessel, by river barge and by canoe; by dog sled and snowshoe; on horseback and in wagons; and many a long mile on foot. He had endured hardships that seem to us almost impossible and which undoubtedly were the foundation of the ills he later suffered. It was to the period of 1844–6 that he referred in a letter to a fellow missionary who was complaining of the hardship of his lot: 'I have been for years a wanderer in the desert. I was three years in the mountains, without tasting bread, salt, coffee, tea, sugar. I was for years without a roof, without a bed. I have been six months without a shirt on my back, and often have I passed whole days and nights without a morsel of anything to eat.'

The results of his labours, from a missionary point of view, were highly successful. The whole Columbia valley had been dotted with infant establishments, some of which had taken on the promise of permanent growth. He had indeed laid the foundation well for a spiritual empire throughout that region, and but for the approach of emigration his plans would have brought forth the full fruition that he expected.

But most important of all, from a public point of view, was the fact that he had become a great power among the Indian tribes. All now knew him, many personally, the rest by reputation. He was the one white man in whom they had implicit faith. The Government was beginning to look to him for assistance. The Mormon, the Forty-niner, the Oregon emigrant came to him for information and advice. His writings were already known on two continents and his name was a familiar one, at least in the religious world.

C and R, p. 57.

If his work had been arduous and dangerous, the results were most consoling. Oregon possessed more than thirty Christian centres. Upon the banks of the Columbia numerous tribes begged for baptism. In New Caledonia and Western Canada more than 100,000 Indians were disposed to receive the word of God. Subjugated by the softening influence of the Gospel, the Missouri Indians gradually conquered their bloodthirsty instincts. The Blackfeet made peace with the mountain tribes, and the Sioux were impatiently awaiting the arrival of the missionary.

Chapter 9

The Sioux

After a rest for a few days in St Louis Father De Smet went to New Orleans to see the Father Provincial. Father Van de Velde, who three years before had succeeded Father Verhaegen as Vice-Provincial, listened with lively interest to Father De Smet's account of the progress the missions were making. The thousands of Indians asking for baptism must be saved. But where to find the missionaries? The priests they had scarcely sufficed for the needs of the Missouri province Another appeal must be made to Europe. Father Elet was about to leave for Rome as Procurator. Every three years each province sent one of its members under the title of 'Procurator' to confer with the Father General. It was decided that Father De Smet should accompany Father Elet.

Father De Smet returned from New Orleans to St Louis early in January 1847, to prepare for his journey. Father Elet had not seen his native land for twenty-six years, and since Father De Smet's last visit to Belgium four years ago, he had received no word from his family. They travelled via Washington, Philadelphia and New York. they crossed the Atlantic – Father De Smet for the sixth time – and landed in London. From there they went to Antwerp, and on to Termonde. After spending some days with his people, Father De Smet accompanied Father Elet to Paris. While there he visited the church of Notre Dame des Victoires, where he returned thanks to his powerful Protectress for the success of the missions. From Paris he returned to Belgium. He then prepared his 'Letters' for publication.

Early in 1848 Father De Smet started on a tour of the principal cities of Holland and Belgium soliciting funds and enlisting recruits for the missions. Despite his warnings of the perilous life of the missions, many young men were won over and said farewell to their families. Among them was Father Charles Elet, brother of Father John Elet, a young priest destined to die a saintly death a few months after his arrival in the United States.

They embarked at Ostend and crossed over to England. On 3 April 1848 they sailed from Liverpool for America. The crossing was a bad one.

> For several days, I suffered from that illness which does not kill, but tries the most patient of men. A mountainous sea tumbled us about, and we staggered around on the deck in grotesque positions. After a wearing day, I sought repose, only to be thrown out of my berth by the violence of the sea.
>
> (Letter to Francis De Smet, New York, 5 May 1848.)

On arriving in New York, the travellers learned that the Revolution that had dethroned Louis Philippe threatened to sweep Europe. In Paris, Rome, Naples, Berlin, Vienna and Prague the people were in revolt. The Jesuits, as usual, were the first attacked, and many sought refuge in America. Hearing that some priests were about to arrive, Father De Smet remained for several weeks in New York to receive them.

He visited Washington and Albany, returning each time to New York. After supplying the Jesuits newly arrived from Europe with funds and starting them safely to their destinations, many for the Oregon missions, he left for St Louis. This time he went west by the Lakes route, via Albany and Troy. He stopped one day to see the sublime Falls of Niagara, then travelled on to Bison, from Lake Erie to Sandusky, then by rail to Cincinnati and finally by steamboat to St Louis, where he arrived on 4 July 1848.

After a few weeks spent in St Louis, Father De Smet left for another mission. It will be recalled that on his return journey from the Rocky Mountains in the autumn of 1846 Father De Smet remained for some time with the Sioux tribes on the Upper Missouri. From that time on he was consumed with a desire to return to these Indians.

In mid-August 1848 he travelled by steamboat up the Missouri towards Council Bluffs. At Bellevue, near the mouth of the Platte River, he joined some agents of the Fur Company. Bellevue was in the territory of the Otoes, 665 miles from St Louis. From there they travelled overland on horseback in the direction of the Niobrara and White Rivers for ten days. The air was very clear, and there were no clouds in the sky. It was pleasant, not too warm, and the horses walked easily through the tall grass. Then for a further twenty-five days they travelled over immense, limitless prairies, where the bison roamed in herds of several hundreds and often several thousands.

In a letter to the editor of *Précis Historique*, Brussels, 3 August, 1854, Father De Smet described the bison lands.

> On my travels I have seen with my own eyes, as far as I could discern on these immense plains, thousands and thousands of these noble animals moving slowly, like an interminable troop, in one direction, and browsing the grass as they progress. They have a fearful appearance; their hairy heads inspire with terror those who are ignorant of the specific habits of this noble quadruped. Indeed, such is their timidity that one man can put to flight the most numerous herd. When alarmed, the tramp of their hoofs, their bellowing and the columns of dust that they raise, resemble the deep murmurs of a tempest mingled with peals of thunder, lessening as they grow more remote.
>
> *C and R, p. 1027.*

Father De Smet gives a vivid eyewitness account of a bison hunt.

> One single Indian, unarmed, is sent upon the best courser in the camp in the direction of the bison, to meet them. He approaches against the wind and with the greatest precaution. At the distance of about 100 paces he envelops himself in a bison hide, the fur turned outside, and also envelops his horse as much as possible in the same manner, and then makes a plaintive cry in imitation of that of a bison calf. This cry attracts the attention of the whole herd; after some seconds, several thousand of them, hearing this pitiful plaint, turn towards the pretended calf. At first they move slowly, then advance into a trot, and at last they push forward in a full gallop. The horseman continually repeats the cry of the calf, and takes his course toward [an] enclosure, ever attentive to keep at the same distance from the animals that are following him. By this stratagem he leads the vast herd of bison to their capture ... As soon as all the bison – several hundred – are captured, they are slaughtered with arrows, lances and knives. Men, women and children all take part in the butchery and the flaying and cutting up of the animals. While men cut and slash

the flesh, the women and children in particular devour the meat still warm with life – the livers, kidneys, brains, etc. They smear their faces, hair, arms and legs with the blood of the bison. Two days after the hunt not a vestige of the carnage remains.

In a letter to the Archbishop of Baltimore dated June 1849, from St Louis University, Father De Smet gives a detailed account of their journey across the prairies.

It is customary to encamp in places where the grass is fresh, which is generally on the border of a stream or pond of clear water. Care must be taken for the safety of the horses at night. To prevent all accidents, they are hobbled, that is; the two forelegs are tied together, so as to prevent their straying too far from the camp. Two or three men remain on guard against any surprise attack from the Indians, too justly renowned as the most expert of horse-thieves. These sentinels also protect us against the bears and wolves that invest the wilderness, and incessantly prowl in the neighbourhood of camps. Horses, on perceiving them, take fright and fly, unless the necessary precautions have been taken, and it sometimes happens that the most careful measures prove futile. Thus we, one day, lost a superb stallion of great value. Every evening he was tied to a post, with a long and heavy halter, but in a fright, caused by the approach of wolves, he darted forward with such velocity after the other horses, as they rushed by him, that on reaching the end of his halter he broke his neck.

C and R, p. 619.

The difficulties of this journey in summer, through the most arid part of the American plains, were many.

In so long a march, through regions so singularly various, two great inconveniences are sometimes experienced – want of water and of wood. More than once we had no other fuel than the dry buffalo-dung, and three times at our camping ground water failed us. This is a hard trial for man and horse, especially after travelling all day under the burning sun of the month of August. Another kind of torment, still less supportable when the heat is most intense, is the appearance of fantastical rivers and lakes in the verge of the horizon, seeming to invite the weary traveller to advance and refresh his wasted strength upon their banks. Fatigue and thirst picture in the distant verdure, shade and coolness awaiting him. The illusion increases the desire of quenching your burning thirst. You hasten onward to reach the goal. Hour succeeds hour; the deceitful mirage heightens in brilliancy, and the panting, exhausted traveller presses on without a suspicion that the phantom flies before him.

Besides the difficulties arising from the nature of the ground, there are others which summer always brings with its myriad of insects. Among these the most to be dreaded is the *gadfly*, the sting of which will make the gentlest horse bound with rage. Happily for the horse in these plains, Providence has bestowed upon him a defender as skilful as devoted; the starling, unalarmed by the presence of man, which, wheeling ever about the rider, lights on the back of the horse or on his load, to dart with wonderful skill upon the malicious insect which is about to attack his travelling companion.

For ourselves, we are obliged to wage a continual war upon the swarms of mosquitoes and their allies the gnats. The latter teased us by day, the former, more cowardly, attacked us by night. These famished enemies, the product of the stagnant waters and decaying plants, at the approach of a convoy rush from their infected abodes, and accompany it with their plaintive buzzing, to the spot where the traveller seeks in vain a brief repose after the heat and hardships of the day. The winged tribe at once sound the trump of war, and darting on their tired victim, sting, harass and pursue him until they have assuaged their sanguinary fury, and obliged the unfortunate traveller, already sweltering in the heat, to seek a stifling shelter under a buffalo robe or a thick blanket. One day I found myself the object of attack of a swarm of winged ants. They came upon me with such a furious impetuosity that in a few seconds I was totally covered. Then I waved my handkerchief about my head, and soon got my horse to leave far behind us this phalanx of black insects, which filled a space of about a quarter of a mile.

In my last letter I spoke of the annoyance resulting from the continual attacks and buzzing of the mosquitoes and *brûlots*. I must add to this harsh music the more fearful and more disagreeable noise of the rattlesnake. These reptiles are frequently met in the region styled Bad Lands, a very remarkable plateau, of which I will hereafter give a description – and where the Little

150

Missouri (Teton or Bad River), the White River and the Niobrara take their rise. Here also are found the many-hued chameleon, the hideous lizard, the horned frog, known by the perhaps more classical name of salamander, and several varieties of small tortoise. I witnessed a singular trait of the instinct of a rattlesnake. The reptile was basking in the sun, surrounded by eight or ten little ones. As soon as she perceived me, she gave the rattle, opened her throat wide, and in an instant the whole brood descended. I withdrew some seconds, and then returned; the young ones had come forth from their living tomb, to which my presence quickly obliged them to seek refuge anew.

Without doubt there will be moments in which the ardour of a burning sun, and the privation of pure water capable of allaying thirst, will force you to remember that the best of earthly joys have their hidden thorns; but these trials are rare and brief. A gentle breeze almost continually refreshes the atmosphere in these vast plains, and the surface is so uniform as to baffle a surprise from the most crafty enemy. The route is one field of verdure, enamelled with odoriferous wild flowers, whose brilliant beauty has no witness but the azure firmament.

The unbroken, arid soil of the Bad Lands, which will ever baffle the most energetic and persevering labours, boasts, however, of several millions of townships, full of life and movement – I mean the villages of the prairie dog – the site of each one of which extends over an area of several square miles of smooth table land, on which the grass is very short and thin. The instincts of this remarkable animal (which bears some resemblance to the squirrel) are at once curious and amusing. The grass that springs up in the neighbourhood of their dwellings they tear up by the roots; but their vandalism has its exceptions. They seem to respect and spare certain flowers that generally surround their little abodes, and give them a much more agreeable look.

They pile up the earth around their dwelling about two feet above the surface of the soil, thus protecting themselves against the inundations which, in the rainy seasons or at the melting of the snows, would engulf them and their little homes. Guided by instinctive foresight, they carefully gather all the straw, which is scattered over the plain and carry them into their subterraneous asylums, to protect them against the rigours of winter. At the approach of a horseman, alarm is rapidly communicated to all the citizens of this singular republic. All quit their habitations, and with head erect, the ears pricked up with anxiety, a troubled stare, remain standing at the entrance of their abodes or at the opening of their conical hills. After a momentary silence, they break forth into one loud and repeated chorus of shrill barking. For some minutes, life, motion and restless agitation reign throughout the extensive field they occupy; but at the first gunshot all is tranquil, every animal disappearing like a flash. A kind of small owl and the rattlesnake appear to entertain amicable relations with the prairie dog, and are commonly found at the entrance of their lodges, and in the general flight the three seek safety in the same asylum. The motives and nature of this singular sympathy are unknown. The wolf and the fox are their greatest enemies.

The Indian word *Mankizita-Watpa*, commonly translated White Earth River, signifies, more literally, Smoking Land River, and in this region there are incontestable and numerous indications that subterranean and volcanic fires have passed there. The water of the river is strongly impregnated with a whitish slime. We encamped on its shore. A heavy rain had recently washed all the ravines and dry beds of the rivulets and torrents, which are abundant throughout the Bad Lands; consequently the water was very similar to thin mud. What was to be done? We must either use this water to prepare our evening repast, or retire without tea or broth. This is no easy sacrifice in the desert, after riding on horseback for ten or eleven hours in the scorching sun. After many fruitless efforts to purify the water, we were obliged to use it as it was. Hunger and thirst make us less dainty. The mixture of mud, tea and sugar was, after all, palatable to our famished stomachs. We set out a pailful of this water to settle over night, and in the morning found it three-quarters full of pure mud. On the morrow we travelled all day and found a delicious spring, where we camped for the night.

The Bad Lands are the most extraordinary of any I have met in my journeys through the wilderness. The action of the rains, snow and winds upon the argillaceous soil is scarcely credible; and the combined influence of these elements renders it the theatre of most singular scenery. Viewed at a distance, these lands exhibit the appearance of extensive villages and ancient castles, but under forms so extraordinary, and so capricious a style of architecture, that we might consider them as appertaining to some new world, or ages far remote. Cupolas of colossal proportions, and pyramids which recall the gigantic labours of ancient Egypt. The atmospheric agents work upon them with such effect that probably two consecutive years do not pass without reforming or destroying these strange constructions. The geologist and naturalist may find abundant material for study and illustration; for here are found curious remains of the mastodon (the largest of known quadrupeds), mingled with those of the mountain-hare. I have seen well-preserved skulls, horns and tortoises, so large that two men could hardly raise them. All of these bore the distinct impress of their primitive nature.

C and R, pp. 619–724.

At the mouth of the Niobrara they came upon the whole tribe of the Poncas assembled there, their favourite haunt during the fruit season and the gathering of the corn harvest. Father De Smet describes his meeting with the Poncas.

The manner in which they accosted my travelling companions augured little good, and was near being attended with disastrous consequences. It appears, indeed, that they meditated an attack upon the little troop of white men whom, numbering but fifteen, escorted a wagon filled with merchandise for the Fur Company. They intended, at least, to pillage the convoy and kill one of the travellers, under pretext that he came from the country of the Pawnee, where one of their warriors had lost his life. I will present you here the laconic formula of reasoning of one of these barbarians, while in the act of taking aim at his victim. 'My brother was killed by a Pawnee! I must avenge his death, or recover the debt (value of his body) in horses or in blankets!' To this degree, unfortunately, has the idea of justice sunk in the Indian mind. Had an Indian fallen by the hand of a white man, every brave of that tribe considers himself justified in retaliating upon the first white man he chances to meet, without regard to his country or part of the world from which he may come. I was in front, but at the first signal of alarm I faced the point of danger. At once the air resounded with reiterated cries of 'The Black Robe has come! The Black Robe has come!' Surprise and curiosity arrest the work of pillage. The chiefs ask for an explanation, and order the spoilers to keep respectfully away, and restore what they had already stolen; then they press around me to shake hands (a ceremony somewhat lengthy, for they were about 600 in number), and conduct us in triumph to our encampment on the shore of the Niobrara. In my turn I made a little distribution of tobacco, which they appeared to appreciate more than anything else. The calumet is smoked in token of fraternal good feeling, and passed from mouth to mouth: they lavish upon me as well as upon my companions the most touching marks of kindness and respect. Such was the happy conclusion of a meeting that at first inspired us with such just fears. But the merciful views of Providence extended further.

They besought me to visit their village, four miles from our camp, in order to pass the night with them. I accepted the invitation the more willingly, as it would afford me an opportunity of announcing the truths of Faith. In fact I lost no time, and shortly after my arrival the whole tribe, numbering more than 1,000 persons, surrounded the 'Black Robe'. This was the first time that the Poncas had heard of Jesus Christ preached by the mouth of his minister. The holy eagerness and attention that they lent to my words induced me to prolong my instructions until late in the night. The next day I baptised their little ones, and when the time of separation arrived they besought me with the greatest earnestness to renew my visit, and to fix my residence among them. 'We will cheerfully listen to the Words of the Great Spirit,' said they, 'and submit to all his commands that he manifest to us.' Until their wishes can be gratified, I considered myself happy to find among them a Catholic half-breed, tolerably well instructed in his religion, who promised me to serve as catechist.

This extraordinary attention on the part of the Indians, and their avidity to hear the Word of God, must appear surprising in a people which seems to unite all intellectual and moral miseries. But the Spirit of the Lord breathes where it will. His graces and light prompt and aid men whom ignorance, rather than perverse and disordered will, renders vicious. Moreover, the same Spirit can also soften the most obdurate hearts, warm the coldest, and produce peace, justice and joy where before reigned iniquity, trouble and disorder.

C and R, pp. 625–6.

A few days after his meeting with the Poncas he passed into Sioux territory. The officers of Fort Bouis and Fort Pierre received him with much hospitality.

After crossing this arid region, Father De Smet at last reached the Sioux camp. The Sioux or Dakotas, divided into several groups, numbered 30–40,000, and formed the most powerful and warlike of the North American tribes. The different Sioux tribes spoke much the same language and were scattered over both sides of the Missouri River north of the Niobrara. When he came upon the Sioux, he found them revelling in all the horrors of their primitive savagery. Several warriors had just returned from a war against the Omahas, carrying thirty-two scalps torn from defenceless old men, and from women and children whose husbands and fathers were away hunting. Rarely did they return from warfare without horses to ride or scalps to boast.

When they re-enter their villages, after the combat, it is their custom to attach these horrible trophies of their shameful victory to the points of their lances or to the bits of their horses. At the sight of these spoils the whole tribe shouts with joy, and everyone considers it the highest gratification to assist at the Scalp Dance and Feast – which is celebrated amid the most discordant yells and fearful gestures. They plant a post daubed with vermilion in the midst of the camp; the warriors surround it, flourishing in their hands the bloody scalps which they have brought back from the field of battle; each one howls his war-song to the lugubrious tone of a large drum; then giving in turn his stroke of the tomahawk on the post, he proclaims the victims that his hatchet has immolated, and exhibits ostentatiously the scars of the wounds which he has received.

Add to the thick shade of heathen darkness a shocking deprivation of manners, and you will have a faint idea of the lamentable position of these wretched tribes. Yet these same men welcomed me with open arms, as a messenger from the Great Spirit!

An event that occurred two days after my arrival at Fort Pierre, contributed much to augment their confidence in me. I give it as it occurred. The tribe of the Ogallalas had entered in a hostile manner on the lands of their neighbours, the Absarokas (or Crows), and had attacked them. The latter defended themselves bravely, routed their aggressors, and killed ten or twelve warriors.

In this affair, the chief of the vanquished nation, named Red Fish, lost his daughter, who was carried off by the Crows into captivity. Melancholy and humbled, he deserted the wigwams of his tribe, which loss of honour and the death of so many of its warriors had overwhelmed with mourning and desolation. He presented himself at Fort Pierre on the morrow of my arrival. The object of his journey was to obtain the liberty of his daughter, through the mediation of the officers of the fort; he offered 80 fine buffalo robes and his best horses for her ransom. In his visit to me, grasping my hand firmly in his, with tears coursing down his cheeks, and heart-broken with grief, he thus addressed me while sobs often interrupted his utterance: 'Black Gown, I am a most unhappy father! I have lost my beloved daughter. Pity me, for I have learned that the medicine of the Black Gown (prayer) is powerful before the Great Spirit. Speak to the Master of Life in my favour, and I will still preserve hope of seeing my child.'

To these few words, which the emotion of the aged man rendered singularly eloquent, I replied that I sympathised with his sorrow, but that he must himself prepare the way for the blessing of heaven – and that by virtuous deeds he might obtain from the Great Spirit the accomplishment of his desires. I added that without doubt the Master of Life had been offended by this unjust attack upon the Crows, of which he himself had been the chief instigator, in his position as Head Chief, and that to himself solely he must attribute the misfortune of his child and all the other miseries which had resulted from that expedition. I exhorted him to abandon in future all unprovoked attacks upon his neighbours, and to persuade his tribe to hearken to the orders of the Great Spirit, which I had come to announce to them.

Red Fish returned soon after to his nation and collected all the principal chiefs, in order to communicate to them what had passed at the fort, and in particular his conversation with me, the Black Robe, concerning his daughter. At that very moment a cry of joy was heard at the extremity of the camp. They ran up from all sides to ask the cause; at length the good tidings are announced, that the captive daughter has escaped safe and sound from her enemies. The old chieftain scarcely dares to believe what he hears. He rises, and on leaving his cabin he has the unspeakable consolation of beholding once more his beloved child, whom Providence has restored. Imagine, if possible, his astonishment and delight, shared with him by his tribe. Every

hand was lifted to heaven to thank the Great Spirit for the deliv-
erance of the prisoner. The report flew quickly from village to
village, and this coincidence, that divine Providence permitted
for the good of the Ogallalas, was to them a certain proof, of the
great power of Christian prayer, and will, I hope, contribute to
confirm these poor Indians in their good dispositions.

C and R, pp. 629–31.

The adventures of the daughter of Red Fish are thus related in a
later letter found in the third edition of Father De Smet's writings.

From the time of her capture by the Crows, the girl had passed
her nights with her hands and feet tied by leather straps to pegs,
strongly driven into the ground. On the night following the Mass
offered at Fort Pierre, a woman untied her bonds, gave her a
little bundle containing food and several pairs of moccasins, and
told her in a low voice 'to get up and start out for her camp,
where her father was waiting for her'. She travelled all that
night. At daybreak, she hid in a hollow tree on the bank of a
river. A few hours later a band of young warriors, following her
trail, breathing vengeance and uttering frightful yells, crossed
the river precisely at the hollow tree. They looked in vain for the
tracks of their destined victim on the farther bank, and finally
returned to camp, much puzzled by the mysterious escape of the
young enemy. When night came on the poor girl resumed her
journey and walked several days and nights in succession with
very little rest. At last she reached her father's camp, a few
minutes after he arrived on his return from Fort Pierre.

C and R, pp. 631–2.

Father De Smet had come to the Sioux to ascertain their moral and
religious dispositions with a view to founding a mission among
them.

The little account that I have the honour of presenting to you
discloses the result of my visit. What I have narrated touching
these inhabitants of the desert offers little encouragement to the
missionary. There is an immense difference between them and
the Flatheads and numerous other nations that occupy the regions
west of the Rocky Mountains. These first children of my apostolate have given me consolations that I should vainly seek

among the Sioux. Would, then, a mission with the latter prove destitute of success? The little experience that I have been able to acquire, and my residence among them, inspires me to trust more confidently in him who holds in his hands the most obdurate hearts and the most refractory wills. I hope that in the course of this year something may be done in favour of these degraded Indians, so long left without aid of religion.

C and R, p. 635.

Winter was now setting in. The dry smell of fall leaves, with their flame fading, filled his nostrils. The brown ferns curled sadly. It was time to leave his neophytes if he was to get back to St Louis. At the end of October, 1848, before the season of rain and snow, Father De Smet quit the uplands of the Niobrara. He set off in a skiff from Fort Bouis, near the mouth of the Little Medicine River. The two shores of the Missouri River teemed with every kind of game.

At Council Bluffs, the sky, which had been hitherto clear and serene, suddenly changed, to give place to wind and tempest, and thick clouds of snow, which accompanied us during the next two days. We took refuge in a dense forest, in order to defend ourselves from the inclemency of the storm. The wild honey which we found there was our principal resource, one poplar alone, which we felled, furnishing us with more than we needed.

We made but little progress during ten days, on account of head winds, rain and snow. Before arriving at the mouth of the Big Tarkio, the Missouri was so covered with floating ice that, in our frail bark, we were exposed to the greatest danger, especially from the many sawyers with which the bed of the river is thickly set, and which discover or conceal their menacing heads on every side. These are trees, or trunks of trees, which the river uproots and washes from its banks, and whose roots get firmly fastened in the muddy bed of the river. Prudence forced us to abandon our boat. I therefore hired a farmer's wagon, which brought us safe and sound to St Joseph, after a drive of two days through a great forest that skirts the Missouri. The steamer *Highland Mary*, last steamboat of the season between St Joseph and Kansas City, which I had hoped to meet there, had departed on the eve of my arrival, and thus the opportunity of a prompt return to St Louis appeared lost to me. I resolved, however, to exert myself to the utmost to overtake the boat: this to many would appear folly; the idea of running after a high-pressure steamboat certainly does appear quite ridiculous. But I relied upon the numerous delays of the boat at the different sandbanks, which were more likely to take place, also, as the season was advancing. I calculated well; in twenty-four hours I was on board at Fort Leavenworth.

For four months I had been night and day exposed to the open air, and, as in all my excursions, with no bed but a buffalo robe. Yet my health had been uninterruptedly good, not even suffering from the slightest attack of cold; but scarcely was I subjected, for one day, to the heat of the stove in the cabin of the steamboat, when I was seized with a violent sore throat – it being my first indisposition through the whole of my long journey.

At length, after four months' absence, I arrived without other accident at the University of St Louis, where, enjoying with my brethren the charms of the community life, I soon forgot the little fatigues of my expedition.

C and R, pp. 636–7.

It was late December 1848.

Chapter 10

The Fort Laramie Council

In 1839 Father De Smet had been appointed Assistant to the Vice-Provincial and Procurator General of the Missouri Province. This latter office related exclusively to the financial affairs of the Church. His great ability in procuring contributions and in managing the unenviable task of their distribution made him admirably fitted for the work.

> I hold the general purse and have to supply all needs; this purse is never full; the greater part of the time it is flat, while I receive demands from all sides.
>
> *C and R, p. 59.*

What he really wanted to do was to spend his days among his dear Indians in the mountains. 'I am like a soldier,' he wrote to a friend. 'When I receive orders I march whither I am sent. Yet, like a soldier, I have my preferences, and I need not tell you that these are decidedly for the Indian country. I miss very much the plains, the Indians and the wilderness with all their privations, miseries and dangers. They were treats indeed compared with the monotony with which I am surrounded.'

In a very feeling letter to the Father General, he implores the privilege of being sent away to some obscure mission there to spend the remainder of his days.

Early in the spring of 1849 Father De Smet, in his new role as Socius, left on an inspection of the Jesuit colleges at Louisville, Bardstown and Cincinnati. When he returned to St Louis he was caught in a cholera epidemic. Over several months 200 victims a day died. In a letter dated 4 July he wrote: 'Often friends whom I have seen in the morning are lying in their coffins in the evening.'

He was constantly on duty, succouring the sick and dying; he had no time even to change his clothes. The roads were silent but for the rattle of the tumbrels and barrows bearing corpses out of the city.

In August he set out to visit several of the Indian missions. He ascended the Missouri as far as Westport. From there he went overland via Fort Scott to the Osage Mission of St Hieronimo on the Neosha River. From there he visited the Miami, the Shawnees and other tribes. For some time he followed the great Santa Fé route on his way to St Mary's Mission in the valley of the Kansas. From there he returned to Westport and back to St Louis.

Early in the spring of 1850 he went with the Provincial to Chicago on affairs of the Province, and then to the Jesuit establishments at Louisville, Bardstowne, Cincinnati and Chillicothe.

In June 1850 he received a letter from Father Schoenmakers, a Dutch missionary working with the Osages, who described them as 'among the most degraded tribes of the desert, idle, filthy, drunkards, corrupted by contact with the whites'. He went on:

> We suffer hunger and thirst and cold and sleep in the open during the wettest season of the year, with only a buffalo skin and one cover by way of bedding.

To encourage the missionary Father De Smet recalled his own sufferings. He replied from St Louis:

> For several years I was a wanderer in the wilderness and during three years I never received a single letter. I lived for two years in the mountains without ever tasting bread, salt, coffee, tea or sugar. During four years I knew neither shelter nor bed; for six months I was without under-linen and often days and nights I have gone without food or drink.
>
> *C and R, p. 57.*

Father Schoenmakers, duly encouraged, endured his rude apostolate for forty years.

Hard apostolate it was for all the Black Robes. When there was an epidemic of smallpox among the Osages Father Bax went from village to village, wigwam to wigwam, carrying help and consolation, until at thirty-three he himself fell victim to his heroic charity. Father Hoeken has left a horrendous account of a journey he made to the Sioux in the depth of winter, through snow fifteen to twenty feet deep, mounted on a lame horse, his feet, nose and ears frost-bitten, his legs stiffened with rheumatism. All the while he was starving. At night storms raged and wolves howled round his camp.

Hard life it was, but that was where Father De Smet preferred to be. He and Father Provincial went on to New Orleans on business for the Society. They visited Springhill College near Mobile, then went to Alabama and back to New Orleans at the end of the year. In January 1851 they returned to St Louis.

In 1851 gold was discovered in California. In a few months the 'gold rush' had begun. Long lines of covered wagons toiled up the Platte River road bound for the newly discovered gold fields of California.

> Adventurers from every country: deserters, thieves, murderers, the scum of the United States, Mexico, Peru, Chili, and the Sandwich Islands, living together, free of all law and restraint.
> (Letter to his brother Charles, 26 April 1849.)

From California the gold-seeking hordes spread to the rich farm-lands of Oregon and Washington. In defiance of all law, they drove out the Indians, forcing them to seek refuge in the mountains. Women and children were driven from their wigwams like dogs. There is no page darker in history than the story of this 'white conquest'. As Helen Hunt Jackson recorded later:

> It would require a volume to recount the injustice, brutality, and murders committed in the last 30 years upon the Pacific coast, the details of which are too horrible to be believed.
> (*A Century of Dishonour*, p. 337)

In exchange for their lands, horses, and furs, the whites gave whisky to the Indians. Drink being the passion of the race, they eagerly seized upon the fatal liquor. We remember the drunken orgies of the Potawatomies; the same scenes were now enacted in Oregon and California. Men slaughtered each other by the hundreds, and the women and children dragged themselves like animals around their wigwams.

Yet fatal as was the effect of alcohol, its action was too slow to satisfy the invaders. They concluded that the revolver was more

Father De Smet as a young man.

PACIFIC
OCEAN

ROCKY

Jasper House

Committees
Punch Bowl

1846

St. Anne †

Fort Assiniboine

Fort Edmonton or
Augustus

Athabasca
Pass

R. Columbia 1845

1845

Rocky Mountain House

BRITISH

MOUNTAINS

1846

1846

Fort Clatsop

Cowlitz

Coeur D'Alenes

Pend D'Oreilles

St. Ignatius †

Blackfoot

1863

R. Columbia

Cayuses

Sacred
Heart

1863

Flatheads

Country

1863

1846

1851

St. Paul

Walla
Wallas

St. Mary †

Fort Owen

O

1841

F

Cou

186

From Europe via Cape Horn 1843

Umpquas

R E G O N

R. Snake

Nez-perces

or

1842

1842

1840

1842

Lake
de Sme

To New York via Panama 1863

Shoshones

1840

1841

The Home of

The Crows

Fort

1851

From New York via Panama 1858

Snakes

1840

Oreg

Root Diggers

Utahs

or

Paiutes

San Francisco

M E X I C A N

P O S S E S S I O N S

Navajos

Los Angeles

Pueblos

PACIFIC

OCEAN

†	Mission Station
⌐ ⌐	Fr. De Smedt's Journeys
— · —	International Boundaries

(Dates and directions are not shown on
those routes he passed over several times)

0   100   200   300   400   500 Km.

0   100   200   300 Miles

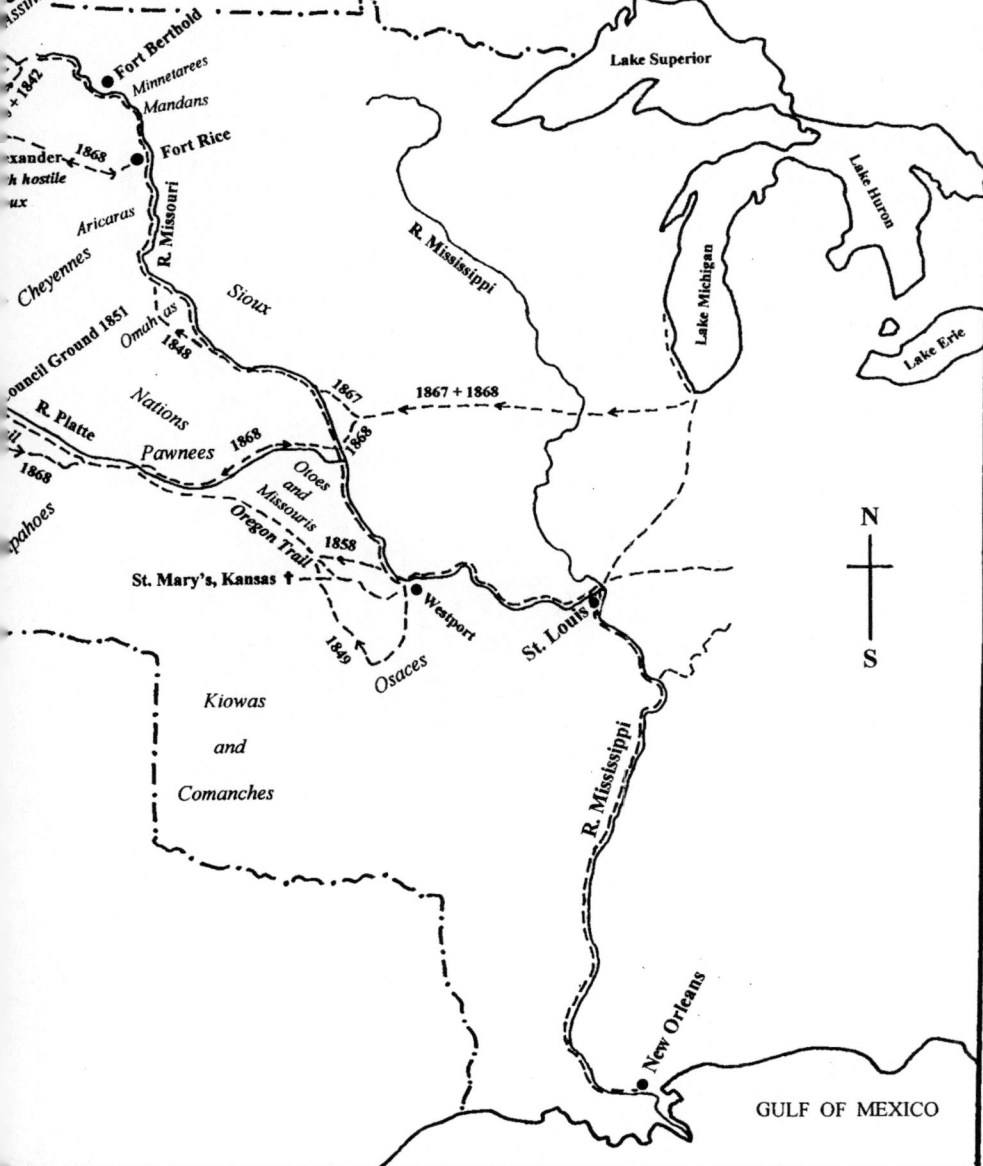

THE TRAVELS OF
FATHER PIERRE-JEAN DE SMET SJ
WEST OF THE MISSISSIPPI

HUDSON BAY

POSSESSIONS

Assiniboines

Fort Berthold

Minnetarees

Mandans

+1842

1868

xander
h hostile
ux

Fort Rice

Aricaras

Cheyennes

R. Missouri

Sioux

Council Ground 1851

Omah'as

1848

R. Platte

Nations

Pawnees

1868

1868

1867

1868

1867 + 1868

Otoes
and
Missouris

Oregon Trail

1858

ahoes

St. Mary's, Kansas †

1849

Westport

Osaces

St. Louis

Kiowas

and

Comanches

Lake Superior

R. Mississippi

Lake Michigan

Lake Huron

Lake Erie

N

S

R. Mississippi

New Orleans

GULF OF MEXICO

St Mary's Mission, among the Flatheads.

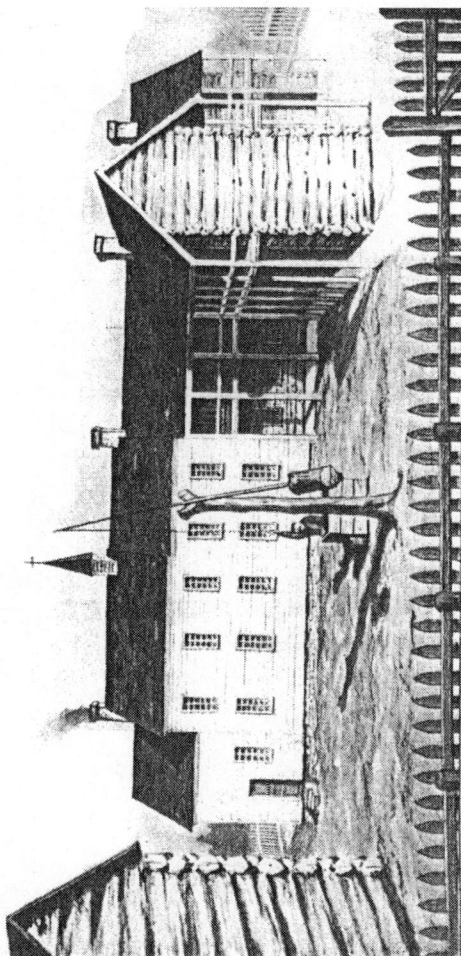

St Stanislaus' Mission, in 1847.

Fr De Smet, wearing the Order of Leopold, awarded to him in 1865 by King Leopold of the Belgians.

Statue of Fr De Smet in Termonde (now Dondermonde), Belgium. The statue was unveiled in 1878, on the fifth anniversary of his death.

Fr De Smet with a delegation of Indian chiefs in Oregon.

expeditious than whisky, and offered twenty dollars for every Indian scalp. Men killed as a training in marksmanship, and to try out their weapons.

Yet still more revolting machinations were resorted to. Arsenic was mixed with the flour and sugar sold to the Indians; their springs, from which they obtained drinking water, were poisoned with strychnine, and clothing reeking with infection was given to them. In one incident, whites decided to destroy an Indian camp; to accomplish their foul purpose they hung from a tree in front of the camp the clothing of a man who had just died from smallpox. The Indians, catching sight of the garments, were enchanted, and proceeded to don them at once. Before long this terrible malady appeared, and of several hundred Indians, only a dozen poor wretches remained to weep over the ravages wrought by the disease. If to these destructive causes are added the evils engendered by the immorality of the whites, one readily understands how the Indian population in California fell in ten years from 100,000 to 30,000 souls.

The Indians, notably the Cheyenne, looked on as the bravest Indians on the prairie, became angry at the invasion by the 'pale faces' of their territory – territory that had been guaranteed by the United States Government. They resented being cheated of their lands. The Cheyenne, implacable enemies of the white man, were known as 'dog-warriors' because of their blood-curdling war chant, like the short, savage barks of a dog. The French settlers who were the first pale faces to encounter the red warriors who barked like dogs when galloping to attack the enemy, referred to them as *chien*, dog in French. Hence Cheyenne. They became restless and discontented as they saw their once undisputed domain slipping steadily from their grasp. It was apparent that trouble might arise at any time. It became necessary to take some measures to avoid it. To that end it was proposed, largely at the instance of colonel D D Mitchell, Superintendent of Indian Affairs at St Louis, to hold a Council at Fort Laramie to discuss compensation to the Indians for the lands taken from them. All the tribes east of the Rocky Mountains were to be represented. The plan was approved by the Government and the year 1851 was fixed upon. Because of his influence with the Indian tribes Father De Smet was invited to the Council. In a letter from St Louis, dated 19 April 1851, Colonel Mitchell, who was entrusted with organising the conference, wrote to Father De Smet:

Should your present duties permit I would like very much for you to take part in the Fort Laramie Council. Your maps and drawings of the prairies and mountains, as well as any information you can furnish with regard to their habits, the history of the country, in fact, all that concerns the Indians, will be of valuable assistance to us, and will be greatly appreciated by the Government.

C and R, p. 1565.

Here was an occasion for revisiting the Sioux and other tribes on the Upper Missouri. Father De Smet's superiors gave their consent. Thus began the long and valuable service that Father De Smet, in the role of peacemaker, rendered the Government of the United States during the remaining years of his life. Father Christian Hoeken, the apostle of the Potawatomies, obtained permission to accompany Father De Smet.

On 7 June, the Fathers left St Louis on board the steamboat *St Ange* and went up the Missouri. Their plan was to visit the Indians camped along the river, and then cross to Fort Laramie, upon the upper course of the Platte. The *St Ange*, one of the finest boats on the river, was commanded by Captain Joseph La Barge, a close friend of Father De Smet, who always lent the aid of his boats to Catholic missionary enterprises. Several members of the fur companies, Canadians, Americans and Europeans, bound for different trading posts in the Indian Territory, were also on board. 'These men,' wrote De Smet, 'were in search of the goods of the world; Father Hoeken and I were seeking the treasures of heaven in the conversion of souls.'

The spring that year was late and wet. Melting snows and continuous rain had swollen the rivers until the muddy waters of the Missouri inundated the land for miles. Father De Smet transmitted this account of his Journey of 1851 to Father General.

We could see the torrent descending with the violence and rapidity of an avalanche, overturning and sweeping away everything with its angry waves.

The *St Ange* used her whole power of steam to stem an almost irresistible current. Several times the boat was carried down; twice, especially, it was a regular contest between the river and the steamer. The latter, for a good quarter of an hour, lay as if motionless in the midst of the angry waters, but thanks to the quantity of tar and resin with which her furnaces were charged, she at last triumphed.

C and R, p. 639.

The boat pushed its way through floating debris, houses, barns, stables, and fences carried along pell-mell, with thousands of uprooted trees. It required skilful steering.

Father De Smet describes an epidemic of cholera that broke out on the boat.

The inundation of the rivers, the continual rains of spring and the sudden transition from heat to cold are, in this climate, sure precursors of malignant fevers. The cholera appears to assume an epidemic type in these regions. Disease in many forms soon appeared on board the *St Ange*. From the moment of its advent a mournful silence took the place of the rude shouts and boisterous conversations of our travellers. Six days had hardly elapsed from our departure, when the boat resembled a floating hospital. We were 500 miles from St Louis when the cholera broke out in the steamer. On the tenth a clerk of the American Fur Company, vigorous and in the prime of manhood, was suddenly seized with all the symptoms of cholera, and expired after a few hours' illness. The following days several others were attacked with the same malady, and in a short time thirteen fell victims to the epidemic.

A bilious attack confined me to my bed for nearly ten days. Good Father Hoeken devoted himself to the sick night and day, with a zeal at once heroic and indefatigable. He visited them; he assisted them in their sufferings; he prepared and administered remedies; he rubbed the cholera patients with camphor; he heard the confessions of the dying, and lavished upon them the consolations of religion. He then went and blessed their graves on the bank of the river, and buried them with the prayers and ceremonies prescribed by the Roman ritual. This beloved brother had naturally a hardy constitution, and was habituated to a life of privation; but the journeys and continued labours of the mission among the Indians had greatly weakened it, and his assiduous and fatiguing attentions to the sick completely exhausted him. In vain I warned him, begging him to spare himself; his zeal silenced every other consideration; instead of taking precautions against exposure, he seemed to delight in it. It gave me great pain to see him fulfilling this heroic work of charity alone; but I was in such a state of debility that I was incapable of offering him the least help. On the 18th, fears were entertained that my illness was assuming the form of cholera. I requested Father Hoeken to hear my confession and give me extreme unction, but at the very moment he was called to another sick person, who was in extremity. He replied, going, 'I see no immediate danger for you; tomorrow we will see.' He had assisted three dying ones that day. Alas! never shall I forget the scene that occurred some hours later. Father Hoeken's cabin was next to mine.

Between one and two o'clock at night, when all on board were calm and silent, and the sick in their wakefulness heard naught but the sighs and moans of their fellow-sufferers, the voice of Father Hoeken was suddenly heard. He was calling me to his assistance. Awaking from a deep sleep, I recognised his voice, and dragged myself to his pillow. Ah me! I found him ill, and even in extremity. He asked me to hear his confession: I at once acquiesced in his desire. Dr Evans, a physician of great experience and of remarkable charity, endeavoured to relieve him, and watched by him, but his cares and remedies proved fruitless. I administered extreme unction: he responded to all the prayers with a self-possession and piety which increased the esteem that all on board had conceived for him. I could see him sinking. As I was myself in so alarming a state, and fearing that I might be taken away at any moment, and thus share his last abode in this land of pilgrimage and exile, I besought him to hear my confession, if he were yet capable of listening to me. I knelt, bathed in tears, by the dying couch of my brother in Christ. To him in his agony, I, made my confession. Strength forsook him: soon also he lost the power of speech, although he remained sensible to what was passing around him. Father Hoeken, ripe for heaven, surrendered his pure soul into the hands of his Divine Redeemer on the 19th June 1851, twelve days after our departure from St Louis. Who would then have foretold it? So ardent were his desires to labour for the glory of God, that he sighed for the wilderness – he thirsted for the salvation of souls! Alas! how many projects annihilated! In any other enterprise it would have proved sufficient motive for discontinuing a perilous journey; but the desire of procuring God's glory endows man with strength that nature denies him.

C and R, pp. 640–2.

Father Hoeken was only forty-three years old when he died.

Father De Smet continues:

> The passengers were deeply moved at the sight of the lifeless corpse of him who had so lately been 'all in all,' according to the language of the apostle. My resolution not to leave the body of the pious missionary in the desert was unanimously approved. A decent coffin, very thick, and tarred within, was prepared to receive his mortal remains: a temporary grave was dug in a beautiful forest, in the vicinity of the mouth of the Little Sioux. The burial was performed with all the ceremonies of the Church, in the evening on the 19th June, all on board assisting.
>
> About a month after, on her return, as the *St Ange* passed near the venerated tomb, the coffin was exhumed, put on board the boat, and transported to the novitiate of the Society of Jesus at Florissant. There repose the mortal remains of Father Hoeken, with those of his brethren. His death, so precious in the sight of God, saddened the hearts of the passengers, but for many it was a salutary sorrow. A great number had not approached the tribunal of penance during long years; immediately after the funeral, they repaired one after another to my cabin to confess.
>
> Five more passengers were also fatally attacked, but received before expiring, the consolations of my ministry. The languor and weakness to which the fever had reduced me quitted me insensibly: after a lapse of some days I found myself perfectly recovered, so that I was able to celebrate Mass on board and devote my whole time to the sick.
>
> *C and R, p. 643.*

As soon as the boat reached the high lands of the Indian Territory, above the floods and into a dryer atmosphere, the boat was unloaded and aired. The fresh, bracing air dispelled the epidemic. The rest of the voyage passed off without further sickness. On its way the steamboat would stop among the several Indian tribes and give Father De Smet the opportunity to visit them. He made numerous trips on horseback to visit their camps.

Eventually they reached the Great Bend of the Missouri, where the boat came to land opposite a camp of the Yanktons, a powerful tribe of the Sioux nation. Here they learnt that another scourge, smallpox, was devastating the homes of the Indians, who were dying in their hundreds. Bodies remained unburied, exposed to the summer heat, and for miles the air was infected with the odour of decaying flesh.

Although barely recovered himself, Father De Smet went ashore, and visited the entire stricken region, where he baptised children, nursed the sick, and ministered to the dying. He spent the night with them. Astonished by his courage and touched by his goodness, the Yanktons, Mandans, Aricaras, and Grosventres listened to the words of the Great Spirit, and invited the missionary to remain among them. Although Father De Smet was obliged to rejoin the *St Ange* and continue his journey, he did not forget these far-off tribes and later laboured to establish a mission for them.

Some days after I was at Fort Pierre, situated on the shore, south of the Missouri, about 1500 miles above St Louis, and near the mouth of the Shicka, or Bad River. The influenza had existed for some time in the fort, and a panic had seized many at the news that the smallpox was in the neighbourhood and the cholera on board. The Indians, awe-struck at the approach of danger from this implacable scourge, were overjoyed at my presence; the children of the whites and of the Indians encamped around the fort were presented to me, to the number of eighty-two, to be regenerated in the holy waters of baptism.

The same inquietude reigned at the post of the Aricaras. Some couriers had announced the approach of the boat, and spread alarm by reporting that there were contagious diseases on board. But when the people saw that all were well, their fears vanished, and they welcomed the boat with the usual demonstrations on such occasions. Cries of joy burst from 2,000 mouths; volleys of cannon and musketry rolled echoing over the plains. The scene was beautiful and imposing. The fort stands on a high hill, nearly a hundred feet above the level of the river. A long row of Indians, in their gayest costumes, their faces daubed with various colours, lined the shore.

I had galloped on in advance of the boat, to have time to instruct the half-breeds and Canadians and baptise all their children. I spent two days among them. A great number of Indians, learning of my arrival at the fort, came to shake hands with me from respect, and to bid me welcome. At the same time they earnestly begged me to grant their little children the same benefit of baptism that I had granted the half-breed children. I yielded eagerly to their wishes, in consequence of the great danger in which they were. The number of baptisms was about 200. Not long after, I heard that the cholera had swept through the village of the Aricaras, and that many of the children had fallen victim.

We now bade farewell to the officers of the fort, to plunge farther into the desert. Ere long we passed the Mandan village, composed of large huts covered with earth. This once numerous nation is now reduced to a few families, the only survivors of the smallpox of 1837. Their village lies 1,800 miles above the mouth of the Missouri, 200 below the mouth of the Yellowstone. Some days after, we stopped at Fort Berthold, to land some goods at the great village of the Minnetarees, or Osier tribe, nicknamed the Grosventres of the Missouri. Their cabins are built like those of the Aricaras and Mandans. Four forks, or rather four forked trees, set in the ground about twenty feet apart, form a square. These are joined on top by crosspieces, over which other pieces are laid obliquely, leaving a great opening in the centre, to admit air and give vent to the smoke; these pieces are woven together with osiers: the whole is covered with hay and earth – not with turf, however. An opening is made on one side to receive the door, which consists of a bison-skin. Before the door is a sort of alley, ten to fifteen feet long, enclosed by pickets, and easily defended in case of attack. In the middle of the lodge, under the upper opening that admits the light, a hole about a foot deep is dug to answer as a fireplace. Around the lodge there are beds, one, two or three feet from the floor, with doeskins as curtains. The whole village is surrounded by a high and strong palisade of large trees, squared.

The other permanent villages on the Missouri are those of the Osages, Omahas, Poncas, Pawnees, Aricaras and Mandans. The great chief of the Minnetaree village, called Four Bears, is the most civil and affable Indian that I met on the Missouri. He begged me to baptise his two little boys and several members of his family.

These tribes evince great eagerness to hear the word of God and to be instructed in our holy faith, whenever a Catholic missionary visits them. In Europe, the preachers and catechists must use a thousand means to win a congregation; here men call priests to instruct them. They are eager for this nourishment of the soul, this word of God, which so many others despise! What an awful account of this heavenly benefit must be one day rendered by men of all ages, especially the young, for whom religious teaching abounds in the churches, colleges and schools of Europe!

C and R, pp. 649–52.

On 14 July the *St Ange* reached Fort Union, situated at the mouth of the Yellowstone. Father De Smet parted with sincere regret from the travelling companions who had shared his trials during the months they had spent together on the *St Ange*. He then began to make all the preparations for his 800-mile journey overland to Fort Laramie. During the fifteen days he stayed at Fort Union he found time to instruct and baptise twenty-nine children, between Fort Union and Fort William, which were only three miles apart. He said Mass daily at the fort, and gave an instruction.

On 31 July they set off for Fort Laramie. It was a common experience in Father De Smet's career that important events in his work occurred on this day, the Feast day of St Ignatius Loyola, the founder of his Order. There were thirty-two persons in the party. There were several Government agents and a number of Indian chiefs, Assiniboins, Minnatarees and Crows, who were repairing to the great Indian council to be held near Fort Laramie.

Two four-wheeled wagons and two carts, for transporting their provisions and their baggage, composed their whole convoy. The four vehicles were in all probability the first that had ever crossed this unoccupied waste. There was not the slightest perceptible vestige of a beaten track between Fort Union and the Red Buttes, which are on the route to Oregon, and 161 miles west of Fort Laramie.

Their route lay across the desolate waste west of the Yellowstone River in eastern Montana to Fort Alexander, on the left bank of the Yellowstone, opposite the mouth of the Rosebud.

After crossing the Yellowstone the caravan entered the heart of the Great Desert, where the rocky soil furnished but meagre sustenance for the horses, and lack of water caused intense suffering to both man and beast.

The mosquitoes tormented us greatly during the day. They especially worried our horses and mules, which were literally covered with them. For us, we had taken measures against their attacks by wearing big gloves in spite of the heat, and covering our heads with sacks formed of coarse gauze.

On the 1st August, at six o'clock in the morning, we resumed our route. We took all possible precaution to avoid meeting any hostile band. The Indians who accompanied us kept their eyes on the earth to discover any recent tracks of an enemy. An extraordinary experience gives them an admirable skill in detecting trails that are imperceptible to others. The foes that our travelling companions dreaded most in the section we were about to traverse, were the Blackfeet and the Sioux.

C and R, p. 654.

At the close of the day they pitched their camp at the base of the Tetons, about thirty miles from Fort Union.

One of the Indians killed a skunk (*Mephitis Americana*). The strong odour of this animal is intolerable to the whites; the Indians, on the contrary, appear to like it, and deem its flesh exquisite.

On the 2nd of August we set out at break of day, and were fanned by a refreshing breeze. Groves of cottonwood, elm and ash, as well as groups of service trees and cherry-trees, offered themselves along the beds of dry rivers and streamlets. We ascended step by step the hills that separate the waters of the Missouri from those of the Yellowstone, like so many insuperable barriers furrowed with profound ravines. We triumphed over these obstacles with great difficulty, and at length attained the summit of the hills. There a most magnificent spectacle unrolled itself before our eyes. On one side is displayed a succession of beautiful prairies, here and there interrupted with groves of stunted trees and shrubs, terminating in verdant hills dotted with groups of cedar and pine; on the other are shapeless heaps of red and white clay and piles of stones, which, viewed at a distance, resemble brick-kilns, from their peculiar colour. The surface was covered with lava and scoriae. Several times, after having gained some miles on the heights, we found ourselves suddenly facing an almost perpendicular descent, formed of rock and white clay, down which we had to let our vehicles by hand.

On the fourth day of our march we descried thousands of buffalo; the whole space between the Missouri and the Yellowstone was covered as far as the eye could reach. Hitherto the mosquitoes had greatly tormented us, but now they entirely vanished. We sought the cause of this phenomenon. The Indians told us that the absence of our winged enemies was owing to the prodigious number of buffalo which were grazing in the neighbouring plains, and which attracted these insects. In fact, we saw these noble animals throwing the earth on their bodies by means of their horns and feet, or rolling themselves in the sand and

171

dust, and thus filling the air with clouds, in the endeavour to rid themselves of their vexatious followers. The lot of these animals appeared bad enough, for they were pursued day and night. During a whole week we heard them bellowing like the noise of distant thunder, or like the murmurs of the ocean waves beating against the shore.

An Assiniboin gave us a singular proof of his dexterity in the chase; I cannot forbear mentioning it. Alone and on foot, he stealthily approached a large herd of buffalo cows. As soon as he was near enough to them to allow of their hearing him, he began to imitate the cry of a young calf. At once the cows ran toward the place of concealment of the ingenious hunter, and he killed one of them. The troop, alarmed, withdrew hastily and in great disorder. He reloaded his rifle and renewed his cry; the cows stopped, returned as if by enchantment, and he killed a second. The Assiniboin assured us that he could easily have taken more by the same stratagem, but thinking two cows were enough for us, he suffered the rest to go.

C and R, p. 658.

On 7 August they crossed lands intersected with numerous ravines and dried streams. Petrified trunks and entire trees frequently met the eye. On the same day they traversed a mountainous elevation which stretched as far as the Owl-head Buttes. The buttes or mounds, in this ocean-like prairie, served as guides to the warrior, the traveller and the hunter, who can perceive them thirty miles off. From the summit of this extensive eminence they observed the White Earth country or clay plains of the Yellowstone ... pillows of red and white hardened clay that rose from 50 to 100 feet. The sulphurous gases which escaped in great volumes from the burning soil infected the atmosphere for several miles, and rendered the earth so barren that even the wild wormwood could not grow on it. The beaver hunters assured them that the frequent underground noises and explosions were frightful. Bituminous, sulphurous and boiling springs were very numerous. Gas, vapour and smoke were continually escaping by a thousand openings, from the base to the summit of the volcanic pile.

On 10 August they left the highlands and advanced about twenty miles, over a barren, rugged space, excavated by rains. Horned frogs, lizards and rattlesnakes were abundant. 'The silence of death reigns in this vast wild,' wrote the missionary. 'Weeks pass without seeing a living creature, but one becomes accustomed to the solitude and ends by liking it. The mind becomes clearer, the faculties are more alive, and ideas spring forth spontaneously.'

On 11 August they arrived at the upper portion of a gently sloping plain. Having crossed it, they found themselves at Fort Alexander, situated on the banks of the Yellowstone, and at a short distance from the little river Rosebud. Fort Alexander was about 200 miles distant from Fort Union, along the dividing ridge.

After remaining six days at Fort Alexander, allowing their animals time to rest, and also awaiting the arrival of a barge belonging to the American Fur Company, which was freighted with some of their effects, they crossed the Yellowstone on 17 August. They passed over a high and very level plain: for a distance of five miles the soil was light, sandy and entirely covered with 'green toads', different kinds of cactus – plants noted for the splendour of their flowers and for their grotesque and varied shapes. The round and the oval, about the size of a hen's egg, abounded in this plain, and were set with long thorns, hard, and as fine and sharp as needles. When trampled by the horses' feet, these thorns spring up and adhere to the legs and belly of the animals, and thus render them furious and unmanageable.

We remarked recent traces of enemies – such as the slain carcasses of very dangerous wild animals, the impress of human feet in the sand, concealed encampments and half-quenched fires. Consequently we redoubled our vigilance, in order to avoid a perilous surprise. A beautiful chief's coat of scarlet cloth, trimmed with gold lace, suspended from the branch of a tree, was perceived waving in the air like a floating banner. There was a race to win the prize; an Assiniboin having carried it off, it was most carefully scrutinised. The conclusion was that it had been offered only the day before by some Blackfoot chief. These Indians, when on the warpath, frequently make such offerings either to the sun or to the moon, hoping thus to render them propitious, so that through their intervention they may obtain many scalps and horses.

C and R, p. 667.

They left the valley of the Rosebud on 22 August and crossed over to the valley of the Tongue river, via sandstone cliffs of a variety of fantastic shapes, the result of the powerful attrition of water and

173

weathering. After advancing about twenty-three miles that day, they camped on the banks of the Tongue River. The next day they entered the watershed of the Powder River, one of the principal tributaries of the Yellowstone, in the valley of Piney Fork. They passed Lake De Smet (named for him on this occasion) on 24 August and reached the Powder River on 27 August.

> Our wagoners will not forget the difficulty of conducting their teams through this vast route, for it was a very miserable, elevated, sterile plain, covered with wormwood and intersected with countless ravines, and they vowed they would never be caught driving a wagon there again.
> The soil, too, was sterile, and as we journeyed on water became scarce – on the fifth day it failed completely, and it did again on the last. The night that ensued was a hard trial, for after so long a march we had not a drop of water to quench our burning thirst.
>
> *C and R, p. 669.*

They crossed the divide between the Powder and Platte Rivers on 1 September.

> On the 1st of September, having traversed three chains of hills, we gradually attained the summit of the Black Hills. We had one cart less, and one heavy wagon so broken that it had to be tied together with strips of raw buffalo-hide. From the summit we were happy to perceive a distant lake. We eagerly hastened in that direction, for we were consumed with thirst, and had serious fears for our beasts of burden, which were slackening their weary pace. To our astonishment, we directly perceived that we were still at a great distance from Fort Laramie. Instead of being near that fort, in accordance with the assurances of the three Crows, we discovered ourselves in sight of the Red Buttes, (near Casper, Wyoming) twenty-five miles off. This is a well-known spot on the Great Oregon Route, and is 160 miles from Fort Laramie.
>
> *C and R, p. 670.*

On 2 September 1851 they were on the north bank of the Platte River at Red Buttes, on the Great Route to Oregon. It was over this route that caravans composed of thousands of emigrants from every country and clime had passed on their way to the rich gold mines of California or to take possession of new lands in the fertile plains and valleys of Utah and Oregon. (The Oregon Trail was first travelled by white men over portions of its course by the Astorians, on their outward and return journeys, in 1811–13. South Pass, the celebrated crossing of the Continental Divide, was discovered about 1824. The route had become well established by the fur travellers before emigration set in. The California Trail, which branched off in the valley of Bear River, did not come prominently into use until after the discovery of gold. The Trail remained the great highway of transcontinental travel down nearly to the advent of the railroads.)

After striking the Oregon Trail the party marched eastward towards Fort Laramie. They followed the great road south of the Platte to the foot of the Black Hills. After eight days' journey along the Platte, they arrived at Fort Laramie without the least trouble or accident. The commander of the fort informed them that the Great Council was to take place at the mouth of Horse River, in a vast plain situated nearly thirty-five miles lower down the Platte. The next day Father De Smet accepted the polite invitation of the respected Colonel Robert Campbell, and took a seat in his carriage. They arrived at the plain of the intended council about sunset. There the superintendent, Colonel Mitchell, received Father De Smet with warm friendship and cordiality, insisting that he should become his guest during the whole time of the council.

In the immense plain mentioned above, there were a thousand lodges, that is to say, 10,000 Indians, representing Sioux, Cheyenne and Arapahos, with several deputations from the Crows, Snakes or Shoshones, Aricaras, Assiniboins and Minnetarees, assembled there to hear the proposition offered by the United States Government. The most complete unity now reigned among these peoples, only yesterday divided by hate and dissension.

During the eighteen days that the Great Council lasted, from 12 to 23 September 1851, Father De Smet remained, advising and assisting at the Council, and giving religious instruction to the Indians. At the Council all features of the troublesome situation were discussed and an earnest effort made to reach some good result.

In *Western Missions and Missionaries*, Father De Smet gives his impressions.

During the eighteen days that the Great Council lasted, the union, harmony and amity that reigned among the Indians were truly admirable. Implacable hatreds, hereditary enmities, cruel and bloody encounters, with the whole past, in fine, were forgotten. They paid mutual visits, smoked the calumet of peace together, exchanged presents, partook of numerous banquets, and all the lodges were open to strangers. A practice occurring but on the most amicable and fraternal of occasions was seen – this is, the adopting of children and of brothers of each side. There was a perfect unanimity of views between Colonel Mitchell, superintendent of the Indian Territory, and Major Thomas Fitzpatrick, and nothing was omitted to foster these germs of peace. The object of the assembly was a distinguished proof of the highest benevolence on the part of the United States Government, as well as of the sincere desire of establishing a lasting peace among tribes hostile to each other, and of obtaining a right of passage through their possessions for the whites, and making the Indians compensation for injuries and losses the latter may have sustained from the whites.

The treaty was signed by the agents of the United States, and by all the principal chiefs of the different nations who were present. Another treaty in favour of the half-breeds and the whites residing in the country was proposed, to wit: That a tract of country be assigned them for their use, in order to form agricultural establishments and colonies, and that they should obtain the assistance of the Government of the United States in the execution of their project.

On the second Sunday of September, Feast of the Exaltation of the Cross, three days after my arrival, some lodges of buffalo-hides were arranged and ornamented as a sanctuary, on the plain of the Great Council. Under this tent I had the happiness of offering the holy sacrifice, in presence of all the gentlemen assisting at the council, of all the half-bloods and whites and of a great concourse of Indians. After my instruction, twenty-eight children (half-bloods) and five adults were regenerated in the holy waters of baptism, with all the ceremonies prescribed by the Church.

They besought me to explain baptism to them, as several of them had been present when I baptised the half-blood children. I complied with their request, and gave them a lengthy instruction on its blessings and obligations. All then entreated me to grant this favour to their infants. The next day the ceremony took place; 239 children of the Ogallalas (the first of their tribe) were regenerated in the holy waters of baptism, to the great joy and satisfaction of the whole nation.

Among the Arapahos, I baptised 305 little ones; among the Cheyenne, 253; and among the Brûlés and Osage Sioux, 280; in the camp of Painted Bear, fifty-six. The number of the half-bloods that I baptised in the plain of the Great Council and on the river Platte is sixty-one. In the different forts on the Missouri, I baptised, during the months of June and July last, 392 children. Total number of baptisms, 1,586. A great number died shortly after, in consequence of diseases that reigned in the Indian camps.

Notwithstanding the scarcity of provisions felt in the camp before the wagons came, the feasts were numerous and well attended. No epoch in Indian annals, probably, shows a greater massacre of the canine race. Among the Indians the flesh of the dog is the most honourable and esteemed of all viands, especially in the absence of buffalo and other animals. On the present occasion it was a last resource. The carnage then may be conceived. I was invited to several of these banquets; a great chief, in particular, wished to give me a special mark of his friendship and respect for me. He had filled his great kettle with little fat dogs, skins and all. He presented me, on a wooden platter, the fattest, well boiled. I found the meat really delicate, and I can vouch that it is preferable to suckling-pig, which it nearly resembles in taste. All must be consumed. This would be impossible were it not for the allowance of the blessed privilege of conducting one or two *eaters* with us. In some of the Sioux camps the guests are permitted just to touch the dish, and then take it home to their cabins.

C and R, pp. 675–9.

In due course the Council concluded. The different articles so long under discussion were finally, one after the other, adopted by the tribes. The treaty was signed by the representatives of the United States and the principal Indian chiefs. By this Fort Laramie Treaty the United States Government was permitted to build roads and military posts within Indian lands. In return the Government would provide $50,000 in annuities for fifty years (later reduced to fifteen years) – a paltry sum for so many tribes. The next day, the United States flag flying from the Superintendent's tent, and the firing of a cannon, announced the arrival of the presents sent by the

Government – a division of which would now take place. The Indians assembled without delay, ranging themselves in a circle around the exposed gifts. The great chiefs were first presented with an outfit of clothing, which they immediately donned. For the first time in their lives the great chiefs wore pantaloons, each arrayed in a general's uniform, a gold-plated sword hanging at his side. All this contrasted with their long, coarse hair, which floated above the military costume, and their faces painted in vermilion. Proud of their new habiliments and courting admiration they proudly showed themselves to the missionary. Thus accoutred, the chiefs then distributed among the members of their tribes the bounty of the Government.

Late in the afternoon of 23 September, Father De Smet shook hands for the last time with the chiefs, and prepared to set out for St Louis with the American delegates and a deputation of Indians en route to Washington. On 24 September, before sunrise, in the dull hour that precedes day, they set off, travelling by the usual route to Fort Kearney. They passed the famous Chimney-Rock. In the course of the day they reached the Platte River, at the place known as Ash Hollow. They turned their steps towards the South Fork, fifteen miles away. From the crossing of the South Fork to the junction of the Great Forks the distance was seventy-five miles, and then another 150 miles to Fort Kearney. They arrived at Fort Kearney on 2 October. Here Father De Smet had a conference with twenty Pawnee chiefs. At Fort Kearney he parted company with Colonel Mitchell and his men. He and Major Fitzpatrick then turned south with a deputation of Indians with a view to visit the Potawatomies at St Mary's Mission on the Kansas River. Father De Smet hoped to give his Indians some idea of the life lived by Indians in a mission ('reduction'); of impressing them with the advantages of agriculture and persevering non-nomadic labour.

We reached St Mary's, among the Potawatomies, on the 22nd October. Bishop Miège and the other Fathers of the Mission received us with great cordiality and kindness.

To give the Indian deputies a relish for labour by the tasting of the various products of farming, a quantity of vegetables and fruits were set before them. Potatoes, carrots, turnips, squashes, parsnips, melons, with apples and peaches, graced the board, and our forest friends did them most ample honour.

We spent two days visiting the mission. The Indian chiefs

quitted the establishment with hearts overflowing with delight, and in the consoling expectation of having similar happiness in their own tribes at no very distant future.

C and R, p. 689.

Upon leaving St Mary's the travellers directed their steps to Westport on the Missouri. The weather was fine and they reached there in three days. Then they embarked on a steamboat descending the great river.

On the 16th of October we took places on board the steamboat *Clara*. Our Indian deputies had never seen a village or settlement of whites except what they had seen at Fort Laramie and at Fort Kearney; they knew nothing of the manner in which houses are constructed, hence they were in constant admiration; and when for the first time they saw a steamboat their wonder was at its height, although they appeared to entertain a certain fear as they stepped on board. A considerable time elapsed before they became accustomed to the noise arising from the escape of steam, and the bustle that took place at the ringing of the bells, etc. They call the boat a 'fire canoe,' and were transported with delight at the sight of another boat ascending with a small boat behind, which they called a 'papoose', or little child. When their apprehensions of danger had subsided, their curiosity augmented; they took the liveliest interest in whatever they saw for the first time. They were in grand costume and seated themselves on the promenade deck; as the boat approached the several towns and villages in her progress, they hailed each with shouts and songs.

On the 22nd of October we reached St Louis. A few days later all the members of the Indian deputation were invited to a banquet given in our university. They were highly pleased at the reception given them by the Reverend Father Provincial, and overjoyed at the encouraging hope that he gave them of having Black Gowns among them – a hope perhaps soon to be realised.

C and R, p. 691.

While at the Council Father De Smet was requested by Colonel Mitchell to make a map of the whole Indian territory, relating particularly to the Upper Missouri, the waters of the Upper Platte, east of the Rocky Mountains and of the headwaters of the Columbia and its tributaries west of these mountains.

179

In compliance with this request I drew up the map from scraps of them in my possession. During the years I spent in the Indian country I occupied myself occasionally in drawing maps of the countries through which I passed. I availed myself of the best information I could obtain from trappers and intelligent Indians who were well acquainted with the mountain passes and the course of the rivers. Not having had instruments with me, the maps were necessarily only an approximation to the true position. The map, so prepared, was seemingly approved and made use of by the gentlemen assembled in council, and subsequently sent on to Washington together with the treaty then made with the Indians.

C and R, p. 1497.

On his return to St Louis Father De Smet wrote to a colleague recalling some of his experiences over the previous five months.

St Louis University, November 13th, 1851.

Reverend Father Helias, SJ St Xavier's Church P. C.

Reverend and Very Dear Father In Christ.

Dear Father, since last I wrote to your Reverence I have suffered much and lost much. I lost my good companion, Father Hoeken, and was left alone like an orphan to find my way through the wilderness, surrounded by a thousand dangers. At my return I found my superior buried, in whom I lost not only a father and brother in Christ, but a faithful friend and a true and sure guide, by his good counsels and examples. The Lord be praised – both died like saints – this consoles and strengthens me in my loss.

Whilst travelling in the plains and mountains, kind Providence has watched over me. I escaped from a dangerous illness, from the attacks of wild beasts and enemies, from the smallpox and cholera. I passed through a camp where people were dying and rotting, alive, unhurt and untouched. I slept among the dying and dead for over a month, handling and attending on the cholera patients, and returned safe and sound. I had the happiness to place the holy waters of baptism on the foreheads of 1,586 children and adults, of whom many have since fallen victims of the two mentioned diseases, and are now forever happy.

The missionary's modesty did not permit him to recall the part he had taken in the success of the Conference, but the United States recognised it, and before long it was admitted in Washington that his mediation had been more effective than that of an army.

Colonel Thomas H Benton wrote on 7 April 1852:

> You could do more for these poor people – more for their welfare and keeping them in peace and friendship with the United States than 'an army with banners'.
>
> *C and R, p. 1566.*

As will be seen, in new conflicts later to occur between the white man and the Indian, he was destined to again fill the role of peacemaker.

Chapter 11

Europe Again

The year 1852 was spent by Father De Smet mainly in St Louis, as Procurator of the Province. In that capacity he made one journey, with Father Provincial, to Louisville, Bardston and Cincinnati.

It had been a lonely time for him, as is expressed in this letter to his three nieces, dated 22 April 1853.

Mes Très Chères Sylvie, Elmire et Rosalie

Exile, even when it is voluntary, or when, rather, it is imposed by conscience or religion, cannot destroy in a man's heart the sweet sentiments there implanted by kinship or love of country. Hence the vacancy I feel within me, for not having received for so long a time any of your letters, always so good and interesting and so consoling to your American exile. But for the last four years I have been worked to death, and have had frequent and long journeys to make.

Every day at the altar I implore the aid and blessing of heaven upon you and all the family. The only thing that I expect from you in return, is that I may always hold the same place in your affections, and that sometimes you will address to God your good prayers for your Uncle Pierre and for the conversion of his poor Indians.

I hope Papa will have received my letter of the 24 of March. Please remember me, and say a thousand things from me, to your dear parents, to your Uncle François, to Charles, Paul, Clémence and all the family at Termonde and Antwerp.

C and R, pp. 1485–7.

But as he was penning that letter, little did he know that he would actually be seeing his family face to face. In the month of April of this year, with the approval of the consultors of the Vice-Province, the Reverend Father Provincial sent him to Europe, in company with the Right Reverend Bishop Miège, then Vicar Apostolic of the Western Indian Territory, east of the Rocky Mountains. His Lordship was to proceed to Rome, himself to France, Belgium and Holland, both on business of the Society.

While passing through Washington en route to New York they were presented to President Pierce by Colonel Thomas H Benton and were kindly entertained. Father De Smet was made bearer of dispatches to various Ministers in several of the great European capitals. They visited Georgetown and Washington Colleges. At New York they were entertained by the Fathers at Fordham and St Xavier.

They sailed from New York on 9 May, on the steamer *Fulton* and made the crossing in eleven days. This was in great contrast to his voyage of 1821, when it took him forty days under sail to go from Europe to America. They landed at Le Havre and proceeded to Paris.

While in Paris Father De Smet gave an address to the young Jesuits at the Sorbonne on his work with the missions. To make the message more effective, he decked out one of them as an Indian chief, much to everyone's amusement.

Father De Smet accompanied Bishop Miège only as far as Paris. While the Bishop went on to Rome, Father De Smet went to Brussels. He then visited all the principal cities of Belgium and Holland.

Among the many stories and adventures he had to relate was the heroic life and death of his great friend and colleague, Father Christopher Hoeken, who had succumbed to the epidemic of cholera just a few months earlier.

On 17 November Father De Smet bade farewell to his family and along with seven missionaries for the Indian missions set out for Paris to meet Bishop Miège, who had five more young recruits for the missions.

In a letter to his brothers Charles and Francis De Smet, dated 1 January 1854, Father De Smet describes the very eventful and disastrous return voyage.

To the violent storms of wind we must add several other disagreeable circumstances: the steam-engine got out of order several times, and the boilers threatened to blow us in the air; the coal was of a bad quality, and that, even, began to become scarce on the twelfth day of our voyage. We were obliged to deviate from our ordinary route, to get a supply of coal at Halifax, a seaport of Nova Scotia. This neglect on the part of the company was extremely fatal in its consequences.

In the forenoon of the 6th of December, about five leagues from port, a fisherman presented himself on board as a pilot, and declared to the captain, who demanded his certificates, 'that his papers were either in his boat, or at his own house.' The captain relied upon his word, and entrusted him with the management of the ship. Against the expressed opinion of the officers, the false pilot changed the boat's direction, and notwithstanding their reiterated remonstrances, he persisted in his obstinacy. An hour and a half afterward, the *Humboldt* struck on the dangerous rocks called 'The Three Sisters', in the neighbourhood of Devil's Island. It was half-past six in the morning – the greater number of the passengers were still in their berths. The shock was terrific: I was walking on the deck at that moment. Discovering directly great pieces of wood floating on the surface of the water, I hastened to warn all my companions of their danger, for they were also still in their beds. Young Hegel having been entrusted to me by his father, I took him by my side as long as the danger lasted, and kept a rope in my hand for the purpose of lowering him into the first lifeboat that should be launched. All had been startled from sleep. Fear had palsied every heart; and while the water was pouring into the vessel by torrents, fire broke out. It was got under by great exertion, through the presence of mind and manly energy of the first engineer, after great efforts, they succeeded in extinguishing it. As if all things conspired to our destruction, a fog arose, so thick that we could not see thirty paces from the vessel. The whole power of the steam engine was exerted in an attempt to gain the shore, six miles distant. The boat soon inclined to the larboard side, where she had sprung a leak, and began to go down. Every arm set to work to aid in launching the small boats. Had not the captain exhibited great presence of mind and an extraordinary firmness, there would have been much tumult and disorder. There was a rush to get in first, but happily we were not obliged to resort to this means of saving ourselves.

While the greater number believed that all was lost, and I among the rest, the ship touched again, in a few fathoms of water, and rested on a Rock. We were saved!'

Immediately after the shipwreck, the fog arose, and we then discovered, for the first time and to our joyful surprise, that the shore was only 100 feet from us. The sea was calm, the wind lowered, and the sun rose majestically. It was the announcement of a return of fine weather, which left us at Havre, and now accompanied us until we reached Missouri. We had the good fortune and the time to save all our trunks, travelling bags and boxes. The loss of the ship and cargo was estimated at $600,000.

We had for travelling companions on the *Humboldt* Jews, Infidels and Protestants of every shade. Some of the voyagers were imbued with very strong prejudices against the Catholic faith, but in particular against Jesuits. The wreck of the *Humboldt* was even attributed to our presence, and it was maliciously proposed to oblige us to quit as soon as possible.

On the 8th December, Feast of the Immaculate Conception, after the celebration of Mass, we heard that the steamship *Niagara*, of the Liverpool and Boston line, was in sight. All the passengers of the *Humboldt*, including those that we took in from England, went on board, making the total of passengers more than 400.

Among those already on the *Niagara*, was a little man, with an ape-like face and a goatee beard, who called himself Francis Tapon, a self-nominated apostle, and self-commissioned to teach a new religion to the universe. Francis declared himself an enemy of all existing creeds, but above all to the Pope and the Jesuits. When quitting Liverpool, he declared openly and aloud that he would *kill* the *first Jesuit* that he might meet on American soil! In fact, he was so violent that the captain prudently took from him his gun, pistols and poniards. The moment I set foot on the *Niagara*, I was informed of these interesting particulars. I advised my young friends to avoid Mr Francis Tapon, and pay no sort of attention to his words or movements. He proclaimed from the deck the program of his new gospel, that 'was to succeed all religions'. Those who heard him shrugged their shoulders, saying, 'the man is crazy'. On arriving at Boston, he made several ablutions, to the great amusement of the passengers, saying that he 'was washing off the last filth of Europe'.

But let us resume our journey. We had fine weather, and a pleasant trip from Halifax to Boston, which we reached at night.

Our Fathers received us with open arms and extraordinary charity, in which all their parishioners joined.

We risked ourselves on the railroad, by Buffalo, Cleveland and Columbus, as far as Cincinnati – a distance of 770 miles – and passed over it in fifty-two hours, comprehending all the delays experienced at the numerous stations. We changed cars six times in this distance. Be not astonished at the word 'risk', for accidents on all the routes are of frequent occurrence, and often frightful. Today it may be that a bridge has been left open – a hair-brained or intoxicated engineer pays no attention, and locomotives and cars are precipitated into the water, tomorrow, two trains will meet in collision, dashing into each other with all the velocity that steam can create. In a word, there are all kinds of accidents. When they occur, a list is given of the killed and disabled, which is often a very considerable one, curious inquiries are made, and some days after there is no further mention of the affair.

At Cincinnati our Fathers were most delighted to see us arriving with thirteen new and youthful companions full of fervent zeal to labour in this vast vineyard of the Lord. As we approached St Louis, I breathed more freely; I was no longer harassed with anxiety – indeed I had but one step to take, and I should be at home. However, this 'step' measured 700 miles, 530 of which were to be passed on the Ohio, and 170 on the Mississippi, and these rivers give an annual list of fearful accidents. We entered the steamer on the Ohio and on the morning of the 21st found ourselves cordially welcomed by our Fathers of Louisville, Kentucky. Continuing our descent on the 22nd, we arrived at the junction of the Ohio and Mississippi without accident.

My young companions were never weary of admiring the graceful and varied scenery of the lovely Ohio, now gratifying the sight by a chain of romantic elevations, then by a succession of rich lowlands, adorned with well-cultivated and extensive farms; and the attention arrested also by a succession of flourishing villages and cities.

The Mississippi is also more dangerous than the Ohio; exacting from its navigators during the winter many precautions, for the river is then low, full of sandbanks, sawyers and floating ice. We were several times in danger, and three different times our boat ran aground, and we believed her lost. On our way we saw the wrecks of five boats.

On the 26th we reached St Louis in safety, and animated with joyful and grateful sentiments on finding ourselves at our destination.

C and R, pp. 703–9.

Father De Smet kept in close touch, not only with his family, but also with his many benefactors and friends in Europe. He named many lakes and rivers that he discovered after his benefactors. He was forever collecting plants, insects, minerals and Indian artefacts of various kinds to send to museums in Europe. He sent family and friends souvenirs of the Far West, such as embroidered moccasins, soft bison robes and suits made of deerskin embroidered with porcupine quills. On 25 May 1854 he is writing to the Agent at the mouth of the Yellowstone to get him an elk-horn bow and arrows.

To Mr E T Denig, Agent, Mouth of the Yellowstone.

You may not forget to tell Crazy Bear, the Three Bears and others, that the old Black Robe thinks frequently of them, and begs daily of the Great Spirit to bless and protect all his Indian friends, to make them happy here in this world and grant them the favour of knowing Him, of loving Him, of serving Him in this world, to be made happy with Him in heaven for all eternity. I will always take great interest in their welfare.

If you have an elk-horn bow to send with a quiver of arrows, I would greatly thank you for it. I promised to procure one for a friend in Europe.

I remain with great respect, Dear Friend.

C and R, p. 1493.

By now the ugly phenomenon of religious persecution had begun to raise its head with more blatant manifestations. In a letter of 16 July 1854 Father De Smet speaks of anti-Catholic persecution.

The anti-Catholic spirit increases daily. All the enemies of our holy religion are leagued against her. As in all persecutions they seek to excite the masses by atrocious lies and calumnies. Within the last few days three Catholic churches have been destroyed.

C and R, p. 935.

The Catholic University of St Louis had to pay an enormous tax of $6,000, whereas the Presbyterian University alongside did not pay a cent in tax.

On 28 November 1854 Father De Smet wrote to his niece Elmire about the persecution against Catholics.

My Dearest Elmire,

... the American liberty and tolerance, so highly boasted, exist less in this Great Republic than in the most oppressed country of Europe. Catholic churches are burned and those who try to prevent it are assassinated. In the city of Ellsworth they snatched one of our Fathers from his abode; despoiled him of all his coats; tarred and feathered him and afterward rode him upon a rail. He was borne up the principal streets of the place, with the most outrageous and indecent insults. All the city applauded it – this horrible scene. They made it a crime for this priest to come and preach and say Mass to the Catholics.

C and R, p. 1453.

In April of the following year Father De Smet referred again to the persecution of Catholics

Dear Charles and Mimi

The Protestant ministers in general, and Presbyterians or Calvinists specially, are the greatest instigators and promoters of all sorts of outrages and of an open persecution of Catholics.

C and R, p. 1454.

He wrote, too, of the expulsion of the Indians from their traditional homelands.

Scarcely seventy years have rolled by since the whole country ... was one continued wilderness, the abode of numerous Indian tribes, which, like the snow before the rising sun, have melted and disappeared at the approach of the ever dreaded foes, the pale-faced European settlers or their descendants.

C and R, p. 1456.

On the 30 December 1854 he wrote from St Louis to the editor of

Précis Historiques, Belgium, of the white take-over of Indian lands.

> They say the whites 'walk in crooked paths to attain their objects'. 'Like Serpents,' said Chief Black Hawk in his famous speech, 'they have glided in among us; they have taken possession of our hearth-stones.'
>
> *C and R, p. 1209.*

Father De Smet had planned to visit the Indian missions in the mountains. But unfortunately circumstances put paid to any such plans. Chief among these events was the Gratton massacre that took place on 19 August 1854, and which resulted in another war with the Indian tribes.

In a letter to his family dated 17 April 1855, Father De Smet wrote:

> I told you in my last letter that I proposed to return to the desert in the course of this spring. That was sincerely my desire and I regret that serious difficulties have come up which compel me to put off my visits to the Indians to more favourable times and circumstances. For you must know, that the grand and glorious Republic is going to appear on the stage of the great Indian desert to give a representation of the lovely fable of La Fontaine (always old and always new) of the Wolf and the Lamb. The moral is, 'The wicked and the strong always find plenty of pretexts to oppress the innocent and the weak; and when they lack good reasons they have recourse to lies and calumnies.' An unpardonable offence, it appears, has been committed in the eyes of our civilised people by the Indians. They had repaired, to the number of 2,000, to the appointed spot at the time fixed by the Government agent to receive their annuities and presents. They waited several days for the commissioner to arrive and in the meantime they ran out of provisions. Then a Mormon wagon train, on its way to the Territory of Utah, came peaceably by the Indian camp. One of the party was dragging after him a lame cow, hardly able to walk. A famished savage, out of pity for his wife and children, and perhaps, also from compassion for the suffering animal, killed the cow and offered the Mormon double value for it in a horse or a mule.
>
> Such an act with such an offer under such circumstances

189

passes for very honest, very fair and very polite, in a wild country. Still the Mormon refused the proffered exchange and went and filed a complaint with the commandant of Fort Laramie, which is in the neighbourhood. Like the wolf who leaped upon the lamb to devour it, crying: 'I know very well that you all hate me, and *you* shall pay for the rest,' the illustrious commandant straightway sent out a young officer, Lieutenant John, with twenty soldiers armed to the teeth and with a cannon loaded with grapeshot He was absolutely determined to capture the so-called robber and make an example of him. The Indians were astonished at the menacing turn the affair of the cow, so frivolously begun, had taken; they begged the officer to take one, two, three horses in exchange, a hundred times the value of the cow, if necessary. They wished at any price to 'bury' the affair, as they express it; that is to arrange it peaceably and quietly, but without giving up to him their brother, innocent according to their code. The officer was inflexible, refused all offers; he must absolutely have his prisoner; and when the latter did not appear, he fired his cannon into the midst of the Indians. The head chief, whom I knew well, the noblest heart of his nation, fell mortally wounded and a number of his braves beside him. At this unexpected massacre the Indians sprang to arms, and letting fly hundreds of arrows from all sides they instantly annihilated the aggressors and provocateurs. Will you in Europe believe this tale of a cow? And yet such is the origin of a fresh war of extermination upon the Indians which is to be carried out in the course of the present year. An army of 3,000 to 4,000 men is being got ready in Missouri at this moment to penetrate into the desert. A very large number of whites will lose their lives without a doubt, but in the end the savages will have to yield, for they are without firearms, without powder and lead and without provisions.

C and R, p. 1217–18.

A little over a year later on 3 September 1855, General Harney, who had been sent out with a military force to punish these Indians, met them in battle on the north shore of the north fold of the Platte opposite the place known on the Oregon Trail as Ash Hollow. The Indians were completely defeated; General Harney then went overland to Fort Pierre where he succeeded in bringing about a general pacification of the tribes.

The letter continues:

Since the discovery of America a system of extermination, of moving the Indians, thrusting them farther back, has been pursued and practised by the whites, little by little, at first – more and more as the European settlers multiplied and gained strength. At this day this same policy is marching with giant strides; the drama of spoliation has reached its last act, both east and west of the Rocky Mountains. The curtain will soon fall upon the poor and unhappy remnants of the Indian tribes, and they will henceforth exist only in history. The whites are spreading like torrents over all California and the Territories of Washington, Utah and Oregon; over the States of Wisconsin, Minnesota, Iowa, Texas, and New Mexico, and latterly over Kansas and Nebraska, which have just been incorporated into the great American confederation. At a very recent epoch, within my own knowledge, all these first-named States and Territories were occupied by Indian nations, and just as fast as the whites settle and multiply there the natives disappear and seem to fade away.

C and R, pp. 1218–19.

On 19 June 1855 an official report on the State of Oregon was sent to the President of the United States by Governor Stevens. This is what he had to say about the mission of St Ignatius among the Pend d'Oreilles.

It would be difficult to find a more beautiful example of successful missionary labours. The mission was established nine years ago, by Reverend P J De Smet, the whole country at that time being a vast wilderness.

For the first two years the missionaries lived in skin lodges, accompanying the natives on their periodical hunts and visits to their fishing grounds.

During this time they found it very hard to live. Their food consisted principally of camas-roots and dried berries, which at best contain very little nourishment. They raised some wheat, which they boiled in the beard, for fear of waste, drying some of the grains to make a substitute for coffee. After this they slowly but steadily increased in welfare. Each year adding to a small piece of their tillable ground. They then obtained pigs, poultry, cattle, horses, agricultural implements and tools.

Before the missionaries came among the Indians, while thus ignorant, it was not uncommon for them to bury the very old and the very young alive, because, they said, 'these cannot take care of themselves, and we cannot take care of them and they had better die'.

The missionaries had an enormous labour before them. The missionaries told them they had a Creator and that he was good. They told them of their Saviour and of the manner of addressing him in prayer.

C and R, pp. 1267–70.

Father De Smet kept in close touch with his colleagues; particularly those working in the missions he had started. One of these colleagues was Father Adrian Hoeken, brother of Charles, one of his earliest travelling companions on his missionary journeys to the Flatheads.

On 18 October 1855 Father Hoeken wrote to Father De Smet from the Flathead camp in the Blackfoot country, giving news of the progress of the mission.

We have found means to build a beautiful church, which has excited the admiration of even Lieutenant Mullan, of the United States Army. This church is sufficiently large to contain the whole tribe, and on Sundays and festival days, when our Indians have adorned it with what ornaments of green boughs and wild flowers the woods and prairies supply; when they sing in it their devout hymns with fervour during the holy sacrifice, it might serve as a subject of edification and an example to quicken the zeal of many an old Christian congregation.

C and R, p. 1229.

He gave the news of the great loss of the Kalispels in the death of their chief, Loyola, 'Standing Grizzly', whom Father De Smet had baptised.

He also gave news of the smallpox epidemic that had hit them.

During the late prevalence of smallpox, hardly any of our neophytes died from it as most had been properly vaccinated by us, while the Spokanes and other unconverted Indians who said the 'medicine (vaccine) of the Fathers was a poison, used only to kill them', were swept away by the hundreds. This contrast of course had the effect of increasing the influence of the missionaries.

C and R, p. 1235.

As Socius or Procurator, holder of the purse strings, Father De Smet was looked upon as a sort of St Nicholas 'who never comes with an empty basket'. In April 1856 Father De Smet had the pleasure of sending by steamship to Father Adrian Hoeken, who was still labouring with the Flatheads, a cargo of tools, clothes and provisions of all kinds. The goods would first go 2,200 miles by boat up the Missouri. Then they would be transported by a barge, which would have to stem a rapid current for about 600 miles. After that they would come 300 miles by land, through mountain defiles, with wagons. So the goods shipped in April would only reach the Flathead mission in October.

On 9 September 1856 Father De Smet left St Louis for Europe yet again. On 20 September he sailed from New York by the steamer *Fulton* on his tenth Atlantic crossing. Four days later disaster awaited them, as Father De Smet later wrote:

Being the time of the autumnal equinoxes, the weather was rather boisterous and the sky foggy and cloudy. The vessel steered for Cape Sable, the most southern point of Nova Scotia. On the third night it was dark and cloudy. To this time the captain had not been able to make any observations, except soundings. For a moment the dark clouds disappeared, the watchman cried out' Land! Land!' the engine was stopped, and captain and officers were soon on deck. They had supposed that the steamer was a hundred miles southeast of Cape Sable. What could be the land they saw, on both sides? And how did the vessel come there? The danger was great. A few minutes more of covering, dark clouds, would have brought us to perish on the dangerous shoals and rocks of Nova Scotia in the Bay of Fundy. The steamer had found its way into this bay, carried on by a strong and setting tide. The land seen on both sides was the rocky, precipitous shore of St Mary's Bay. This happened on the night of the 24th of September.

C and R, p. 695.

They arrived at Le Havre on 3 October. The next day Father De Smet reached Paris. He took a stroll in the city,

> to see as much of its wonders as possible. I was facing the Rue Rivoli, toward the Champs Elysées, when the great Lion and Lioness made their unexpected appearance in an open carriage. I had a good view of Napoleon III and of the Empress Eugénie, at a distance of hardly twelve feet.
>
> *C and R, p. 695.*

From Paris he went to Brussels. He spent the rest of the year visiting the larger towns of Belgium and Holland.

On 21 April 1857 he embarked at Antwerp on the steamer *Leopold I* for New York. In a letter to the editor of *Précis Historiques* Father De Smet gave an account of the journey:

> They weighed anchor between nine and ten in the morning. The weather was superb. The large and beautiful ship *Leopold I*, was full of animation. A multitude of emigrants, from Germany, Holland, Switzerland, Belgium, Russia, France, etc., etc., were already on board, and were occupied with an infinity of petty cares and arrangements.
>
> We took but a day to reach Southampton, and remained there until the next day, to take in English and Irish passengers. Our number increased then to more than 620 persons. During the whole of this day the air resounded with the songs of the Germans and Hollanders, collected on the deck; several parties executed dances, to the sound of the violin and guitar.
>
> On the 23rd April, at half-past four in the afternoon we left Southampton. We soon lost sight of the Isle of Wight and of the English coast. Though the wind was moderate and the weather fine, we met a high, swollen and agitated sea, which tossed the vessel violently to and fro. This day and the two following were like days of mourning, without a song or a dance, without fun or any animation whatever. The dinner table was almost deserted, and appetite and gaiety had both left together. Here and there groups of men, women and children were observed, leaning over the side of the vessel, with haggard looks and pale faces, paying their tribute and forced respects to the sea. Those especially who had revelled most freely, and perhaps looked too deeply into the wine cup, wore the most melancholy and lengthened faces; they

looked absolutely like old parchment. Neptune was at his post; this inexorable toll-gatherer exacted the very last portion of his tribute; willingly or unwillingly, it must be paid.

Though this was my eleventh trip across the Atlantic, I was not exempted from the general seasickness. I endeavoured to resist, but all in vain. I was, therefore, obliged humbly to submit, and share the common misery.

This little shadow past, the remainder of the passage was unclouded. The weather was favourable from that day forward. The winds were sometimes a little contrary, but the ocean was calm and tranquil, until within six days' distance from New York.

On Sunday I said Mass in the grand saloon, where more than a hundred persons could conveniently find places; several Protestants asked permission to be present. Hymns were sung, during the sacrifice, in French, Latin, Dutch and German. It was certainly a rare spectacle on the ocean, where one is much more habituated to hearing blasphemies than the praises of God.

On the 2nd day of May, when near the Banks of Newfoundland, the sea became covered with a dense fog. It continued thus during four days, so that the captain could not make an observation. We could not distinguish anything a few feet from the boat. The misfortunes of the *Lyonnais* and of the *Arctic* are still recent. We were in continued danger of coming in contact with some sailing vessel pursuing the same route. As a precaution, the great whistle of the steam engine was heard day and night, in its loudest and most piercing tones, in order to give the alarm to vessels that might be in our passage. By means of this manoeuvre we were able to advance with our ordinary rapidity, ten or twelve knots, or four leagues, an hour.

However, as we were rapidly approaching land, and the fog increased in intensity, it appeared that we were progressing more or less at random; and as the observations of the meridian had become impossible, we were not without anxiety. We, therefore, had recourse to heaven, and we said our beads together. Our prayers appeared to have been heard. Some hours after, the fogs had vanished, and we had one of the most glorious evenings that can be witnessed at sea. The full moon, reflected on the waves, shone in its splendour from the starry and cloudless firmament. The next day the sun rose majestically. All eyes were stretched westward. We beheld in the distance, above the horizon, a long and foggy line, as of dark rising vapours and clouds. Spyglasses were then applied, a close examination made. From a hundred mouths, from one end of the vessel to the other, re-echoed the ever-joyous cry, Land! Land! Land! No mistake! First the outline of the hills and bluffs; next the forest trees and houses; at last, men riding and walking, bands of horses and herds of cattle, were seen browsing the rich herbage in the beautiful meadows along the shore. Songs and exclamations of joy were simultaneously offered by all hearts. The emigrants, grouped upon the upper deck, all saluted the New World, the land of promise, which bore in its bosom all their hopes and all their future prospects. Before the end of this beautiful day, on the 7 of May, at four in the afternoon, we anchored off Staten Island, in the bay of New York.

One duty remained for us to fulfil. In the name of all the passengers of the first and second cabins, who amounted to more than a hundred persons, I presented to the worthy commandant of the steamship, Monsieur Achille Michel, and to all his officers, a document signed by all, to express our cordial gratitude and sincere thanks for their assiduous attentions, their great kindness and politeness in regard to all the passengers; and, at the same time, to compliment them for their naval skill in the management of the large and noble ship, *Leopold I.*

On the 8th of May we disembarked with our baggage and lodged at St Xavier's College and St John's, Fordham, until the 18th of May. On the 19th May we took the cars in New York, via Buffalo, Cleveland, Indianapolis, Terre Haute, and arrived in St Louis on the 21st May a little after noon.

C and R, pp. 712–14.

This visit to Europe had not been a pleasant one for the much-travelled priest. He wrote: 'The journey comes wonderfully hard on me on the present occasion. I find consolation only that it is undertaken by obedience.' Reluctant as he had been to go, he was very happy to get back. 'I embraced the floor of my room on entering it,' he wrote, 'and from my innermost heart thanked the Lord.'

In December 1857 a sad bereavement completely prostrated Father De Smet. Father Duerinck, a cousin, was drowned near Independence, Missouri. He was descending the Missouri in an open boat with six men. The boat was wrecked on a snag. Father

Duerinck was learned in the natural sciences and had turned down a Chair at the University of Cincinnati.

Some days after the unfortunate accident the captain of a steamboat had seen a dead body on a sandbank, near the place of the accident, and buried it. Early in 1858, when he heard this news, Father De Smet went to Leavenworth to recover the body. He visited the solitary grave, on the bank of the Missouri, near the town of Liberty. But the body was not that of Father Duerinck. The clothing suggested it was a deck hand on one of the boats. Father De Smet recalls:

> I was very much grieved. Our petitions have so far not been heard. It would be a consolation if we could find the lost remains of Father Duerinck and inter him in consecrated ground, beside his brethren who have preceded him.
>
> *C and R, p. 1194.*

Back in St Louis, Father De Smet continued to receive news from the other missionaries. A letter from Father Adrian Hoeken, dated 15 April 1857, gave news of the Flathead Mission.

> Here in our missions, we already observe all the conditions stipulated in the treaty concluded last year by Governor Stevens, at Hellgate. Our brothers assist the Indians and teach them how to cultivate the ground. They distribute the fields and the seeds for sowing and planting, as well as the ploughs and other agricultural instruments. Our blacksmith works for them: he repairs their guns, their axes, their knives; the carpenter renders them great assistance in constructing their houses, by making the doors and windows; in fine, our little mill is daily in use for grinding their grain, *gratis;* we distribute some medicines to the sick; – in a word, all we have and all we are is sacrificed to the welfare of the Indian. The savings that our religious economy enables us to make, we retain solely to relieve their miseries. Whatever we gain by manual labour and by the sweat of the brow, is theirs! Through love of Jesus Christ, we are ready to sacrifice all, even life itself. Last year we opened our school, but circumstances forced us to close it. Next spring we shall have a brother capable of teaching and we intend opening it a second time; but in the interval we shall not earn a cent.
>
> We have done, and shall continue to do, all that lies in our

power for the Government officers. Still our poor mission has never received a farthing from the Government. Do not think, Reverend Father, that I complain – oh no! You are too well assured no earthly good could ever induce us to work and suffer as we do here. As wealth itself could never recompense our trials, so privations are incapable of leading us to renounce our noble enterprise. Heaven, heaven alone is our aim. Yet all is not less true, that, if we had resources (humanly speaking), our missions would be more flourishing.

C and R, pp. 1245–6.

In a letter to Lieutenant John Mullan, of the United States Army, headed 'St Louis University, 31 March 1858', Father De Smet wrote:

The missions of Father Hoeken, near the Flathead Lake, of Father Joset among the Coeur d'Alènes, of Father Ravalli at the Kettle Falls, are getting on slowly but prosperously.

In a temporal way the Fathers are sorely pinched and they sent me long lists of objects that are much needed. I am sorry that our private means in St Louis, owing to the hard times, are in a condition that we are unable to relieve them fully. Two thousand dollars would hardly buy what they call for. I shall, however, do what I can to come to their assistance, and the little I shall be able to collect I will forward by the boats of the American Fur Company.

C and R, p. 1501.

Chapter 12

Chaplain to the Army (1858–1859)

It was six years since Father De Smet had been to Indian Country. He was contemplating a trip among the Missouri and Flathead Indians. He got his wish, but from quite an unexpected source.

At the time the Mormon rebellion of 1857–8 was in progress. The Mormons had migrated to the Salt Lake Valley when that region was still a possession of Mexico. But after the war with Mexico it was transferred to the United States. Brigham Young and his people opposed all Federal interference. The Government was not at all disposed to trouble them; and to make interference as light as possible, Brigham Young was himself made first governor of the territory. The movement of people along the California trail had brought to the States the first real knowledge of the condition of things in Utah, and a feeling of prejudice against the Mormons gradually assumed formidable proportions. The polygamous fanatics were accused of atrocities upon poor, peaceable immigrants. In 1857 the incoming administration at Washington appointed a new governor, Alfred Cummings, to succeed Young. The ex-governor and his people rebelled and decided that the change should not take place. They announced that the day had arrived to avenge the death of their prophet Joseph and his brother, and to retaliate the wrongs and acts of injustice and cruelty of which they claimed to have been the victims in the States of Missouri and Illinois, whence they had been forcibly expelled by the inhabitants. To make good their threat they prepared for active resistance.

It became necessary to send a military force to protect the governor and other new officers in the discharge of their duties. Albert Sidney Johnston was sent in command of the expedition. The Mormons at first got the better of the federal troops, destroyed large quantities of their supplies, and so crippled the usefulness of Fort Bridger as a base that the expedition was threatened with starvation when the winter of 1857–8 approached. Thereupon the Government assumed both a commanding and a conciliatory tone. It organised a new military expedition, and it sent commissioners offering amnesty to such of the Mormons as ceased their resistance.

The commander of this second expedition was General William S Harney. He asked to have Father De Smet accompany the expedition as chaplain. On 9 May 1858 Father De Smet wrote to the Provincial from St Louis University.

Right Reverend and Dear Father

General Harney is ncw in St Louis with General Smith. I paid him a visit at the Planter's House. He seems really to have been in earnest in asking for a Catholic chaplain for the Utah army.

C and R, p. 715.

In his letter to the Father Provincial De Smet added that he was just preparing a journey among the Missouri and Flathead Indians of the Upper Missouri.

On 13 May 1858, Father De Smet received this letter from the War Department in Washington.

Sir

The President is desirous to engage you to attend the army for Utah to officiate as chaplain. In his opinion your services would be important in many respects to the public interest in the present condition of our affairs in Utah. Having sought information as to the proper person to be thus employed his attention has been directed to you, and he has instructed me to address you on this subject, in the hope that you may consider it not incompatible with your clerical duties or your personal feelings to yield to his request.

Should you conclude to accept this invitation you are requested to advise me of the fact, and proceed to the headquarters of General Smith at Fort Leavenworth.

Very respectfully

Your obedient servant

John F Floyd,

Secretary of War.

C and R, p. 1569.

So Father De Smet was appointed army chaplain to the army of Utah, fighting against Brigham Young's Mormons. He would have the rank of Major and be paid $1,200 a year plus expenses.

On 20 May 1858 Father De Smet set off from St Louis to join the headquarters of General Smith at Fort Leavenworth, Kansas Territory. Leavenworth was the principal town of Kansas Territory, with a population of about 10,000, even though it had only sprung into existence in the last six years. It was beautifully and advantageously situated on the Missouri. It had a bishop, two Catholic churches, a convent, a boarding school and a day school. Father De Smet hoped that he might be able to proceed from Utah to the Flathead Mission to confer with the Fathers there about a new mission for the Blackfeet.

In a letter to his Provincial dated 1 November 1859, Father De Smet later described his introduction to the army.

On the very day of my arrival I took my place in the Seventh Regiment, composed of 800 men, under the command of the excellent Colonel Morrison, whose staff was composed of a numerous body of superior officers of the line and engineers. General Harney, the commander-in-chief, and one of the most distinguished and most valiant generals in the United States, with great courtesy, installed me himself at my post. General Harney then shook hands with me, with great kindness, bade me welcome to the army, and assured me that I should be left perfectly free in the exercise of my holy ministry among the soldiers. He kept his word most loyally, and in this he was seconded by all the officers. During the whole time that I was among them, I never met with the slightest obstacle in the discharge of my duties. The soldiers always had free access to my tent for confession and instruction. I had frequently the consolation of celebrating the holy sacrifice of the Mass early in the morning, and on each occasion a large number of soldiers devoutly approached the holy table.

On 1 June 1858 Father De Smet left Fort Leavenworth with the Seventh Regiment, commanded by Colonel Morrison. They ascended the valley of the Little Blue River for three days, covering a distance of fifty-three miles. At a distance of 275 miles from Fort Leavenworth they left behind the waters of the Little Blue. Father De Smet was amazed at how much the countryside had

changed since his earlier travels in those parts. In his letter he
details some of those changes.

A space of 276 miles was already in great part occupied by white
settlers. No further back than 1851, at the time of my return
from the Great Council, held on the borders of the Platte or
Nebraska River, the plains of Kansas were almost entirely
without inhabitants, containing only a few scattered villages of
Indians, living for the most part by the chase, by fishing and on
wild fruits and roots. But eight years have made an entire
change: many towns and villages have sprung up, as it were, by
enchantment; forges and mills of every kind are already very
numerous; extensive and beautiful farms have been established
in all directions with extraordinary rapidity and industry.

The face of the country is entirely changed. In 1851, the antelope, the wild deer and the wild goat bounded at liberty over
these extensive plains. nor it is much longer ago that these fields
were the pasture of enormous herds of buffalo; today they are in
the possession of numerous droves of horned cattle, sheep and
hogs, horses and mules. The fertile soil rewards a hundredfold
the labours of the husbandman. Wheat, corn, barley, oats, flax,
hemp, all sorts of garden stuff and all the fruits of the temperate
zone, are produced in abundance. Emigration tends thither, and
commerce follows in its tracks and acquires new importance
every day.

C and R, p. 720.

Continuing the journey they crossed elevated prairies for a distance
of twenty-six miles, and entered the great valley of the Platte
River, at a distance of fifteen miles from Fort Kearney. This river,
up to its two forks, is about 3,000 yards wide, its waters yellowish
and muddy in the spring freshets, and resembling those of the
Missouri and the Mississippi. It is not so deep as those, but its
current is very rapid. Fort Kearney was rather insignificant. It
consisted of three or four frame houses and several made of *adobe*,
a kind of coarse brick baked in the sun.

A great number of Pawnee Indians were encamped a little
distance from the fort. Father De Smet came near to witnessing a
battle between them and a war party of Arapahos. He describes
what happened.

The Arapahos, favoured by the night, had succeeded in approaching the camp unseen almost forty strong. The Pawnees had just let their horses loose at break of day, when the enemy, with load cries, rushed into the drove, and carried away many hundred with them at full gallop. The alarm immediately spread throughout the camp. The Pawnees, indifferently armed and almost naked, rushed to the pursuit of the Arapahos, caught up with them, and a combat more noisy than bloody took place. A young Pawnee chief, the most impetuous of his band, was killed and three of his companions wounded. The Arapahos lost one killed and many wounded. Desirous to stop the combat, I hurried to the scene of battle with an aide-de-camp of the general, but all was over when we arrived; the Pawnees were returning with their dead and wounded and all the stolen horses. It was a harrowing scene. The deceased warrior was decorated and painted with all the marks of distinction of a great brave, and loaded with his finest ornaments. They placed him in the grave amid the acclamations and lamentations of the whole tribe.

The next day the Pawnee Loups invited me to their camp. I found there two French Creoles, old acquaintances of mine, of the Rocky Mountains. They received me with the greatest kindness, and desired to act as my interpreters. I had a long conference on religion with these poor, unhappy Indians. They listened with the most earnest attention. After the instruction they presented me 208 little children, and very earnestly begged me to regenerate them in the holy waters of baptism. These Indians have been the terror of travellers obliged to pass through their territory, for many years their character has been that of thieves, drunkards and ruffians, and they are brutalised by drink, which they readily obtain, owing to their proximity to the frontiers of civilisation. This accursed traffic has always and everywhere been the ruin of the Indian tribes, and it leads to their rapid extinction.

C and R, pp. 721–2.

The Pawnees dressed in the skins of animals they killed in the chase. They cultivated maize and squashes, using a shoulder blade of the bison as a substitute for the plough and hoe. On the march, the old and infirm and ill were left behind if they could not keep up.

If, on the long journeys which they undertake in search of game, any should be impeded, either by age or sickness, their children or relations make a small hut of dried grass to shelter them from the heat of the sun or from the weather, leaving as much provision as they are able to spare, and thus abandon them to their destiny. Nothing is more touching than this constrained separation, caused by absolute necessity – the tears and cries of the children on the one hand, and the calm resignation of the aged father or mother on the other.

This practice was common to all the nomadic tribes of the mountains. The Pawnees, one of the few aboriginal tribes, descending from the ancient Mexicans, were guilty of offering human sacrifices. Father De Smet was in the neighbourhood when one such barbarous sacrifice took place. The victim was a young Sioux girl, aged fifteen years, who had been taken prisoner six months previous to her immolation.

In the neighbourhood of Fort Kearney they met their first herds of bison.

The sight created great excitement among those soldiers who had not visited the plains before, and they burned to bring down one or two. Armed, as they were, with the famous Minié rifles, they might have made a good hunt, had they not been on foot; it was therefore, impossible to get near them. They fired, however, at a distance of 200 or 300 yards.

C and R, p. 723.

Two days' march above Fort Kearney, at a place called Cottonwood Springs, Father De Smet came upon thirty lodges of the Ogallalas, of the Sioux or Dakota tribe. At their request be baptised all their children.

During the months of June and July, tempests, and falls of rain and hail, were almost daily occurrences in the valley of the Platte, an area known for storms and whirlwinds. They had their share of torrents of water that drenched the valleys, and volleys of hail that crushed the herbs and flowers. They passed many graves of those adventurers who had risked their lives in the search for gold. The sight Father De Smet found most remarkable were the long wagon trains engaged in transporting provisions and stores of war for Utah. Each train consisted of twenty-six wagons, each wagon drawn by six yoke of oxen. On the plains the wagoner assumed the style of 'captain', being placed in charge of his wagon and twelve oxen. The master-wagoner was 'admiral' of this land-fleet. He had control of twenty-six captains and 312 oxen.

> The Quartermaster-General made the calculation and told me that the whole train would make a line of about fifty miles. We passed every day some wagons of this immense train. Each wagon is marked with a name, as in the case of ships, and these names serve to furnish amusement to the passer-by, the caprices of the captains in this respect having imposed upon the wagons such names as the *Constitution,* the *President*, the *Great Republic*, the *King of Bavaria, Lola Montes, Louis Napoleon, Dan O'Connell, Old Kentucky*, etc., etc. These names were daubed in great letters on each side of the carriage.

At a distance the white awnings of the wagons had the effect of a fleet of vessels with all canvas spread. Father De Smet continues his narrative.

> On leaving Leavenworth the drivers look well enough, being all in new clothes, but as they advance into the plains their good clothes become travel-stained and torn, and at last are converted into rags. The *captains* have hardly proceeded 200 miles, before their trail is marked with rags, scattered and flying along the route. You may often remark also on the various camping grounds, even as far as the Rocky Mountains, and beyond, the wrecks of wagons and the skeletons of oxen, but especially the remains of the wardrobe of the traveller: legs of pantaloons and drawers, a shirt-bosom, the back or the arm of a flannel vest, stockings out at toe and heel, crownless hats, and shoes worn through in the soles or uppers, are strewed along the route. These deserted camps are also marked by packs of cards strewed round broken jars and bottles: here you see a gridiron, a coffee-pot or a tin bowl; there a cooking-stove and the fragments of a shaving-dish, all worn out and cast aside.
>
> The poor Indians regard these signs of encroaching civilisation with an unquiet eye as they pass them on their way. These rags and refuse are to them the harbingers of the approach of a dismal future for themselves; they announce to them that the plains and forests over which they roam in the chase, their beautiful lakes

and rivers swarming with fish, and the repair of numerous aquatic birds; the hearth which witnessed their birth, and the soil which covers the ashes of their fathers – all, in fine, that is most dear to them – are about to pass into the hands of the rapacious white man: and they, poor mortals, accustomed to roam at large and over a vast space, free like the birds of the air, will be enclosed in narrow reserves, far from their cherished hunting grounds and fine fisheries, far from their fields of roots and fruits; or driven back into the mountains or to unknown shores. It is not surprising, then, that the savage seeks sometimes to revenge himself on the white man; it is rarely, however, that he is the aggressor: surely, not once out of ten provoking cases.

The wagons are formed every evening into a *corral*. That is, the whole twenty-six are ranged in a circle, and chained one to the other, so as to leave only one opening, to give passage to the beasts, which pass the night in the centre, and are guarded there by several sentinels under arms. Under the protection of a small number of determined men, the wagons and animals are secure from any attack of undisciplined Indians, in however great numbers. When the travellers neglect this precaution, and camp at random, not infrequently a hostile band of Indians will provoke what is called a *stampede*, or panic among the cattle, and carry them all off at once. The travellers go into camp early, and at break of day the beasts are let loose in the praire that they may have plenty of time to graze. Grass is very abundant in the valley of the Platte, and on the neighbouring acclivities.

C and R, pp. 725–7.

Between Fort Kearney and the crossing of the South Fork of the Platte, they met over 100 families of Mormons on their way to Kansas and Missouri, with the intention of settling there. They appeared delighted at being fortunate enough to escape safe and sound from the famous Promised Land of Utah; thanks to the influence of the new Governor, and the presence of the United States troops. They confessed that they would have escaped long before, had they not been afraid of falling into the hands of the Danites, or Destroying Angels. These composed the bodyguard of the Prophet; they were said to be entirely and blindly at his disposal, to carry out all his plans, meet all his wishes and execute all his measures, which often involved robbery and murder. Before the arrival of the United States soldiers, woe to anyone who manifested a desire to leave Utah, or abandon the sect.

Couriers and Pony Express messengers often crossed their path on the plains. The Pony Express was a remarkable enterprise. The eastern forwarding terminus was at Pike's Peak Livery Stables in St Joseph. Twenty-nine days later mail would be delivered in San Francisco, 2,000 miles away. The express riders would cover eighty miles between exchange posts in eight or nine hours. Horses were exchanged every twelve miles. One man would do about 400 miles without real rest or sleep, riding across prairie and mountain range, through flash floods and rivers in spate. He would ride more than 300 miles before snatching some sleep out of the saddle. He would sing and shout to keep himself awake. He rode the last miles while asleep in the saddle, his eyes shut because he couldn't keep them open any longer. Passing a rider travelling in the opposite direction greetings were caught in the wind of their passing. However, when in October 1861, words were spun along ribbons of wire with the invention of the telegraph, the days of the Pony Express were numbered.

The expedition against the Mormons was brought to a halt before reaching Utah. The commanding general and staff were already at the crossing of the south branch of the Platte, 480 miles from Fort Leavenworth, when he received the news that the Mormons had submitted, or laid down their arms. The troops were ordered back to their States. The conclusion of peace brought a change in Father De Smet's eventual destination; gone were his hopes of a little diplomatic mission to the Indian tribes of Utah.

Father De Smet returned to Fort Leavenworth with General Harney. Before leaving Fort Leavenworth for St Louis, Father De Smet made a small excursion of seventy miles to visit his colleagues at the Mission of St Mary among the Potawatomies. He then went to St Louis to resign his commission. He, at last, reached St Louis at the beginning of September, after an absence of three months and a journey, to and fro, of 1,976 miles.

But his plan to resign his commission was aborted by events taking place in the far distant Oregon, the familiar field of his labours in years gone by. As he later described events, in a communication to *Précis Historiques*:

Upon my arrival in St Louis in the early part of September 1858, I tendered to the Secretary of War my resignation of the post of

Chaplain to the Army of Utah. It was not, however, accepted, because of fresh difficulties that had arisen with the Indian tribes west of the Rocky Mountains. The papers announced that a powerful coalition of Indians had been formed, and that Colonel Steptoe had been attacked, and two officers, a sergeant and several soldiers of his company killed in the first engagement. A general rising was feared of all the tribes in that section – the Palooses, Yakimas, Skoyelpi, Okinagans, Spokans, Coeur d'Alènes, Kalispels, Kootenais and Flatheads. All these Indians, hitherto quiet and peaceable (especially the four tribes last named) had of late become more or less disturbed and irritated, chiefly through the incursions of white emigrants into the Indian lands on the southwest of the territories of Oregon and Washington, where, without the least ceremony and without any preliminary arrangement or agreement, they had taken possession of the most fertile lands and the most advantageous sites.

The mountain Indians, especially, had become alarmed and had resolved to oppose the entry of whites and their further advance into the land. The Indian force that was on foot consisted of 800 to 1,000 warriors. They had just won a victory: the hasty retreat of the brave Colonel Steptoe, who was hardly expecting an attack from the Indians and had only 120 soldiers, appeared to them a flight. He had even abandoned to them all his train and provisions. Swollen with pride and presumption, the Indians henceforth believed themselves invincible and capable of resisting and withstanding the whole United States Army. Accordingly they issued their defiance of the whites. The Government at any rate thought their opposition quite a serious matter, and decided to send out General Harney, who had covered himself with laurels on various occasions in Indian warfare in Florida, Texas, Mexico and the plains of the Missouri.

C and R, pp. 730–1.

General Harney asked once more to have Father De Smet as chaplain and envoy extraordinary for the Government. Knowing the missionary's influence over the Indians, he believed his mediation would put an end to hostilities. It was General Stanley who stated that, 'Father De Smet, alone of the entire white race, could penetrate to these cruel savages and return safe and sound.' The mission was a delicate one. What would the Indians think when they saw the missionary attached to the army that had come to make war on them?

But peace in Oregon meant the saving of the 'reductions'. Father De Smet hoped he might be of some use to the mountain tribes and once again be among his brethren in the difficulties that the war would bring upon them. With the consent of his superiors, he accepted the post of army chaplain.

Father De Smet was notified by telegraph to proceed to New York and to embark there with General Harney and his staff. In order to avoid crossing the wilderness, General Harney decided to go across the Isthmus of Panama and enter Oregon through the mouth of the Columbia. The journey from New York to Idaho and Montana by way of Panama, San Francisco and the Columbia River was long, but it was easier and more sure and made in less time than by the Missouri River. The voyage by way of the Missouri, if made favourably and without the least obstacle, took ordinarily, three months. By way of the Pacific it took from New York to Panama ordinarily nine days; from there to San Francisco, twelve days; from San Francisco to Vancouver, on the Columbia River, four days; from Vancouver to Walla Walla, three to four days; from Walla Walla to the Mission of the Sacred Heart among the Coeur d'Alènes, six days – in all just over a month.

On 15 September Father De Smet left St Louis by rail. In fifty hours he covered the 1,100 miles and reached New York. On 20 September he embarked, together with the general and his staff, on the steamer *Star of the West*. Their first destination was Aspinwall, a small place on the northern side of the Isthmus of Panama, about 2,000 miles from New York. They passed San Salvador, the first land reached by Christopher Columbus 12 October 1492, then the eastern tip of Cuba, then San Domingo. They came in sight of Jamaica, into the Caribbean, finally reaching Aspinwall. They made this distance in eight days. It was the time of the equinox, and they were accordingly accompanied by high winds, squalls and some small tempests, especially among the dangerous Bahama Islands. The trip was a very fortunate one; no serious case of sickness appeared on board, which was quite unusual in the topics. The passengers were 640 in number, bound mainly for California, the great Eldorado of the West.

Father De Smet gives an interesting description of his journey across the Isthmus of Panama.

The Isthmus of Panama is thirty-six miles in width, and the railroad that joins the two oceans forty-seven in length. This railroad may be cited as a wonder, for the boldness of the undertaking and the success with which it was carried out. It traverses dense forests and crosses one handsome river, over which a bridge of the most solid construction has been thrown. It is indeed a gigantic work and must have cost an enormous sum.

There is no sign of human habitation along the way, save two or three little villages, consisting of a few poor huts of bamboo.

Formerly, to reach the farther shore, it was necessary to travel three or four days afoot or on horseback, amid privations and difficulties of every kind. Today you are softly transported in less than three hours from Aspinwall to Panama.

C and R, p. 733.

On 30 September 1858, Father De Smet was able to celebrate Mass in the Cathedral of Panama.

On 2 October they left the Bay of Panama and set off for San Francisco, more than 3,000 miles away. They coasted along almost the entire shoreline of Costa Rica and Nicaragua. By the sixth day they had covered 1,500 miles and had reached Acapulco, where they stopped to receive mail and to take on provisions, coal and water. On 10 October they espied the summit of the volcano Mount Popocatépetl, the loftiest peak in the Sierra Madre, at 19,623 feet. On 15 October they perceived Point Conception, 250 miles distant from San Francisco; they saluted from afar Santa Barbara, San Luis and Monterey. On the evening of 16 October they arrived at San Francisco. Father De Smet was glad to find himself in a house of the Society and in the company of his brethren: especially so after having been shut up in a ship among 1,300 individuals of all nations, 'all with their morals infected with the yellow (or golden) fever and who think, speak and dream of nothing but mines of gold and the earthly happiness which their wealth is to procure them, hereafter – and often this "hereafter" never arrives.'

Father De Smet was much taken with San Francisco.

A dozen years ago San Francisco was nothing but a very little seaport, with only a handful of inhabitants. Today it is the marvel and the port *par excellence* of the whole Pacific Ocean. The population of at least 60,000 comes from all corners of the earth, with 4,000 Chinese preserving faithfully the manners and customs of their fatherland, including the long queue [pigtail]. They almost all live in a separate quarter and they are quiet and industrious, though charged with great immorality.

C and R, p. 738.

On 20 October 1858 they left San Francisco for the mouth of the Columbia River. They skirted the coast of Oregon. On 23 October they passed over the dangerous bar of the Columbia which he had crossed for the first time in 1844. A large lighthouse shone its beacon from Cape Disappointment. Indians, formerly so numerous along the coast and river, had almost entirely disappeared.

Every approach of the whites thrusts them back, by force or otherwise; they go upon the reservations, in a strange land, far removed from their hunting and fishing grounds and where drink (alcohol), misery and diseases of every sort mow them down by hundreds.

They passed the little town of Astoria, picturesquely established on the slope of a steep hill, surrounded with thick forests of Canada balsam.

They arrived back at Fort Vancouver on 28 October. As in the case of the Utah expedition the actual campaign was over before General Harney arrived on the ground. Upon his arrival, the General heard, to his great surprise, that peace had been made. Wishing to avenge Steptoe's defeat, Colonel Wright left for Walla Walla at the end of August and, through his clever tactics, routed the united forces of the Coeur d'Alènes, Spokanes, and Kalispels early in September. Disconcerted by this prompt reprisal, the tribes were ready to make peace. They gave hostages, and, moreover, surrendered several Indians, guilty of having assassinated Americans, to be hanged.

The Indians were vanquished but not reconciled. Father De Smet records:

The task remained of removing the prejudices of the Indians, soothing their inquietude and alarm, and correcting, or rather refuting, the false rumours that are generally spread about after a war, and which otherwise might be the cause of its renewal.

C and R, p. 72.

The season was too far advanced to permit troops to set out for the mountains. Father De Smet offered to go alone to spend the winter

211

with the Indians and consolidate the peace and return in the spring to give his report to the General. For the accomplishment of such a task there was no other individual so well equipped as he. It was decided that he should visit the upper tribes among whom his name was held in affectionate reverence, and use his efforts to bring about a general pacification.

On 28 October 1858 Army Headquarters issued the following notice:

Headquarters, Department of Oregon

Fort Vancouver W T

October 28th, 1858

Special Order No 4.

1. The Reverend P J De Smet, chaplain, etc., being about to proceed to the Coeur d'Alène Mission under instructions from the general command; officers commanding posts and stations in his route are directed to furnish the Reverend Father with every facility and means for prosecuting his journey securely, and in an expeditious manner. Orders will, therefore, be given to provide such guides, interpreters, escorts and animals to Father De Smet as will attain the object of this order.

2. The assistant quartermaster at Fort Walla Walla will defray the expenses of such expressmen as may be sent to that post, from time to time, by Father De Smet.

By Order of Brigadier General Harney

A Pleasonton

Captain Second Dragoons A A Adjt-Gen.

C and R, p. 1575.

The next day Father De Smet left Fort Vancouver to go among the tribes of the mountains. Four hundred miles lay between him and the nearest mission, that of the Coeur d'Alènes.

Thirty-six miles above Vancouver, and at the distance of 132 miles from the sea, the Columbia River passed through the mountainous Cascade Range. For a stretch of five miles it was strewn with great masses of rock, accumulated in a quite narrow place, which formed those rapid and insurmountable currents called the Cascades. The view of the mountains on each side of the river was truly breathtaking and grand. Their flanks were covered with trees and high brush, and especially now in the autumn the different coloured foliage, bright golden and scarlet, augmented greatly the beauty and magnificence of these picturesque places.

After sixty miles of navigation above the Cascades they reached the Dalles, another fall on the Columbia. Boats cannot pass here. Father De Smet visited the Catholic soldiers at Fort Dalles. On 2 November he left the fort at the Dalles and made for Walla Walla in an ambulance. The journey took eight days. They camped on the Des Chutes, John Day and Umatilla Rivers, where there was wood for camp fires. Again he visited the Catholic soldiers of Fort Walla Walla. At the fort Father De Smet met the hostages and prisoners taken previously by Colonel Wright. Fearing they were in danger of being corrupted, Father De Smet asked that the Indians might be allowed to return with him to their country. 'Impossible,' replied the Colonel, 'without express authorisation from General Harney.' 'Very good,' said Father De Smet. 'I will answer for it that you will not be reproved by him for acceding to my request. I know well the Spokanes, Coeur d'Alènes, and the Kalispels. They are my children, and I will answer for their loyalty with my head, which will be at the disposition of the General should these Indians be untrue to their word.' The Colonel no longer opposed the departure of the hostages, who set out with their Father, happy as souls escaping from limbo.

This arrangement furnished Father De Smet with guides and travelling companions, and, above all, assured him a welcome from the tribes.

After three days' journeying in the plains and after crossing a high mountain covered with a dense forest of cedars and pines, they arrived, on the evening of 18 November, at the great Coeur d'Alènes Lake. On 21 November 1858 he arrived at the Sacred Heart Mission among the Coeur d'Alènes. He was enthusiastically welcomed as the friend, father, and liberator of the Indians. After an absence of twelve years, the missionary again found himself in the midst of those to whom he had given the light of faith. The 'reduction' had steadily prospered, possessing now a beautiful church, comfortable houses, a mill, workshops, rich pastures, and fields of prodigious fertility. But even their prosperity was a menace, for the whites began to covet the mission lands. The thought of being obliged one day to leave the place where reposed the ashes of their fathers and all those they loved, and their hunting and fishing grounds, plunged the Indians into black despair. 'The Indian sees nothing ahead of him but a dark and sombre future. That is the present state of all tribes of these parts.' Father De Smet vigorously denounced the conduct of the immigrants, and the Christian Indians promised to have no further dealings with them. Moreover, he assured the Government that while repressing the violent acts of the Indians, it must at the same time defend their rights.

The bad season had commenced, and it was not long before the snow had filled the passes of the mountains, and heavy ice began to float on the rivers and lakes. Father De Smet was therefore compelled to abandon, for the time being, his project of going to the mission of the Flatheads and Pend d'Oreilles, who were located six days' journey to the northeast, in one of the loftiest valleys of the Rocky Mountains.

In *Prècis Historiques* Father De Smet records:

At the beginning of winter, the snow piles up on the plateaux and in the mountain gorges to a great depth. They never become practicable, either for ordinary footwear or for snowshoes, until after a good thaw and rain, followed by a hard freeze; only then can the intrepid traveller venture upon a passage. Without this precaution, a man is risking his life. It is rare for a foolhardy or imprudent adventurer to escape the danger. I tried it in 1845. I then crossed, on snowshoes, the Saskatchewan Mountains at the sources of the Columbia, for a distance of about ninety miles, over snow five to twenty feet in depth. I shall never forget the good and brave Indians who served me as guides at this time: but for them, certainly I should never have gotten out of the bad place I had so rashly engaged myself in. The danger that I ran on this occasion has made me more prudent.

C and R, p. 759.

Father De Smet remained at the Coeur d'Alène Mission over the winter. On Christmas Eve he celebrated Midnight Mass in the handsome church.

All men, women and children, intoned together the Vivat Jesus, Gloria, Credo and several other canticles composed in their own tongue. All, with a few exceptions, approached the Lord's table to partake of the bread of angels.

Father De Smet was there until February 1859. In that time they had forty-three days and forty-three nights of snow, more or less abundant.

Impatient to visit the other tribes, Father De Smet departed from the mission on 18 February for St Ignatius' Mission. The 'reduction', founded fifteen years before, near the mouth of the Clarke River, was transferred in 1854 to a more favourable situation some miles north of St Mary's and became part of St Francis Borgia's Mission. He was accompanied by Father Joset, who stayed with him until he met Father Hoeken, who had promised to meet them on Clark's river.

> The ice, snow, rain and winds impeded very much our course, in our frail canoes of bark, on the rivers and great lakes: we often ran considerable risk in crossing rapids and falls, of which Clark's River is full. I counted thirty-four of these in seventy miles.
>
> *C and R, p. 764.*

The joy of seeing his neophytes again, and the hope of effecting peace, rendered Father De Smet indifferent to fatigue and dangers. Finally he arrived with the Kalispels, who received him with joyful demonstrations befitting the Black Robe who had been the first to give them the knowledge of the Master of life. This, the most prosperous of the Oregon Missions, counted 2,000 Christian Indians. Less exposed to contact with the whites than the St Paul or Sacred Heart missions, this tribe, under Father Hoeken's watchful care, still adhered to its first fervour.

On 11 March 1859 Father De Smet arrived at the Mission of St Ignatius among the Pend d'Oreilles of the mountains.

> The Kootenais, a neighbouring tribe of the Pend d'Oreilles, having heard of my arrival, had travelled many days' journey through deep snow to shake hands with me, to bid me welcome, and manifest their filial affection. In 1845 I had made some stay with them. I was the first priest who had announced to them the glad tidings of salvation, and I had baptised all their little children and a large number of adults. They came on this occasion,

with a primitive simplicity, to assure me that they had remained faithful to 'the prayer', that is, to religion, and all the good advice that they had received. All the Fathers spoke to me of these good Kootenais in the highest terms. Fraternal union, evangelic simplicity, innocence and peace, still reign among them in full vigour. Their honesty is so great and so well known, that the trader leaves his storehouse entirely, the door remaining unlocked often during his absence for weeks. The Indians go in and out and help themselves to what they need, and settle with the trader on his return.

C and R, p. 765.

Only the Flatheads now remained to be visited.

On 18 March he travelled across deep snow for a distance of seventy miles to the abandoned mission of St Mary's in Bitter Root Valley, the scene of his first labours with the Flatheads. Father De Smet had left it in a flourishing condition in 1846. But in 1858 the mission was abandoned. 'The why and the how, I could, I think, pretty well guess at,' wrote Father De Smet on 1 May 1858. 'But we are left in the dark as to what actually happened.' Father De Smet was naturally sad.

For fifteen years the Oregon tribes had lived peacefully and happily under the watchful eyes of the missionaries. Great numbers were baptised. All were taught agriculture, harvests were abundant, the mills worked regularly, and new ground was tilled for cultivation continuously. But things changed after the discovery of gold in 1851. White men invaded the west. From California this gold-seeking army spread to Oregon, trading whisky for land. The whites seized the lands under cultivation; the villages, given over to debauchery and drunkenness, because theatres of the worst excesses: gambling, stealing, illicit dealings, divorce. The villages were reduced to the conditions they were in before the arrival of the Black Robes. For three years Fathers Vercruysse and Ravalli contended with the invaders for the souls of their neophytes. Finally the mission was abandoned at the close of 1858, and the Fathers, with a few remaining Christians retired to the Coeur d'Alènes. But Father De Smet's spirits rose again when he visited the new mission of St Ignatius in Mission Valley near to Great Flathead Lake.

Following the example of the Coeur d'Alènes, the other Christian tribes promised not to begin war. The Flatheads and Kalispels boasted of never having spilled the blood of the white man, and of having entered the coalition solely for the defence of their rights.

The pacifier encountered greater opposition from the pagan tribes, but Father De Smet's uprightness and touching kindness so influenced the Indians that he succeeded in modifying their defiant attitude. The Spokanes, Yakimas, Palooses, Okinagans, and the Chaudières promised to accept the Government's conditions.

On 16 April, in accordance with the orders of General Harney, Father De Smet left for Vancouver, accompanied by nine Indian chiefs, delegated by their respective tribes to sign a treaty of peace with the agents of the Republic – the General and the Superintendent of Indian Affairs. The chiefs were, Alexander Temflagketzin, or Man-without-a-horse, great chief of the Pend d'Oreilles; Victor Alamiken, or Happy-man (he deserved his name, for he was a saintly man), great chief of the Kalispels; Adolphus Kwilkweschape, or Red-feather, chief of the Flatheads; Francis Saxa, or Iroquois, another Flathead chief; Dennis Zanamtietze, or thunders-robe, chief of the Skoyelpi or Chaudières; Andrew and Bonaventure, chiefs and braves among the Coeur d'Alènes, or Skizoumish; Kamiakin, great chief of the Yakimas; and Gerry, great chief of the Spokanes. Alone and unarmed, a Jesuit priest had been able to do more to restore peace in the country than the entire American army.

Father De Smet's efforts on behalf of peace were crowned with success, but the journey had been a most difficult one. It required more than a month's travel to reach general headquarters.

In a letter to the Father General, dated 1 November 1859, Father De Smet wrote:

We suffered much and ran many dangers on the route, on account of the high stage of the rivers and the heavy snow. For ten days we had to clear a way through thick forests, where thousands of trees, thrown down by storms, lay across one another, and were covered, four, six and eight feet with snow; several horses perished in this dangerous passage. My horse stumbled many a time, and procured me many a fall; but aside from some serious bruises and scratches, a hat battered to pieces, a torn pair of trousers and a *soutane* or black gown in rags, I came out of it (the 'Bad Forest') safe and sound. I measured white cedars in the wood, which were as much as six or seven persons could clasp at the base, and of proportionate height. After a month's journey we arrived at Fort Vancouver.

C and R, p. 767.

On 18 May the meeting took place with the General, the Superintendent of Indian Affairs and the Indian chiefs. The chiefs renewed their assurances of submission, asked for the friendship of the Americans, and expressed regret for the blindness that had led them to taking up arms. They promised, moreover, that no further molestations would be made upon the whites crossing their lands, if the Government in turn would consent to give the Indians 'reserves', and engage itself to protect them.

The Indian chiefs were then given about three weeks to visit the interesting points in the territory in the hope that an acquaintance with the number and power of the whites would be a wholesome restraint upon further outbreaks. The visit that appeared the most to interest the chiefs, was that which they made to the prison at Portland and its wretched inmates, whom they found chained within its cells. They were particularly interested in the causes, motives, and duration of their imprisonment. Chief Alexander kept it in his mind. Immediately on his return to his camp at St Ignatius Mission, he assembled his people, and related to them all the wonders of the whites, and especially the history of the prison. 'We,' said he, 'have neither chains nor prisons; and for want of them, no doubt, a great number of us are wicked and have deaf ears. As chief, I am determined to do my duty: I shall take a whip to punish the wicked; let all those who have been guilty of any misdemeanour present themselves, I am ready.' The known guilty parties were called upon by name, many presented themselves of their own accord, and all received a proportionate correction. The whole affair terminated in a general rejoicing and feast.

Before leaving the parts of civilisation, all the chiefs received presents from the General and Superintendent, and returned to their own country contented and happy and well determined to keep at peace with the whites. The whites would conciliate important chiefs by presenting them with medals, bearing the impression of the President. Father De Smet's mission was now finished.

Feeling that he could be of no further service on the expedition, the objectives of which were now accomplished, Father De Smet asked permission to return to the States by way of the mountain missions and the Missouri River. The General replied as follows:

Headquarters, Department of Oregon

Fort Vancouver, W T

June 1st, 1859

My Dear Father

The General Commander instructs me to enclose a copy of his special order, No 59, of this date, authorising you to return to St Louis, through the different tribes of the interior, which you are so desirous to visit once again, for the purpose of confirming them in their good disposition toward the whites, as well as to renew their zeal and intelligence in the elements of Christianity, – the means so signally productive of goodwill and confidence, in your labours of the past winter, requiring such self-denial and resolution.

The General is anxious that I should communicate to you the deep regret with which he feels your separation from the service.

By the campaign of last summer submission had been conquered, but the embittered feelings of the two races, excited by war, still existed, and it remained for you to supply that which was wanting to the sword. It was necessary to exercise the strong faith which the red man possessed in your purity and holiness of character, to enable the General to evince successfully toward them the kind intentions of the Government, and to restore confidence and repose to their minds. This has been done; the victory is yours, and the General will take great pleasure in recording your service at the War Department.

Your most obedient servant

A Pleasonton.

Captain Second Dragoons A A Adjt.-Gen.

Headquarters, Department of Oregon

Fort Vancouver, W T.

June 1st, 1859.

Special Orders No 59
The Reverend P J De Smet, chaplain, etc., having accomplished in a highly satisfactory manner the important duties confided to his charge in Special Orders No 4 of October 28th, 1858, from these headquarters, and being now desirous of returning to his

219

clerical station at St Louis, visiting the various Indian tribes of the interior on his route; he is authorised to do so. Commanders of posts and others belonging to this Department will afford every facility and assistance to the Reverent Father, when called upon by him to aid in his mission of peace to the unfortunate race whose confidence he has always most generously maintained.

By order of General Harney

A Pleasonton

Captain Second Dragoons A A, Adjt.-Gen.

Reverend P J De Smet

C and R, p. 1577, 1581.

Father De Smet left Fort Vancouver on 15 June with the chiefs to return to the mountains. He passed the 7, 8 and 9 of July at the Mission of the Sacred Heart, among the Coeur d'Alènes. Thence he continued his route for St Ignatius with Father Congiato, and completed the trip in a week; not, however, without many privations, which deserve a short mention here. It was no easy task to cross the mountains that separated the Sacred Heart Mission from that of St Ignatius, especially as Father De Smet was now fifty-eight years old. As he wrote in his letter to Father Provincial, 10 November 1859:

Imagine a dense virgin forest, the ground strewn with thousands of uprooted trees. The paths are hidden and obstructed by these barricades that imperil the life of horse and rider at every step. To these obstacles must be added immense fields of snow which have to be crossed, and which are at times from eight to twelve feet deep. Two large rivers wind through the forest, whose beds are formed by boulders of fallen rock and glistening stones deposited by the rushing water. The path crosses the first of these rivers thirty-nine times, the other thirty-two times. Often my horse stood in water to his breast and at times even over the saddle, but one is lucky to escape with only soaked legs. A mountain of 5,000 feet lies between the two rivers, with here and there vast plateaux covered with eight feet of snow. After eight hours of painful climbing we arrived at a beautiful plain enamelled with flowers, where, sixteen years before, during my first journey, a cross had been erected. In this beautiful situation, after so long and rude a course, I desired to encamp; but Father Congiato persuaded me that in two hours more we should reach the foot of the mountain, and induced us to continue the march.

The two hours passed, then four hours, and night overtook us in the midst of a thousand difficulties. Mounds of snow and barricades of fallen trees were again encountered. Sometimes we were on the edge of sheer precipices of rock, sometimes on a slope almost perpendicular. The least false step would precipitate us into the abyss. Without a guide, without a path, in the most profound darkness, separated one from the other, each calling for help without being able either to give or to obtain the least assistance, we fell again and again, groped our way on all fours. At last a gleam of hope arose; we heard the hoarse murmur of water in the distance: it was the sound of the waterfalls of the great river that we were seeking. Each one then directed his course toward that point. We all had the good fortune to arrive at last, but one after another, between twelve and one o'clock in the night, after a march of sixteen hours, fatigued and exhausted, our dresses torn to rags, and covered with scratches and bruises; but without serious injuries. While eating our supper, each one amused his companions with the history of his mishaps. Good Father Congiato admitted that he had made a mistake in his calculations, and was the first to laugh heartily at his blunder. Our poor horses found nothing to eat all night in this miserable mountain gap.

C and R, pp. 767–71.

He arrived at St Ingatius on 16 July. He left this mission a week later by way of the Mullan road for Fort Benton, 200 miles away. On 26 July he crossed the mountain which separated the sources of the Clark River from those of the Missouri, at the 48th degree of north latitude and the 115th degree of longitude. He reached Fort Benton on the Missouri on 29 July, visiting the Great Falls on the way. The last time he had been at Benton was in 1846, when the post still bore the name of Fort Lewis. It had been his intention on leaving General Harney to travel all the way to St Louis on horseback in the hope of meeting a large number of Indian tribes, especially the large and powerful tribe of Comanches. But he had to forego this project, for my horses were entirely worn out, and unfit for making so long a journey; they were all more or less saddle-galled, and, not being shod, their hoofs were worn in crossing the rocky bottoms of the rivers, and the rough, rocky mountain roads. In this difficulty, I ordered a little skiff to be made at Fort Benton; worthy Mr Dawson, superintendent of the Fur Company, had the very great kindness to procure me three oarsmen and a pilot. On the 5th August I bade adieu to Fathers Congiato and Hoeken, and dear Brother Magri, and embarked on the Missouri, which is celebrated for dangers of navigation – snags and rapids being numerous in the upper river.

We descended the stream about 2,400 miles in our cockleshell, making fifty, sixty, and sometimes, when the wind favoured us, eighty miles a day.

C and R, p. 774.

At Omaha City they came across a steamboat and made the rest of the journey to St Louis by that means. The steamer made about 700 miles in six days. On the way Father De Smet met with thousands of Indians – Assiniboins, Minnetarees or Grosventures of the Missouri, Mandans, Crows, Aricaras, Sioux, Poncas and others.

Everywhere I was received with the greatest kindness and affection by these poor, unhappy and long abandoned tribes, still longing to hear and know the word of God, and, at every distant chance they get, listening with the utmost attention. I had the great consolation to regenerate hundreds of their little children in the holy waters of baptism.

C and R, p. 1502.

On 23 September, vigil of Our Lady of Mercy, he reached St Louis. He had travelled by land and river over 8,314 miles, and 6,090 miles on the sea. He says of the manner in which they lived:

During this long trip on the river we passed the nights in the open air, or under a little tent, often on sandbars to avoid the troublesome mosquitoes, or on the skirts of a plain, or in an untrodden forest. We often heard the howling of the wolves, and the grunting of the grizzly bear disturbed our sleep, but without alarming us.

Our wants were constantly supplied; yes, we lived in the midst

222

of the greatest abundance. The rivers furnished us excellent fish, waterfowl, ducks, geese and swans; the forest and plains gave us fruit and roots. We never wanted for game; we found everywhere either immense herds of buffalo, of deer, antelope, mountain sheep and bighorn, or pheasants, wild turkeys and partridges.

C and R, pp. 74–5.

At the end of the year Father De Smet received this letter from the army in Fort Vancouver.

We all miss you so much; I have not met an officer of your acquaintance who has not expressed great regret at your departure, and we all feel indebted to you for the good understanding that exists between the poor Indians and the whites at this time. No disturbance of any kind has occurred and I feel confident there will not be any.

A Pleasonton

Captain Second Dragoons

Fort Vancouver

November 9th 1859

C and R, p. 1580.

Chapter 13

The Civil War

As Procurator of the Missions Father De Smet had to provide for the needs of the Province and find men and money for the mountain missions. In all he secured 100 apostles for the New World and over $200,000 in money.

In September 1860 he left St Louis for Europe. As part of his fund-raising and drive for novices, he would regale his audiences with tales and adventures from the Far West. The following true anecdote greatly amused his audience:

Surprised one night in the depth of the forest by a snowstorm, Father De Smet climbed a tree, and, in searching about for a safe spot in which to spend the night, discovered that the tree was hollow. 'Aha!' said he, 'here I will be safely sheltered,' and proceeded to descend inside. Arriving at the bottom, he felt something move under his feet, which turned out to be a brood of harmless young cubs. Soon, however, the sound of heavy grunts reached him. The mother bear was returning; her claws were already on the bark. She climbed up, then down she came, backward. What was the next move? With great presence of mind the missionary seized her tail with both hands and pulled it violently. The frightened bear quickly climbed up again and disappeared into the forest. Master of the lodging, he remained there quietly until daylight permitted him to continue on his way.

In listening to these tales the children saw before them only a kindly old man who entertained and amused them, little dreaming that this priest was one of the greatest explorers of his time and the protector of the Indian race. That he knew how to move and impress the seminarians is evident from the numbers he gained to the apostolate. Yet he never forced a vocation, nor did he endeavour to directly influence anyone to accompany him. His method was to speak frankly of the missions, and affectionately of his dear Indians. This awakened interest in them, and the rest followed naturally. He would also read letters, such as the following from the chief of the Assiniboins.

Black Robe, Father and Friend,
I was so happy to become acquainted with you at Fort Union in the summer of 1851 ...

Our Great Father [Colonel Mitchell, superintendent of Indian Territory] told us that some Black-gowns would come and live among us in the course of four or five years. Black-gown, five years are long to wait! In this interval I and many of my children may have entered the land of spirits. Take pity on us! The Black-gowns ought not to delay their coming so long. I am growing old ... If to hasten the project pecuniary aid be wanting, I will cheerfully give a portion of the annuities of my tribe to meet this deficiency.

I see the buffaloes decrease every year. What will become of us without help? If our children are not instructed in time, they will disappear, like the game.

Father De Smet left Belgium on 27 March 1861. This time, it was with much foreboding that he neared the American shore, for it had become known to him before sailing that the standard of rebellion had been raised by the South. For a long time there had been division between the South, anxious to maintain slavery, and the North, the champion of emancipation. The election of President Lincoln, a strong abolitionist, had precipitated the conflicts. A few hours before arriving in New York on the night of 14 April,

the great American metropolis had been thrown into the wildest excitement and consternation by the tidings that Fort Sumter in South Carolina and several arsenals, had been taken by the Rebels, and that the Stars and Stripes, the far-and-wide honoured flag of the great Republic, had been battered down by the enemies of the Union – once Union men themselves – reduced to mere shreds, a rag! Unpardonable outrage! – one which I fear will be avenged in a deluge of blood. On hearing the sad news of the insulting and arrogant deed, tears flowed freely from many an eye among the passengers of the *Fulton*, and were followed by loud imprecations and threats against the

Secessionists. The North retaliated by arming 200,000 men – city boys, ribbon clerks and the like, and proclaiming a blockade of the coast States in revolt. I am not a man for war and am averse to its horrors and bloodshed; but I was deeply moved at the scenes I witnessed on the day of my landing on the shores of my once happy and beloved adopted country. I prayed and prayed most earnestly, that the Lord in his mercy might allay and soften the rising passions, and that peace might again be restored in this now distracted land.

C and R, pp. 76–7.

Father De Smet hastened to St Louis on 17 April. He notes that:

On the long stretch of over a thousand miles nothing was heard but the clang of arms and the war cry repeated in every city, town, and hamlet; while from every house and spire, and on every mountain top and hill, and in every breeze, waved the insulted Stars and Stripes.

C and R, p. 77.

Father De Smet was a loyal citizen, a Union man; but he was not what he later calls a radical. His views were doubtless modified by the atmosphere of St Louis, which was his home, and he saw more clearly the other side of the question than people of the North generally did. His prayers were for peace, but as between the North and South his sympathies were with the North. At one time he frankly doubted that the North would succeed, for he felt that so great a section of people of the Anglo-Saxon race could not be subdued. As the war progressed and the power of the North became more autocratic, he dissented from some of its extreme measures; but there was never a shadow of doubt of his unswerving loyalty to the Government.

A passionate advocate of peace and liberty, he deplored the military regime to which the country was subjected. The press and telegraph were under Government control, newspapers suppressed, railway lines cut, canal and river transportation intercepted.

Up to this time no one could predict the final result. Numerous battles had been fought without leading to any decisive result. Missouri, being on the border between the free states and the slave states, was the scene of the worst excesses. In a letter to his brother Francis, on 4 December 1861, Father De Smet wrote:

My very dear Francis,

You have read of the horrors of the French Revolution and the civil wars of different centuries and countries; but all that gives only a faint idea of the condition to which Missouri is reduced. Her own children, divided between the North and the South, tear one another to pieces and burn and sack one another's houses, while enemies from without overrun the State to satisfy their hatred and thirst for pillage. To this condition has Missouri been reduced by detestable Secession, and yet we are only at the first page of its history.

C and R, p. 1432.

Murders were on the increase in St Louis; in two months there were seventy. The rumour spread that Father De Smet had been rescued by an armed force from being burned to death, but the report was unfounded. Yet he was none the less horrified at what was taking place under his eyes. The city he had seen built, and the University he and Father Van Quickenborne had founded, seemed destined to early ruin.

Only a few months ago business flourished and the population was increasing. Since then 40,000 people have left St Louis and thousands of houses and stores are vacant. Landed property has fallen to one-fourth its value, our great river is blockaded, and hundreds of steamboats are lying idle along the levee. Farm products rot in barns and sheds. The college has opened with only a third of its pupils. When and how will it all end? No man can predict.

Lavaille, p. 301.

Father De Smet intended to visit the missions in Oregon in 1861. But the death of the Provincial, Father Druyts, delayed his departure until the following spring. In the meantime he sent by steamboat fifty ploughs, a mill, tools, and household utensils. He took pleasure in the thought of the joy these articles would give to the missionaries. Shortly after came the sad news that both boats and all the cargo were destroyed by fire.

The war brought new problems for the Jesuits, such as conscription, which made no exception in favour of priests. In the autumn of 1861 Father De Smet went to Washington. He saw President Lincoln, among others, on many pressing issues. He pointed out that the

Jesuits were few in number, and in addition to their priestly duties nearly all of them were teachers in institutions of learning. The Society was poor and had no funds to hire substitutes for their priests either in the field or in the schools. Besides this, they were on principle opposed to war. He succeeded in gaining some exemption under the rigid terms of the law. In the spring of 1863 Congress passed a law calling to the colours all men old enough to bear arms. Neither secular nor regular clergy were exempt. In fact, two Jesuits – Father Verdin and Brother Flanigan – were called up. Father De Smet felt compelled again to intercede. The Jesuits, while willing to expose their lives in the interests of their country, did not feel at liberty to go against ecclesiastical orders. 'We are ministers of peace,' writes Father De Smet, 'and from all times the sacred character of the priesthood has been judged incompatible with war and the shedding of blood. It is a law of the Church, and one binding on our consciences.' The authorities had no power to exempt the two priests directly, but they were told to remain at their work and they would not be ordered to the front.

At the time Father De Smet was in Washington the disastrous Battle of Bull Run occurred. From the heights overlooking the city he heard the cannons roar. After a bloody conflict the Federal troops began to give way and were finally routed. But defeat in no way diminished the courage of the North. A call was made for 500,000 men and for 500 million dollars, and the war continued with varying success for both the combatants.

When the war was at its height, Father De Smet was given special permission to cross army lines to visit the tribes on the Upper Missouri and to re-victual the Oregon Missions.

Towards the end of February 1862 he went again to Washington to argue for payment of the accounts payable to the Indian missions among the Potawatomies and Osages. A sum of over $18,000 was due to the missions. Father De Smet argued to the officials that the subsidies were guaranteed by treaties, and a longer delay would antagonise the Indians, who up to the present had shown themselves faithful subjects of the Union. Should the missions, for want of funds, be forced to send the hundreds of children back to their families, the tribes might make common cause with the Rebels. The argument evidently worked, for $11,000 was paid at once and a promise given that the rest would follow soon.

In passing through Washington, Father De Smet had several interviews with President Lincoln. Between the emancipator of the slaves and the defender of the Indians a friendly understanding was easily established. The President showed himself well disposed toward the Indians and promised support.

> During my short stay in the capital I had the honour of being presented to President Lincoln and of talking with him about the present state of our Indians and our missions. He showed himself very affable and well disposed towards us and promised me he would favour and aid us in our efforts to aid the unhappy lot of the Indians. *C and R, p. 1507.*

Everywhere the missionary was well received. Statesmen invited him to their tables. Mr Blondeel, the Belgian Ambassador, invited him to dinner along with the French, Spanish and Russian Ambassadors. In a letter to a colleague dated 17 February 1862, Father De Smet writes:

> All the ambassadors were resplendent with their orders, (grand cordons). I had a frock coat well worn and with two buttons gone. However, it all went off very agreeably. I did the best I could among these great personages. These kind of dinners made a great contrast with the Indian feasts in which I have so often taken part; where they offer you with their hands a chunk of roast dog or bear, or a stew of meat hashed with their teeth. I will admit I am more at my ease among the latter. *C and R, p. 1507.*

One day in 1862 Father De Smet received a letter from a friend, Mr W H Campbell, of Sacramento River. He asked the priest to give him information and maps on the gold bearing regions of the Rocky Mountains.

In 1840 Father De Smet had passed over the site of the famous gold mine of Alder Gulch, Montana, the richest of all gold placers. In a letter to his brother Charles, he had written on 26 April 1849:

> I climbed a lofty mountain a few days travel from the Sacramento. The bed of a stream that came down from it seemed to be of gold sand. It was so abundant that I could not believe the thing was real, and I passed on without examining it. Today I have little doubt that it was really the precious metal. *C and R, p. 1421.*

On another occasion he learned from a reliable Indian that on one summit in the Black Hills the tilted layers of the rocks were filled with golden sand, bright, yellow, shining. But he kept the discovery secret. He appreciated only too well the great harm a gold rush would do to his beloved Indians: they would be driven off their lands in the wild stampede of whites.

De Smet would keep his secret as long as he could. He also swore the Indians to secrecy, explaining to them that if they revealed it they would be dispossessed of their lands.

He replied as follows to Mr Campbell.

You ask me for information and maps of certain gold localities in the mountains, should I be at liberty to make disclosures on the subject. You can, dear friend, appreciate my motives and reasons for the silence I have hitherto kept on this matter. They still exist and I could not in conscience deviate from the course I have hitherto pursued.

C and R, p. 1511.

But despite his keeping his discovery to himself, the location of the gold bearing deposits soon got abroad. As Father De Smet explained:

The mountains will now be thoroughly searched; the results may reach the expectations of the gold hunters, and the massacres in California of Nomecult Valley, of Matole near Cape Mendocino, of Humboldt Bay, etc., will be once more renewed among the Indian tribes of the Rocky Mountains. For their safety I have kept my secret for these twenty years past.

In a letter to the Belgian Ambassador, Blondeel, dated 4 May 1862, he wrote:

The mines of the Rocky Mountains, on Salmon River and its tributaries of Lewis River in the Kootenai country, which I have known for twenty years, have been discovered anew and thousands of miners are going up at present to take possession of them.

C and R, p. 1510.

Two years later Father De Smet wrote to a colleague:

The numerous gold mines that have been discovered in this new Eldorado in the last three years are drawing thousands of inhabitants and their number is continually growing. Today the miners are spread over the country from the Gila to the Fraser and from the Pacific Ocean to the sources of the Columbia, the Missouri, the Colorado and the Rio Grande Del Norte. While some, starting from the shores of the Pacific, push their search eastward, others begin in Pike's Peak and the Rocky Mountains and advance toward the West. From both sides they come together in Oregon, in the Territories of Washington, Nevada, Idaho and Utah, in the Caribou Mountains and in Arizona, and an immense population is sure to come to fill up all these countries.

C and R, p. 1518.

Early in May 1862 Father De Smet left St Louis on the steamboat *Spread Eagle*, of the American Fur Company, bound for Fort Benton, in the Rocky Mountain region, and upwards of 3,000 miles by the Missouri. His purpose was to revisit the tribes of the Upper Missouri, baptise their children, take supplies to the mountain missions and study the prospects for new missions. The captain of the boat, Charles Chouteau, one of the first pupils of St Louis University, offered his former professor yearly free transportation for himself and for supplies destined for the missions. The captain had had a little chapel prepared on board so that Father De Smet had the great consolation of offering Mass every day during the long voyage.

The river was bank-full at the time and a great deal of power was required to stem the current. They were six weeks in making the journey. In a letter to Father Boone, Father De Smet describes his journey:

At various places or stations we found more or less numerous camps of Indians on the banks of the river. The boat would stop to distribute among the Indians the Government gifts or yearly pensions, and I would seize all these precious moments to visit them in their buffalo-skin dwellings or cabins; and on all these occasions I passed my days and nights among them. I was welcomed everywhere – they met me most eagerly, with the calumet of peace in their hands, and showed me a most simple but hearty kindness. They listened to my teachings with much diligence and attention. It was most touching and consoling to have the poor Indian mothers come to me, leading their little children or carrying them in their arms or on their backs, and to hear them say 'O Black Robe! Oh, bless our little children and offer them to the Great Spirit,' signifying in their simple language that they would have them regenerated in the holy waters of baptism. Thus I had the consolation, in these various meetings and visits, of giving baptism to more than 900 infants – a great triumph, if one remembers that three-fourths of the children of these tribes died before attaining the age of reason, and a good number of the sick and aged.

The following little anecdote, connected with the last baptisms administered, may perhaps not be without interest. It was among a band of Yankton Sioux; I had finished the ceremonies of a large number of baptisms, and night was falling. I was about leaving the place for my lodging, when I saw something moving, some distance off, dragging itself along the path. I stopped, in doubt, to see what this strange animal or moving mass might be. On approaching it, I was surprised to behold a poor old Indian woman, covered with wretched rags of buffalo-skin – a cripple, having lost the use of her hands and feet. She had heard the news, that the Black Robe had arrived in their camp and was baptising the children, and she, too, desiring that happiness as well, had dragged herself a considerable distance from her lodge to come to me. On seeing me, the good old woman raised her two palsied hands and cried 'Oh, my father, have pity on me – I too wish to be the child of the Great Spirit – oh, pour water on my forehead and speak the holy words! The whites call me Marie – it is the name of the good and great mother in heaven; when I die, I wish to go to my good mother.'

I instructed the poor Indian Marie and she received baptism, with the most pious sentiments and in transports of joy and happiness.   *C and R, p. 783–4.*

When Father De Smet left St Louis it had been his intention to spend three months evangelising the Sioux, numbering between 30–40,000. But, as he wrote in a letter to Father General, dated 18 August 1862:

An unfortunate incident prevented my doing it. A few days before my arrival at Fort Pierre, the head chief of the Sioux tribes had been killed by his own people, because of his friendship for the whites. Consequently the country was in confusion and much agitated against the whites. It was impossible for me to obtain an interpreter or guides to accompany me into the interior of the country where they dwell, which is very vast. I have put off this visit and mission to next spring.

War had just broken out between the Sioux and the Americans. The conference held at Fort Laramie in 1851 had guaranteed to the Sioux tribes the undisputed possession of their territory, on two conditions. The different Sioux tribes occupied a vast quadrilateral, bounded on the north by Canada, on the west by the Rocky Mountains, and on the east by the Sioux and Red Rivers. The Missouri with its tributaries flowed through this desolate region. One condition was that the highways should be left open and the other was that a certain number of forts could be built there, along the river-front, to protect the fur trade and maintain relations with the Indians. The United States agreed to pay the Indians an annuity of $50,000 for fifty years. However, the Senate, without consulting the Indians, changed the provisions of the treaty and limited the payments to fifteen years.

The rapidly increasing white colonies in the West began to invade the virgin solitudes of the central districts. Agricultural land was seized and other tracts were overrun by gold seekers. The whites often obtained entire countries for a song. The Osages ceded 29 million acres for an annual payment of a thousand dollars.

Towns sprang up, roads were made, and the Pacific Railway spanned the continent. By 1860 30,000 miles of rail track was in regular use: the 'Iron Horses' with their wide-funnelled smoke-stacks and large cow-catchers in front, thundered their way across the continent, their parallel lines of steel crossing canyons on high trestles, tunnelling through rock faces, curling round mountain shoulders, bringing white immigrants by the thousands. For hundreds of years the Indian had hunted bison in the lush grasslands. Now with the coming of the white man, with his stagecoaches and railroads moving up the Yellowstone Valley, the thunder of the bison had been stilled. The tribes fought for the increasingly dwindling herds of bison. White hunters killed the bison, leaving the red man hungry, his squaws and papooses without food. It was feared that the last of the bison might be disputed in a last fight between the remnants of those tribes. The region of the Upper Missouri became part of the United States and formed the Territories of Dakota, Wyoming and Montana. In exchange for the lands they had been cheated of, the Indians often received lessons in lying and immorality.

Tracts of land called reservations were given exclusively to the Indians. An agent was stationed among them to keep peace, to punish all whites that harmed the Indians and to inform the Government at Washington of any untoward happenings. More often than not, however, the agent swindled the Indians he was supposed to care for. He retained a large part of the indemnities meant for the Indians. The Indians on the reservations were destined not to enjoy for very long their restricted domains, for valuable mines discovered on what was thought to be waste land attracted hordes of fortune-seekers to the country. The Indians resisted the invaders and exchanged shots. Then the Federal troops intervened, new treaties were imposed on the tribe, and again they were forced to retire to a new reservation, often far distant, and destined in turn to become the ground of similar disputes.

The Sioux, resolved to guard their independence, retired farther and farther into the wilds and lived by hunting. With rage in their hearts, they watched the steady advance of the colonists and from day to day their complaints became more bitter.

Chief Black Hawk complained:

Like serpents, the whites have crept into our midst and taken possession of our homes; the opossum and deer have fled at their approach. We are dying of hunger and want. Contact with them has poisoned us.

Lavaille, p. 320.

Matters came to a head in 1861 when the hostilities broke out between the North and the South. The Indians judged this moment propitious for repelling the invasion of their lands and for redressing the many injustices they suffered. They believed the Civil War had so crippled the Government that it could not make effective resistance. Swindled, robbed and maltreated, unable to obtain any justice against their oppressors, the Indians, driven to extremity, finally uttered their terrible war-cry against the whole race of the enemy, war hatchets were unearthed, the tomahawk brandished and eagle feathers prepared to decorate their hair (every feather standing for a scalp taken).

Forthwith the United States sent an army against the Indians.

The Indians were beaten in several battles in the latter part of 1862. Hundreds of Indians were taken prisoner. A military commission tried these prisoners and sentenced over 300 to be hanged. All but thirty-nine were reprieved.

Learning of the fate of the prisoners Father De Smet wrote, on 12 December 1862, an appeal to the Honourable Mr Mix of the Indian Department, Washington, to ask to have the prisoners kept as hostages, for he hoped in this way to save the lives of the whites who were still in the power of the Sioux. Father De Smet's petition was refused. Thirty-eight of the prisoners were hanged on 26 December 1862. Before the execution a priest (Father Ravoux) visited the condemned in prison. All but five asked for baptism. A few were sufficiently instructed to make their first communion on Christmas Day. As he saw them calm, almost joyful, in the presence of death, the missionary was unable to restrain his emotions: 'It is thus,' he said, 'that Christians of a day meet death.'

Father De Smet was deeply grieved and alarmed at the state of things as he found it among the tribes of the Missouri, particularly the Sioux nations. He had never before seen them so hostile and it was evident that they were on the eve of an outbreak against the whites. In fact he had scarcely returned to his home in St Louis when the storm burst. The historic Minnesota Massacre took place from August 18–21, 1862. The massacre was an outburst of Indian rage and vengeance over the wrongs they had suffered at the hands of the whites and the evident fate that awaited them with the progress of settlement. In the three days that the massacre lasted, nearly 1,000 lives and two million dollars' worth of property were destroyed.

The Fathers in the Oregon missions considered Father De Smet the main support of their 'reductions'. He collected funds and sent yearly from St Louis ample provisions of foodstuffs, clothing, grain, farm implements, and tools. He obtained authorisations and subsidies from the Government, and he never left Europe without bringing back with him several missionaries.

On his return to St Louis Father De Smet made new purchases and on 9 May 1863 went up river on the American Fur Company steamer *Nellie Rogers*. He took with him two brothers and a cargo valued at $3,000, destined for the missions. For several days they travelled through country infested with bands of secessionists, and in several places they passed dead bodies lying on the riverbank.

Safety required that all travellers should be armed, and a heavy cannon was stationed in the prow of the boat. 'As for myself,' says the missionary, 'I make use only of spiritual arms. I offer the Holy Sacrifice in my cabin, and the Brothers as well as myself are filled with confidence in protection from on high.'

The heat was often very great, even stifling; The Fahrenheit thermometer registered more than 100° on several occasions. The heat of the summer had already dried up the streams. When they reached the mouth of the Milk River, the water was too low to permit the steamboat to navigate further. The entire load (200 tons) of freight and all the ninety passengers had to go ashore in the forest that covers the mouth of Milk River, 300 miles from their destination, Fort Benton. Here they had to wait until wagons from the Fort came to fetch them and their baggage. Father De Smet describes the journey:

> Every passenger chose a spot for himself in the forest and bestowed himself as best he could. General Harney had made me a present of his big camp tent before I left St Louis; I had my little chapel, my little kitchen, the necessary bedding and provisions, and in less than an hour, with the help of the two brothers, we were properly established, under the shade of some big cottonwoods.
>
> *C and R, p. 791.*

While encamped on the banks of the river for several weeks awaiting transportation from Fort Benton, Father De Smet worked assiduously among the Crows, Assiniboins, Grosventres, Mandans and Aricaras. He baptised more than 500 people, and arranged for the founding of a new mission near the mouth of the Yellowstone.

> On the 4th of July, as the camp was making ready to celebrate the great day of American Independence, we had an alarm, and escaped a great danger as if by a miracle. A war party of hostile Sioux, of some 600 warriors, discovered our camp and attempted an attack. Two of our men were wounded; one received two arrows, in the fleshly parts of the arm and thigh, and the other was shot in the body with an arrow that went in up to the feather. Immediately every man seized his arms and made ready for a desperate defence, with the chances plainly against us, by reasons of our small number.

Without thinking long of the danger, but full of trust in God I went outside to meet the scouts of the hostile band. Fortunately, I was recognised, and they expressed their astonishment by cries and gestures. One of the first 'partisans' who took my hand exclaimed: 'This is the Black Robe who saved my sister.' It was the son of Red Fish, head chief of the Ogallalas. This meeting was truly providential. I talked to him and his companions for about an hour. On leaving them I made them a little present of coffee, sugar and sweet crackers, and I saw them depart with no further thought of attacking our camp. Other travellers were less fortunate than we. Several steamboats that left St Louis at about the same time as ours had to withstand sundry attacks from the Indians, in which they lost several men. One large keelboat was sunk and all its crew destroyed. We understood better then that the war cry was really ringing all along that river, over which our passage had been so quiet and peaceful.

C and R, p. 792.

The perils of navigation on the Missouri in 1863 can hardly be overstated. The Sioux tribes were uncompromisingly hostile. With good reason. In 1863 a joint campaign under Generals Sibley and Sully had been planned. General Sibley proceeded west to the Missouri, driving the Indians before him, while General Sully was to go up the east bank of Missouri with a large force and intercept them, forming a union with Sibley. The most constant vigilance was required by the boats to get through at all. A Mackinaw boat containing twenty-one men and three women was attacked at the mouth of Apple Creek just before General Sibley arrived there, and all the passengers were killed. Captain La Barge with the *Robert Campbell* lost three men near Fort Berthold.

At last, on 30 July, after a month's weary waiting, the passengers saw a long line of carts approaching from Benton to transport the freight of the boat. There was also a carriage which the Fathers of St Peter's Mission, among the Blackfeet, had sent in which Father De Smet and the two brothers were to make the 300-mile journey. It was a long tedious journey, in the heat of summer, over parched plains where the grass had almost entirely disappeared. Not a drop of water had fallen for months.

All the rivers were dry, leaving only here and there a little pool of stagnant salty water – altogether, this passage was no small affair for the travellers and for their horses and oxen as well; the whole region bore the imprint of desolation.

We encamped every evening beside one or several of these water holes, which supplied us with fish in abundance. Our cattle and horses scattered over a vast expanse, to graze on the dry and scanty herbage. By night we formed a corral, or circle of wagons and carriages, wherein to keep the animals in safety, protected against attack from horse-thieves, whether white or Indian, by whom this region is infested. On the way our hunters procured from time to time buffalo, elk, deer, bighorn, beaver, prairie chickens, wild ducks and geese, furnishing us more or less our portion of meat. We crossed three branches of Milk River, the *diviére au François* (Willow Creek?), the Beaver and the Sureau (White Horse Creek?), the Marias and Teton Rivers, tributaries of the Missouri, and passed below the Little Rocky and Bear Paw Mountains, two isolated chains standing in the plains, east of Benton.

After a somewhat painful journey we arrived at Fort Benton, 3,000 miles above St Louis, on the Feast day of the Assumption of the Holy Virgin.

C and R, p. 793.

While at Fort Benton Father De Smet formed one of a party that visited the Great Falls of the Missouri. On this occasion he had an unexpected meeting with two Italian Jesuits, Fathers Giorda and Imoda, who were on their way to meet him at Fort Benton.

They stayed in Fort Benton for several days, to recover from their fatigue as well as to instruct and baptise a goodly number of Crow or Absaroka children. They then went to the Mission of St Peter, founded a year earlier on the left bank of the Missouri, with more than 700 Christians. This was the mission of the Italian Fathers and Brothers.

In a letter to Father Boone S J, Father De Smet writes:

I found them in a rather bad way, lacking, in fact, almost every-thing, even necessaries, and I had expected as much. Thanks to a remnant of the funds obtained in Belgium (in 1860–61), I was enabled to bring them assistance. I had the great consolation to find them safe and sound, and to procure for them, in good order, a fine assortment of church ornaments and sacred vessels, victuals for nearly a year, garments and bed coverings, which they sadly needed, agricultural and carpenters' tools, several ploughs, some picks and shovels, an ambulance and a wagon – all of which were absolutely necessary, in a new establishment among 10,000 nomadic savages, whom it is desired to Christianise and civilise.

These worthy brothers are labouring among the Blackfeet with tireless zeal and courage. At the time of my visit they had been barely six months in that country, and the number of baptisms inscribed on the register came to upwards of 700 children and adults. I had thus far fulfilled the wishes of my superiors; I had brought two Italian Brothers to the first Rocky Mountain mission.

C and R, pp. 786, 794.

Father De Smet could now return to St Louis – but by a different route.

The reports that reached us every day, of robberies and massacres committed by the Indians of the plains, on one hand – and on the Salt Lake route by marauders and murderers of another species, the off-scourings of civilisation, living by robbery and assassination on the unhappy travellers whom they meet – caused me to take the resolution of returning to St Louis by the Pacific Ocean. That is not only the safest route, but also the most prompt, with its regular line of steamships, by the way of the Isthmus of Panama and Aspinwall.

C and R, p. 794.

He left for San Francisco on 3 November, crossed the Isthmus of Panama on 18 November and took the steamer *North Star* for New York, which he reached on Thanksgiving Day, 26 November. He writes:

The day following, I offered the holy sacrifice of the altar, as a thanksgiving service for all the benefits received from heaven in my long, painful and dangerous tour, upon rivers and seas and in diverse lands, through numerous bands of hostile Indians, in the mountainous portions of Idaho infested by white marauders and assassins of the lowest and vilest sort, and on the two great oceans, the Pacific and Atlantic, ranged at present by hostile ships of the American Confederacy.

Lavaille, p. 314.

It must be remembered that in all these extensive travels Father De Smet was getting to be an old man. He was now sixty-three years of age.

On 9 December he left New York. On his way west he called at Washington. The Secretary of the Interior and the Commissioner of Indian Affairs took advantage of his presence to request him to go to the Sioux, and in the name of the United States make proposals for peace.

The most scientific strategy failed against 6,000 warriors who were determined not to give battle until they had the advantage in numbers and position. Their wives and children were safe far from the scene of hostilities; they had no towns, forts, or arsenals to defend; no line of retreat to cover, and they were not encumbered with either baggage or beasts of burden. Mounted on fiery horses, they unceasingly harassed the enemy's troops and always escaped pursuit. Although in sight, they were never overtaken.

The campaign of 1862–3 had cost the United States more than $20 million, and yet the end was not in sight. It added a heavy weight to the strain of the Civil War. The spectators, contractors and *ejusdem generis* of the region did what they could to protract this unlucky war, because it was so much money in their pockets. It was proposed that Father De Smet be appealed to as a mediator. Five years before he had accomplished the pacification of Oregon, and it was believed that he alone could induce the Missouri tribes to lay down their arms. He was to act in concert with the commander-in-chief of the troops and the various Government agents. Moreover, the expense of the journey and a large financial compensation were offered him by the Government.

It was a difficult role that Father De Smet was asked to fill. His mission had always been one of peace. On the banner that he carried were only the mild emblems of Christianity. No weapons of slaughter ever accompanied him to the wigwams of the Indians. Now he was asked to accompany a military expedition to be sent against them. While it was the chief desire of his heart to stop the war, he felt that he would be compromising his entire influence among the Indians if he went to them in company with armed soldiers, or under the flag which they looked upon as a symbol of ruin to their people.

I fear I would lose all caste among the Indians. They have hitherto looked upon me as the bearer to them of the word of the

Great Spirit and have universally been kind and attentive wherever I have met them. Should I present myself in their midst as the bearer of the word of the Big Chief of the Big Knives in Washington, no longer their Great Father but now their greatest enemy, it would place me in rather an awkward situation.

C and R, p. 85.

In a letter he wrote, 'surely my black robe would then cease to be a passport into Indian country. I tried to make the Commissioner of Indian Affairs see this'.

I have written to the Commissioner that if I can go, I will go on my own hook, without pay or remuneration; visit the friendly Sioux first, and in their company try to penetrate among their fighting brethren and do my utmost to preach peace and good will to them, and to make them come to a good understanding with the general in command and the agents of Government.

C and R, p. 85.

The Government recognised the wisdom of Father De Smet's plan, and accepted his terms.

First, of course, the priest would have to have the agreement of his superiors. Father De Smet continued his journey back to St Louis.

For many months the Jesuits in St Louis had been without news of the missionary. They had heard only of his enforced landing at Milk River, but not of his arrival at Fort Benton. Could he with his companions have fallen under the hatchets of the Sioux? 'What increases our anxiety,' writes Father Arnould from Belgium, 'is that the provisions he had with him might have excited the cupidity of the Indians. Moreover, the crucifix by which the Indians recognised him, which he always wore on his breast, had by mistake been left in St Louis.'

When winter came and he did not return, all hope was abandoned and the *suffrages* (prayers and masses for the deceased) were said for the repose of his soul.

One can imagine the astonishment of the community when, on 17 December, he suddenly appeared. In eight months he had travelled 11,400 miles without suffering injury from the bands of secessionists or from the Indians in revolt against the whites.

In a letter to his brother Francis and nephews Charles and Paul dated 24 December 1863, Father De Smet described his many travels.

Mr very dear Brother (Francis) and my very dear Charles and Paul:

I wish you a very happy New Year, filled with all the benedictions of heaven. I have just reached St Louis after a long journey of about eight months and after having covered a distance of nearly 4,000 leagues. I have passed through many dangers, the details of which I will give you later. I set out from St Louis at the beginning of last May. I went up the Missouri River for 2,400 miles, as far as the mouth of Milk River. I then continued my route on horseback for some 1,200 miles, visiting our various missions east and west of the Rocky Mountains. During my mission I had the consolation of baptising upward of 400 Indians. At Walla Walla, a city of some 2000 souls, in the Territory of Washington, I embarked upon the Columbia River for Portland, the principal city of Oregon – distance 400 miles. From Portland I went to Victoria, the capital of Vancouver Island; thence to San Francisco in California; then to Acapulco in Mexico, and thence to Panama; distance 4,500 miles. I crossed the Isthmus of Panama, 47 miles; at Aspinwall I took ship for New York, 2,000 miles, and from New York came to St Louis 1,200 miles. Upon arriving in St Louis I found your good, dear letters of the 29th of July and 23rd of November. I am very grateful to you for them. My health is not good, but that is generally the case after each long journey I make. The cessation of fatigues uses me up more or less and it takes me some little time to get back into my ordinary equilibrium. I will write you more fully later.

C and R, p. 1516.

Such a journey had entailed excessive fatigue, and the traveller returned to St Louis broken in health, tortured with neuralgia, and crippled with rheumatism, contracted as a result of long nights holed up in damp hideouts.

On 14 March 1864 he wrote from St Louis University to his niece Silvie:

I am broken down with all sorts of troubles; I suffer particularly with my head; it is seldom I can leave my room.

The next day he wrote to his nephew Gustave:

I can seldom leave my room and go out of the house. For some time past my greatest privation is to be unable to celebrate Holy Mass. It is the first time since I was ordained priest in 1827.

C and R, pp. 813–4.

Three months later he wrote:

I am now in my sixty-fourth year, and I have an inward conviction that my end is near.

To his ardent nature, death was preferable to inactivity: 'after enjoying robust health for so many years, and after so many years of travel, I find the change hard to bear. But we are in God's hands.'

In keeping with the Flemish proverb 'When the legs creak, the heart is good', Father De Smet's health slowly improved. 'Though my legs are unsteady, my heart is still strong.' To while away the weary hours he wrote long accounts of his journeys to the Father General and to his Belgian friends.

As soon as he was able to get about he began to prepare a $3,000 shipment for the Oregon missions.

But he was destined never to serve these missions again. God called him to another scene of action. The Sioux, the tribe that he had dreamed of evangelising for twenty years, and which had declared an implacable war against the whites, were to henceforth absorb his untiring efforts and bring him his greatest triumphs.

Chapter 14

Peace Mission to the Sioux 1864

Early in 1864 Father De Smet received a letter from the Commissioner, Department of the Interior, Office of Indian Affairs, requesting him to act as a peacemaker between the Government and the warring Sioux tribes.

> It is believed that you can safely visit them in their camps and convey to them any message that the Government may wish to send them either from the Interior or War Departments.
>
> *C and R, p. 1583.*

Father De Smet's Superior feared he was sending him to certain death, alone and unarmed to encounter the enraged tribes, drunk with carnage. On 20 April 1864 Father De Smet took passage on a steamboat leaving for the Upper Missouri. The captain, Mr Charles Chouteau, offered his former teacher the cabin de luxe, in which an altar had been prepared where he might daily celebrate Mass. The water was low and sandbars numerous, so that after eight days they had advanced only a few miles. To pass the time, Father De Smet continued his studies on the river Missouri. He prepared descriptions of the river, the steamboats that plied it, the perils and dangers of its navigation. These observations are the most complete that have come down to us.

The Sioux continued to terrorise the country. On 10 May news came that 3,000 were armed and lying in wait to stop every steamboat they surprised on the river, and that they possessed two cannons, many guns, and an abundance of powder and bullets. 'In a few days,' writes Father De Smet, 'we shall be able to judge of the truth of this information. I placed myself in God's hands, and under the protection of the holy Virgin, our good Mother. I came

244

here under obedience, to carry words of peace. Of a truth the time is critical; but if God is with us, who can be against us.'

Nor was his confidence betrayed. The steamboat advanced unimpeded, save for the sandbars that several times obliged them to stop near the forts, in order to land a portion of the cargo. At last, on 9 June, they reached Fort Berthold, near the mouth of the Little Missouri. Not far away there were living together in a single village, the Grosventres, the Aricaras, and the Mandans. These three nations had not entered into the revolt against the whites, so Father De Smet decided to remain with them, and await an opportunity of getting into relations with the Sioux. He sent a messenger to the Sioux chiefs, announcing the object of his visit, and inviting them to a conference. While awaiting their arrival he preached the word of God to the friendly tribes.

In a letter to the editor of *Précis Historiques* Father De Smet describes events:

I collected the principal Mandans and Grosventres in one of their big lodges or earthen houses; they are about 150 feet around and can contain over 600 persons. I made known to them the motives of my visit, which were to announce to them the word of the Great Spirit, to baptise the little children, to penetrate, if possible, among their enemies, the Sioux; and to endeavour, in the name of the Great Spirit, to make them relish the words of peace of which I was the bearer from the President of the United States, Mr Lincoln. I spoke for two hours, and they listened with the greatest attention and the liveliest interest. The chief, Manchoute, 'Soaring War Eagle,' (he is six feet six inches in height) addressed me in reply, in fitting and well-chosen words, accompanied by a really remarkable oratorical bearing and gestures. This facility in speaking seems to be natural to the Indians of the plains.

After the advice and the speeches, the Indian mothers came into the lodge with their babies, and placed themselves in a double and triple circle. What a consolation! Two hundred and four children were regenerated in the holy waters of baptism. Everything passed off in the best of order, though not altogether without noise. During the ceremonies, we were honoured from time to time with a deafening chorus. All that was needed was for a young baby, seized with terror at the approach of the Black Robe, to exhibit the strength of his young lungs in piercing yells, to set all his comrades going in the same key. It was really enough to split one's ears. The dogs on the outside added to the uproar by reinforcing the cries of the children with their frightful howls and roars. But all in all, the 10 June was for me a beautiful and consoling day.

C and R, p. 828.

A providential event contributed largely to enhance the value of the religion Father De Smet taught. The preceding year a long drought had destroyed the crops. Not discouraged, the Indians had put under cultivation a thousand acres of land with no implements save hoes, broken spades, crooked sticks, and the shoulder blades of bison. But again this year, a dry spring threatened ruin to the crop. The distressed Indians had recourse to Father De Smet. 'Black Robe,' they said, 'you who have such power, can you not also make a little rain come?' He answered them that he had not that power. 'Let us implore Him together and offer him our hearts. I will say the greatest of prayers (the Mass)!' The next day the clouds gathered and rain fell for twenty-four hours. A few days later, after renewed prayers, a heavier shower followed, the fields became green, the grain formed in the ears, and everything portended a rich harvest. These favours from on high made a deep impression on the Indians. They followed assiduously the missionary's instructions. Mothers brought their children by hundreds to be baptised; the chiefs themselves undertook to eradicate vice and do away with superstition.

In the meantime the news of the great Black Robe's arrival had reached the Sioux, and on July 8 they encamped about 300 strong on the opposite side of the Missouri. Their presence terrified the whites who were defending the fort.

It was clearly a risk to cross over to their side. Contrary to the advice of all the whites in the fort I went to meet them. They received me with unmistakable tokens of friendship and respect. They had repaired to the spot for the express purpose of having a conference with me. The council lasted nearly three hours. The great chiefs spoke favourably with regards to peace, and heard with pleasure and satisfaction the words I addressed to them on the part of the Government. Our interview concluded in the most favourable manner.

C and R, p. 833.

A week after his return to St Louis, on 4 October 1864, Father De Smet left for Europe yet again. He embarked at New York on the steamer *China* on 20 October, to make his fourteenth crossing of the Atlantic. He landed in Liverpool about the end of October. He visited the Jesuit Public School at Stonyhurst and then travelled on to Rome, where he arrived on 19 November. He was received with great consideration by Pope Gregory XVI. While in Rome he had the privilege of assisting at the beatification of Blessed Peter Canisius, a former General of the Jesuits, who was prominent at the Council of Trent in 1549. 'I shall never forget that ceremony,' Father De Smet wrote.

Before leaving Rome he visited the celebrated basilicas and the places consecrated by the blood of the martyrs, and on the feast of St Cecilia he descended into the catacombs. Several times he was received in audience by the Pope, who showed great affection towards him and bestowed many favours on his mission.

In December he returned to Belgium. During his stay there he gave only a few days to his family, and set out in the depth of winter upon his arduous begging tour. Several times he was forced by illness to interrupt his travels. Nevertheless he canvassed Holland, Luxembourg, England, Ireland, and his native country. The sight of this old missionary, who had come from such a distance to ask for help, created a profound impression. Contributions flowed in, and many young men answered the call to the apostolate.

Such self-sacrificing devotion commanded the respect of even unbelievers. Charles Rogier, one of the ministers of Leopold I, and anything but clerical in his feelings and opinions, expressed great esteem for Father De Smet. He invited the missionary to his table and lent a willing ear to his discourses upon religion; he marvelled that a man could travel such distances and suffer such fatigue and privation for what he called the salvation of souls. 'If you should hear some day that I was on my death-bed and that I had asked for you, would you cross the ocean for that?' 'I would not hesitate an instant,' replied the Jesuit; upon which Rogier threw himself upon the missionary's neck and embraced him before the assembled guests. Several years later when the statesman felt his end approaching, he called for a Jesuit (Father Delcourt), and was reconciled with God.

In June 1865 Father De Smet was honoured by King Leopold of the Belgians as Chevalier of the Order of Leopold. This decoration was received with his usual modesty by the missionary.

At his family's insistence he consented to have his portrait painted, wearing the distinguished decoration, and after that nothing more was heard of it. To the last he wore no other cross save that of the missionary, the cross that had redeemed the world, and to which he owed his best achievements.

The time for departure was drawing near. His labours had borne abundant fruit. Besides great financial assistance and other gifts, he had gained twelve new missionaries for America, of whom five were Belgians, four Dutch, and three Irish. Four Sisters of Notre Dame de Namur also accompanied him to the New World. Before sailing he wrote the following lines:

> Here I am once again leaving my country, my family, friends, benefactors, and brothers in religion. A fond farewell to all, perhaps, forever, until the last meeting in heaven. This separation – why should I not own it? – gives me no small heartache; but I hope to be able to work yet a little longer for the glory of God and the salvation of souls; this is the supernatural magnet which draws me so far away from dear Belgium and the affection that I have found there. When I am not with my dear Indians, I feel as if something was lacking, and, despite the kind reception that I receive everywhere, there is a void within me, until I get back to my beloved Rocky Mountains. Only then am I satisfied and happy. *Haec requies mea.* I have spent the best part of my life among the Indians and to them I wish to consecrate my few remaining years; in their midst I wish to die.

Father De Smet reached New York on 19 June 1865. On 21 June he celebrated the feast of St Aloysius Gonzaga. He left New York on 26 June and reached St Louis four days later. He remained in St Louis for the rest of the year.

Upon his return to America Father De Smet's name was again mentioned for episcopal honours. The Catholics were becoming so numerous in the West that the Archbishop of St Louis asked the Pope to create an apostolic vicariate in Montana, and, desiring that the incumbent be a Jesuit, proposed Father De Smet. The latter immediately wrote a letter to the Father General, which reveals his profound humility.

> If, as the Reverend Father Provincial assures me, my name figures among those sent by Archbishop Kenrick, it is only, I imagine, to

complete the list, which usually comprises three names. In the sincere belief that I possess neither the virtues nor ability that such an office demands, and not doubting your Paternity will be consulted in regard to an affair of such importance, I am not uneasy. My sole desire is to live and die faithful to my vocation and to the obedience I owe my Superiors, and from this determination, thanks be to God, nothing can move me.

Providence granted his wish, and Father De Smet was spared the burden he had feared would be imposed upon him. His mind now at ease, his great preoccupation was the distribution of the money and goods he had brought back from Europe.

On 9 April 1866, he left St Louis on the *Ontario* for Fort Benton, the post nearest to the mountain missions. This meant a journey of more than 3,000 miles, through a country at war with the whites. But with his usual confidence and faith, he placed himself under the protection of the Blessed Virgin, and asked that a lamp should be kept burning day and night before her picture until he returned.

The spring thaw had brought about a sudden rise in the river: enormous blocks of ice crushed steamboats, trees were uprooted, and houses carried away. From the outset the boat had to contend with the excessively high water, and with high west winds, which often made it impossible to proceed. The Missouri was bank-full and beginning to overflow into forests and lower valleys. Consequently progress was much retarded. In many places all the power of the boat's two engines was exerted, without being able to make head against the impetuosity of the current. To breast the current, the captain had recourse to a windlass, but the cable broke and the boat swept along in the eddies until she crashed against a hidden rock. The shock was great and caused a heavy leak. For a few moments the salvation of the *Ontario* was despaired of; she was filling rapidly. Several of the officers thought her lost and were for abandoning her, but others redoubled their efforts to repair the injury, and with the aid of all the pumps they kept her afloat, and she resumed her course.

In a letter 10 June 1866, Father De Smet describes an interesting scene.

Thousands of buffalo were cropping the tender grass as we approached. As soon as they got wind of man's proximity and heard the noise of the steamer, they rushed precipitately to the nearest bluffs, whose slopes were fully 60° with the horizontal, and by pushing on and climbing stoutly in zigzag lines, they gained the summit. The dark, living, winding lines, the columns of dust that followed them, from the bottom to the top, and the noise of their tread and their dull bellowing, furnished the spectators a most charming and imposing spectacle, and moreover a revelation concerning the agility, muscular strength and capacity for endurance of this mighty animal of the American desert.

But the buffalo had not yet showed all their accomplishments; as in all spectacles a farce is usually the closing piece, so here three old buffalo bulls gave us one after their kind. The spot chosen was an almost vertical hill (something like 75° slope, and nearly a thousand feet in height). The bulls found themselves just about in the middle of the slope; it was hard to see how they could have got there. At the approach of the boat they made prodigious efforts to clamber up and gain the top. All eyes were fixed upon them; our cheers were a powerful encouragement to high speed. One reached the goal, and received the applause of the spectators; his two companions strained their best, but still they slipped down; and beginning to slide with their enormous weight, they rolled head over heels, and by a long series of bumps and pirouettes, at a height of 400 or 500 feet, they came tumbling into the river within a few yards of the boat. The entire descent was accomplished in less than a minute. We supposed they were killed; but not the least in the world – to our great astonishment and admiration they rose to the surface and, snorting, blew the water from their nostrils. Their life was granted them – for the reason that our larder was well stocked. We saw them both reach shore, shake the water from their shaggy heads and necks, and each triumphantly hoisting his standard (his tail), they disappeared at full gallop.

C and R, pp. 850–1.

As they were about to enter the Sioux country a cannon was placed ready, and every night sentinels stood guard – a needless precaution, as the enemy gave no sign of life. 'Our arms,' writes Father De Smet, 'have been used only to kill game, which is served on our already abundant table.'

It was evident that Providence was caring for the travellers. 'We have passed thirteen boats that started from ten to fifteen days ahead of us. We have been carried as on the wings of angels.' And yet our missionary's life was not wholly satisfactory. Far from his brothers in religion, and with little in common with the mercantile interests of the boat's passengers, he felt lonely.

He used his leisure to reread the letters of St Francis Xavier, his model in the apostolate.

This book fills my heart with consolation: two passages especially have touched me: 'Among other intercessions, I have recourse to the children I have baptised and whom God, in His infinite mercy, called to Himself before they had stained their baptismal robe. They number over a thousand, and I invoke them to obtain for me the grace to accomplish God's will in the way He wills it, upon this earth of exile and misery.' 'You can imagine what my life must be here, not understanding what is said to me, and unable to make myself understood. Yet I baptise new-born children, for which ceremony I need no interpreter, nor do I need one in my ministrations to the poor, who can make me understand their sufferings and misery.'

It is not surprising that Father De Smet should share the sentiments of this illustrious apostle, for his own life was a continual service of charity and devotion. Even on the boat he found an opportunity to bring souls to God. He baptised a Protestant, and prepared several passengers to make their entrance into the Church. The Catholics attended Mass and received Communion every Sunday.

But the Indians were ever his special care. Now more than ever were they deserving of pity. In many places the whites had left them but barren lands, where even wild beasts could not exist. The annuities were not paid regularly, and the agents sometimes retained a part of them, or substituted barrels of whisky or useless goods in place of money. The winter was long and severe, and many families died of hunger; others, after they had killed their horses and dogs, lived on wild roots, and were happy when they could pick up refuse from the soldiers' kitchen at Fort Sully, or rats that had been thrown over the stockade.

At Fort Sully Father De Smet met many of the Sioux tribes; they laid before him all their wrongs and sufferings. They were still in hostile mood. Father De Smet relieved this misery as much as lay in his power. He spoke to them of the Great Spirit, of the future life and of the joys reserved for those who have shunned lies and injustice. He baptised nearly 500 children, the greater number of whom he was persuaded would die before attaining the age of reason. 'The regeneration of these poor little ones is for me a subject for rejoicing. I have a deep conviction that baptism has opened heaven to numberless souls whom I have had the happiness of meeting in my long sojourns among the Indian tribes.'

At last on 7 June 1866, after a 57-day journey, he arrived at Fort Benton. But alas! he did not find his fellow missionaries from St Peter's Mission. A fresh and furious war had broken out between the whites and the Blackfeet, 'in which again the whites have given the first provocation'. The Fathers had had to retire, for a time at least, to St Ignatius' Mission. The church ornaments and sacred vessels that he had brought for the missions, he left for safe keeping with the officers at the Fort, and then returned to St Louis.

On 9 April 1866 Father De Smet received a passport from General Sherman, authorising all military authorities to give him every possible assistance in his travels through their territories.

Passport from General Sherman to Father De Smet:

Headquarters Military Division of the Mississippi, St Louis, Mo, April 9th, 1866.

All officers of the Army with this Military Division are required, and all citizens are requested to extend to the bearer of this letter, the Reverend Father De Smet, a Catholic Priest, who had heretofore travelled much among the Rocky Mountains and is now en route for missions under his control, all the assistance and protection they can enable him to fulfil his benevolent and humane purposes.

He has always been noted for his strict fidelity to the interest of our Government, for indefatigable industry and an enthusiastic love of the Indians under his charge.

W T Sherman, Maj.-Gen.

C and R, p. 845.

In descending the Missouri Father De Smet stopped for several days with the Yanktons, who were encamped near the mouth of the James River. The Yanktons consisted of nearly 3,000 souls, and belonged to the Sioux nation. He gives a revealing account of the Yankton camp.

When one enters an Indian camp, whatever be the size of it, 100 to 200 or 800 to 1,000 souls, one is struck by the order and tranquillity that prevail. Among them as everywhere else the children are playing with all their might at their little innocent games, their bows and arrows or balls, or running races. The women are about their usual housework which is various and ample enough. They do the cooking, cut the wood and go for water. They work the skins of the animals killed in the chase – that is, they remove the hair from the hide, dry it, scrape it, tan it and paint it; they soften the skins to be used for garments, which they afterward embroider with porcupine quills or beads of various colours. Besides all this, they have the entire care of their little papooses or children; they are always and everywhere industriously occupied. The men look after the horses, make bows and arrows, prepare and dry their smoking herb (*kinikinik*) or busy themselves about useful or purely fanciful matters. Their favourite occupation is to smoke the calumet of peace, eat a good piece of broiled buffalo or deer then take a nap or else chat over the news of the day and the future movements of the camp. Though less perhaps than civilised countries, still the Indian camps also have their idlers and loafers, their good-for-nothings who kill time before the mirror, daubing their faces with colours and adorning themselves from head to foot.

C and R, p. 1058.

On his first night his dugout was swarming with famished rats; 'they came and laughed in my very face'. Another enemy that assailed him were the fleas and other insects.

I was awake and up all night, making play with my hands, fingers and nails to defend myself against the fleas and their comrades in evil-doing, the mosquitoes, the bedbugs, the ants, the spiders, *et omne genus muscarum*.

C and R, p. 1282.

The chief of the tribe was Pananniapapi, 'the man that Strikes the Ree'. He was one of the noblest types of men of his race. A small arrowhead had been lodged in the small of his back for sixteen years. He had met Father De Smet for the first time in 1844 and had attended his instructions, receiving from him the Miraculous Medal. From that time he had added the practice of admirable

253

virtues to his invincible courage, and he professed toward the Blessed Virgin a touching piety. During the cholera epidemic he exposed his miraculous medal in the camp, and, following his example, the Yanktons, 3,000 in number, assembled to venerate it. The same day the plague disappeared.

Time and again the Methodists who endeavoured to penetrate to the tribe were kept at a distance by the chief, who said to them: 'You wish to enrich your wives and children at our expense. The Black Robe has neither wife nor child; his heart is not divided; he lives only for God and the happiness of the people who surround his cabin.' And the old man remained obdurate.

For twenty-two years he had looked forward to the day when he should receive baptism. The hour of grace had now struck. Father De Smet completed his instruction and received him into the Church. Once a Christian, Pananniapapi's only thought was to procure the same happiness for his people.

Thus the great missionary, in the twilight of his years, realised his life's dream, the evangelisation of the Missouri tribes. A rich harvest was promised; not a single Indian refused to hear the word of God, not a wigwam remained closed. The Grosventres, Aricaras, and Mandans asked repeatedly for a Black Robe. The Yanktons offered to contribute two or three thousand dollars yearly to the support of the missions.

General Sully himself now asked for a missionary, as he foresaw that the Sioux could only be conquered through the Gospel.

One evening the Grass Dance was performed in Father De Smet's honour. Each member of the tribe carried a long bunch of grass, the emblem of abundance and charity. It is the grass that nourishes their horses and domestic animals, and fattens the bison, deer, elk, bighorn and antelope of the plains and mountains.

The sexes are never mingled. The men dance by themselves and the women form a ring around them. All their movements are in strict time to the sound of drum, tambourine, flute and gourd filled with pebbles. When they leap and dance with fantastic gestures and capers the ground trembles beneath the beating of their feet. While they jump up and down each brave in turn sings his *Dowampi*, recording his lofty deeds of valour or his heroic charities. These savage dances certainly exceed in propriety many dances in civilised countries.

C and R, p. 1060.

Father De Smet was back in St Louis by 20 July. He remained there for the rest of the year.

A torrid summer had followed a rigorous winter; the thermometer stood at 100°F in the shade, and cholera was raging. A colleague, Father Louis Dumortier, died while attending the epidemic. The sudden change from pure, high-mountain air to the stagnant air of a pest-ridden city seriously affected Father De Smet's health. For several months he suffered from overpowering fatigue, excruciating rheumatic pains, and, even worse, deafness threatened him.

Autumn, however, brought him some measure of relief. With his customary cheerfulness, he writes to one of his nephews, on 26 November 1866:

> My health, thank God, is fairly good now. I seldom consult a doctor or take medicine. For three months two little bottles, delicate attentions from the druggist, have been standing on my chimney piece. Until now I have only looked at them, but I have taken the precaution to see that they do not evaporate, for they may be useful some day. I will soon enter upon my sixty-seventh year, an age when man's garments cover a multitude of infirmities. Yet I shall end by believing that I carry my years lightly, for every one tells me so, and people laugh when I say my end is drawing near.

In the meantime the war against the tribes in revolt was still going on, and while Father De Smet, at the price of unspeakable fatigue, laboured to bring about peace, the Americans seemed to take pleasure in thwarting his efforts. Soldiers and colonists alike increasingly exasperated the Indians. The tribes of the neighbourhood of Fort Berthold remained friendly to the whites. The Government, wishing to protect them against hostile bands, sent them troops; these were under no restraint and gave themselves up to brutality and libertinage. 'During the whole winter,' writes Father De Smet, 'the Indians have been the sport of the captain, whose sole object seemed to be to torture them. When women with their starving children approached the Fort, to gather disgusting refuse from the soldiers' kitchen, they were chased away by having boiling water thrown on their ragged, emaciated bodies.'

In February 1867 he visited Washington and New York and returned to St Louis. On 12 April he left St Louis to visit the up-country missions. He first went to the Yellowstone River where he arrived on 28 June. On the way he visited various tribes. He then returned to St Louis at the beginning of August 1867, where he remained for the rest of the year.

Chapter 15

Peace Commission of 1867 and 1868

The Indian Affairs of the Government were at this time in critical shape and required the constant efforts of the War and Interior Departments to prevent further outrages and to arrive at some peaceful solution of existing troubles. The Indians in revolt numbered several thousand. Every day new tribes joined the coalition and now the Cheyenne and the Blackfeet had combined with the Sioux and it was imperative to check the progress of the red rage that swept the plains. The years 1867 and 1868 were the most important in Father De Smet's life because of the part that he took in this work of pacification. He had greater influence with the Indians than any other living white man. His natural sympathies were with the Indians and they knew it, and this was the secret of his wonderful influence over them. The Government appealed to Father De Smet. On 13 February 1867, Colonel Bogy, the Commissioner of Indian Affairs, wrote to him:

> Your relations with the Indians and your marvellous influence over them are well-known facts. It is certain that your presence in their midst will obtain the best results. No special instructions will be given you and I leave you at liberty to take your own measures.

And the Secretary of the Interior requested him to go to the hostile tribes:

> To endeavour to bring them back to peace and submission and to prevent as far as possible, the destruction of property and the murder of the whites.
>
> *Lavaille, p. 341.*

Father De Smet accepted the commission on condition that he was to receive no personal remuneration. 'I prefer,' he said, 'to be entirely independent in the matter of money: my sole desire is to be of service to the whites and above all to the poor Indians.' He accepted money only to cover the expenses of his journey and that of his interpreter.

On 12 April 1867 Father De Smet left St Louis for Chicago, the principal city of Illinois, 280 miles away. He left, however, not without apprehension as to the result of his undertaking.

Shall I be received by those proud Indians, whose tomahawks are uplifted against the whites, from whose lances hundreds of scalps dangle, serving as decorations for the warriors and their steeds? The conviction that fervent prayers accompany me gives me courage. Knowing my own nothingness, I place myself unreservedly in God's hands and under the protection of our good Mother, the Immaculate Virgin.

Letter to Father Terwecoren, 30 April 1867.

To avoid the dangers and delays of high water in the spring, Father De Smet travelled by a different route from that followed heretofore; he went overland to Sioux City by way of Chicago. This was the first time he had crossed the undulating plains of Iowa.

All this region resembles an agitated sea, suddenly become motionless. Day after day the same monotony. Like waves, hills succeed valleys interminably. Only here and there a clump of trees along the streams and in some deep valleys and ravines in the higher portions. In summer this region is an ocean of verdure, adorned with flowers, in autumn fire burns everything and the land is covered with the sad black veil of mourning; then comes winter with its mantle of snow. Spring is just now beginning, and the snow that lay from two to four feet deep is melting and rapidly disappearing, and only a few glistening white patches are seen on the hillsides.

Letter to Father Terwecoren.

At Boonesboro came a long delay. In addition to the sudden melting of the snows, an extraordinary downpour of rain some days previously had swollen the rivers and streams and transformed them into rushing torrents, which had washed out tracks and all the bridges. There was nothing to do but be patient and wait. On 16 April the railroad took him ninety miles further to the little village of Denison. Five travellers joined him in hiring a wagon that took them the 100 miles to Sioux City. On 30 April 1867 they took a steamer, the *Guidon*, at Sioux City and continued their journey up the river. With Father De Smet were twenty-six Yankton Sioux, an interpreter, and their chief Pananniapapi, with whom the missionary had long enjoyed the most cordial friendship. The destination of the Indians was the Yankton Agency near Fort Randall.

Many of the passengers were soldiers journeying to the different forts. In his capacity as envoy extraordinary, Father De Smet had been gven the rank of Major – 'a title singularly out of place for a Jesuit, nevertheless it gives me free access to the soldiers, many of whom are Catholics, and to them I devote much of my time, not in my capacity of officer, but of priest. It is like a little floating mission, and my days are spent in teaching the catechism or hearing confessions.'

But the soldiers were not the only ones to benefit. At every landing Father De Smet visited Indian villages or Canadian families, instructing them, performing marriage ceremonies, baptising in all 900 children. On 24 May, the feast of Our Lady, Help of Christians, a rustic altar was erected in the open country, and under an azure sky, surrounded by his neophytes, he celebrated the Holy Sacrifice.

But his solicitude for the salvation of souls in no way interfered with the worldly object of his mission. The tribes along the river had not yet taken up arms, but a revolt was imminent. In concert with Pananniapapi, Father De Smet endeavoured to maintain their good relations with the whites, although the latter had committed crying injustices against the Indians. It was evident to these tribes that they could not long withstand the United States Army. The missionary argued with them that rather than make common cause with the hostile bands, it was wiser to assure them of the protection of the Government, which engaged itself to do what was right and admit all just claims.

The boat took six days from Sioux City to the Yankton reservation, a distance of 260 miles. Father De Smet stopped a few days at Fort Randall until the *Bighorn* arrived, with provisions on board for the long journey across the plains.

The Yankton interpreter and agent, Mr Alexis Gion, provided

Father De Smet with a small apartment in his frame cottage. Here he set up his altar and ministered to the spiritual welfare of the Indians.

In a letter headed 'Fort Burford, at the mouth of the Yellowstone, July 8, 1867', Father De Smet describes events.

On 17th May 1967, the steamboat *Bighorn*, thirty-three days out from St Louis, arrived at the Yankton agency, and landed in good order my wagon, my little travelling necessities, my two mules and my saddle horse. These three animals, on coming ashore after so long an imprisonment, performed capers without end. The attractive perfume of the fresh grass caused them delirium of joy; they threw themselves down with all four feet in the air, rolled right and left on the sod, jumped and skipped, and carried on at such a rate that they were near playing the mischief with the spectators, assembled to admire their leaps and exploits. Still, these four-legged humorists did not forget the matter of refreshment; in a short time each was going around with a rounded paunch, looking like a bag of hay.

The captain of the steamboat deserves thanks for the care he had taken of my animals. Despite his watchfulness, however, the horse on one occasion got loose from his halter and managed to get off the boat, while it was in motion, and tranquilly went for a swim. His escape was not discovered for an hour afterward. At once the boat was turned back down river, in search of my courser, and he was found safe and sound at the foot of a bluff too steep for him to climb; otherwise he would have got to the woods and that would have been the last of him. The deckhands brought him on board again.

Three days were required to bring our quadrupeds into tractable shape. One of the mules showed himself nothing less than bull-headed, and revolted whenever the bridle was passed over his ears. After several attempts, all of them fruitless, the driver, to punish the balky animal and get a little respite himself, left him the bridle, but took away the bit; the mule appeared satisfied and the driver had no further need to resort to the whip to keep him quiet.

On May 21st I left the Yankton agency, together with the good chief Pananniapapi and his band. My little caravan was composed of a Sioux interpreter, a guide, a horse herder and a hunter. For seven miles, the route lay across an elevated country, through lovely smiling prairies, slightly rolling. Then we came down on the bottomlands, the valley proper of the Missouri. There the Yankton chief called Iron Horn and his little band have some cultivated fields. I gave baptism to all the little children. Six miles farther on, at the *Sentier de bois à proue*, (Prow-wood Landing?) I baptised several others. We had much difficulty in crossing the muddy stream opposite Fort Randall: all the baggage had to be carried to the farther bank on men's shoulders; all arms were required to help the two mules and the horse pull the empty wagon out of the sticky mud. Three miles farther, on the bank of the Missouri and on the land of the chief Magaska, or Swan, we camped for the night, at a distance of 17 miles from our starting-point.

On May 22nd I regenerated in the holy waters of baptism a half-breed family, mother and seven children, who had prepared themselves several years before to obtain this favour.

On May 23rd we set up our tent on the bank of Pratt Creek. The Sioux chief of the Brûlé tribe, Katanka-Wakan, or Ghost Bull, joined us on the road and we camped together at the foot of hills at Bijou. Here a Canadian has built his cabin. I baptised his five children.

On 26th May we arrived at Fort Thompson, about seven in the evening. There we set up our tent, at a short distance from the Missouri. I made my call on the officers of the fort, and we spent an agreeable evening. The officers of the American army are, in general, *gentlemen* in the full force of the word.

The next day Father De Smet met Indians of the Brûlés, Two Kettles and Yanktonnais.

The object of my mission from the Government had already been announced to them; they received me with affability and confidence. I convoked the principal chiefs and the braves in council. As the names they bore may interest you, by reason of their singularity, I will give you a few of them; besides, they are my spiritual children and my friends: I take pleasure in making you acquainted with them. They are, Mazoéâté or Iron Nation; Istamanza or Iron Eyes; Tawagoekeza-numpa or Two Lances; Tchêtauska or White Hawk; Mantowa-Koua or Hunting Bear; Gougounapia or Knucklebone Collar, and Mantâtska or White Bear.

261

Thirty-six chiefs and braves attended the council. I opened the session with a solemn prayer to the Great Spirit. The chiefs kept their hands raised toward heaven throughout this invocation. Then I laid before them at some length the object of my mission, the desires and wishes of the Government in regard to them. In their speeches in reply, the chiefs made solemn promises to listen to the advice of the Great Father, the President of the United States, and to keep peace with the whites. They laid before me, quite simply, their delicate and critical position. On the one hand, they alleged their nearness to and relations with the fighting bands, who are their own blood and kin; and the invitations of the latter to take up the hatchet against the whites in defence of the land of their birth; invitations always accompanied with insults and menaces. On the other – I will quote their own words: 'Commissioners and agents of the Government come to us every year; they are affable and prodigal of speeches and promises on behalf of our Great Father. What is the reason that so many fine words and pompous promises always come to nothing, nothing, nothing?' The council lasted several hours, with every indication of a good and fortunate outcome.

On May 28th I said Mass late in the morning and gave an instruction at Fort Thompson. The garrison is principally composed of Irish, Germans, and French, all Catholics. It was the first visit they had received from a priest. Accordingly a good number made haste to profit by my presence to approach the sacraments. I spent part of the day with them, and employed the remainder in conferences with the Indians, which was the main object of my mission.

On May 29th early in the morning I became aware that one mule and my horse had strayed away during the night. I was not altogether easy about them: it was quite possible that the hostile Indians, who often roam this region, especially in the dark, had carried them off. I had recourse to the good Saint Anthony, and to my great joy, the two fugitives were brought back to me a short time after my prayer.

On May 30th the glorious day of the Ascension: I offered holy Mass for the conversion of the Indian tribes. On leaving, at seven in the morning, the wagon got mired in the deep mud of Chapelle Creek. As at the muddy stream near Fort Randall, we had to unload and carry everything over on our shoulders. We succeeded with difficulty and by main force in disengaging our vehicle from its embarrassed situation, and took up our march anew for twenty-five miles. We camped at old Fort Sully, now abandoned; about five in the afternoon, I found myself among 220 lodges of Indians, who received me with every demonstration of the warmest cordiality.

May 31st. As at Fort Thompson, I convoked the chiefs and braves in a grand council. Allow me to give you a second list of our Nestors of the plains. Their names, as in ancient times, are characteristic and significant; they have reference to some remarkable action in their lives. For the most part, they are names illustrious among the tribes of the Great Desert. They are as follows: Nâgi-wakan, or Chief Ghost; Tchêtangi, or Yellow Hawk; Zizikadaniakan, or Man who Soars Above the Bird; Tokayâketé, or Killed the First One; Matowayouwi, or Dispersed the Bears; Tokaoyouthpa, or Took the Enemy; Wawantaneanska, or Big Mandan; Wagha-tshawkaeyapi, or Serves as a Shield; Wâmedoupiloupa, or Red Tail Eagle, and a great number of others.

As soon as they comprehended the object of my visit, they paid the closest attention to my words. They complained bitterly of the bad faith of the whites, of the commissioners and agents of the Government, always so prodigal of promises and always so slow in fulfilling them, if they ever do so. This conduct sticks in their minds; they propose to wait a while longer and see. In their speeches and in private conversation they declared themselves favourable to peace with the whites and ready to call on their young warriors to bury the hatchet and withdraw from the fighting bands. They expressed also a lively desire to settle on reservations and cultivate the soil. But until such time as their fields produce abundance, they choose to continue to lead the nomadic life and to range the plains peaceably in search of animals, roots and fruits.

In the evening of the 5 June a terrible hurricane, accompanied by continuous lightning, turning night into day, and a roll of heavy thunder like the discharge of a thousand cannon, burst over our camp. One would have thought the last day was at hand.

The hurricane lasted several hours. A large number of tepees were blown down. Wagons were taken off in haste by the wind. The violence of the gusts came near carrying away my tent; it took three strong men to hold it upright. The play ended with a deluge of rain and hail, which flooded all the country.

C and R, pp. 870–9.

On 6 June Father De Smet met Generals Sully and Parker, the Peace Commissioners who had been instructed to record the complaints and grievances of the Indians, near Fort Peter. They decided to travel with him as far as the mouth of the Yellowstone as they realised what great services Father De Smet could render them. General Sully, who had formerly refused the Jesuit's mediation, now deemed himself fortunate to be able to approach the Indians under his protection.

Then began a peace campaign that affirmed in a striking degree the prestige of the Black Robe. Father De Smet, the Generals, and the faithful Yanktons stopped at Forts Sully, Rice, Berthold, and Union, and wherever they found a group of lodges they sought out in each place the chief, and asked him to convoke a council. When the warriors had assembled, and the calumet had been passed around, the priest would address the gathering, declaring the object of his mission and making known the advantages of an agreement with the whites. Then pointing out the Commissioners, he explained: 'Your Great Father desires to know your grievances in order to remedy them.' The Generals in turn invited the chiefs to speak openly, telling them that their complaints, formulated in council, would be sent to Washington and submitted to the President.

Ranged in a circle, the warriors listened in silence. Then arose a chief of gigantic stature, proud of mien, and of stately tread, his head ornamented with eagle feathers, and his feet encased in rich moccasins. He was Iron Shield, chief of the Miniconjous. Placing himself in front of the Commissioners, he lifted his hand, called for attention, and began to speak.

'When the Great Father sends honest men to my country I am glad to speak to them. Among you is one known to me, a man of God: I and my people love him. You tell me that the Great Father loves his red-skinned children, that he wishes to be just to them and make them happy. Formerly we were happy, because the whites that came to us to hold council did not deceive the Indians. If the Great Father really loves us, why has he sent agents into our country who lie to us? Since the coming of these men all is changed, prosperity and goodness have disappeared. Even the climate, which before was pleasant, has become bad.

'We have never troubled your lands, and you come to ours to sow unhappiness. Why do you do this? You have built four railroads through our country and driven away the wild animals. You refuse us powder and bullets, and why? The game has become so shy that my bow and arrow are useless. I now need powder and lead.

'Since the white man has come here and deceived us we cannot live in contact with him. I am ashamed to put my foot in a white man's lodge or to receive him in mine. Also, the soldiers have treated us badly. If the Great Father would recall them and leave us only the traders whom we need, happiness would return and the climate would again be good. He must also do away with all the railroads built on our lands. This is my country; it does not belong to you, and we have no intention of surrendering it. We do not wish to inhabit the lands you offer; we wish to live here, and I and my warriors choose rather to fight and die in defending our rights than to leave our country and die of starvation. Moreover, we swear to scalp every white man that falls into our hands, if the Great Father does not withdraw the soldiers and restore to us our lands. I have spoken.'

C and R, p. 880.

General Sully made known to him that the soldiers had been brought into the country by the massacres that had taken place in Minnesota and on the plains of the Missouri; that if these murders and massacres continued, the number of soldiers would be increased, until they would cover the country as grasshoppers cover their fields. 'Bury that hatchet,' said the general, 'and the soldiers will return whence they came.'

The Indians remained defiant. Father De Smet alone had any influence over them, and that through private counsels rather than by haranguing them. He finally succeeded in calming them, assured them of the sincerity of the Commissioners, and restored their confidence in the good intentions of the Government.

Everywhere Father De Smet heard the same story: 'The Government agents visit us frequently. They are amiable and prodigal of words and promises, but why do such professions come to nothing?' The Indians would then enumerate the evils of which they were the victims. 'Notwithstanding, we still hope that our appeals will reach the ear of the Great Father and touch his heart, and that he will take pity on us. The Black Robe's words today strengthen our hope.'

Father De Smet's interviews with them were everywhere satisfactory and it seemed to him that peace was clearly in sight if the Indians could be assured of fair treatment on the part of the whites.

He writes:

> I am firmly convinced that if the just claims of the Indians are attended to; if the agents and other employees of the Government treat them with honesty and justice; if they are supplied with the necessary tools for carpentry and agriculture – the tribes of the Upper Missouri will maintain peace with the whites; and the warlike bands who today infest the plains of the Far West and the valley of the Platte, where there is so much destruction of property and loss of life, will promptly cease their depredations and would not be long in joining the stay-at-home tribes.

This was undoubtedly the case; but the conditions named by Father De Smet were impracticable. The onward rush of immigration could not be checked, and it was that that made the difficulty. It drew all the lesser evils in its train.

On 16 June Father De Smet arrived at Fort Rice. He sent several embassies to the hostile Indians and succeeded in getting upward of a hundred chiefs and warriors to come to Fort Rice and meet Generals Sully and Parker; but owing to the delay of the arrival of these two officers, the Indians were compelled to leave, on account of lack of provisions, without having seen them. They sent back word that they were very anxious to see them and that they were desirous of peace. 'On June 19 we left Fort Rice early in the morning. The distance to Fort Berthold is 175 miles. We arrived there without the slightest incident.'

At Fort Berthold De Smet performed a very brave and gallant act. A party of Sioux appeared on the opposite bank of the river. He crossed to meet them, contrary to the advice of everyone in the post. He was well received and found that they had come there for the express purpose of seeing him. He remained with them for nearly three hours. The chiefs received with ready ear the message he brought from the Government and the conference was entirely satisfactory.

While at Berthold Father De Smet learned that the Santee Sioux, who were mainly instrumental in the Minnesota massacre, and who were then hovering on the British frontier, would like to see him and hear what the Government had to say to them. De Smet thought he ought to go, but before doing so felt that he must consult General Sully, who was coming up the river with a strong military force. He descended the river to meet him and told him what he proposed; but the General thought that it was his duty to deliver a blow to these Indians that they would remember, and that it was best to talk peace only after they had been punished for what they had done.

> In consequence of the General's declaration and the circum-
> stances of the case, my errand of peace, though sanctioned by
> the Government, became bootless and could only serve to place
> me in a false position – that of being face to face with the Indians
> without being able to do them the least service. So I took the
> resolution of returning to St Louis.

Shortly after his arrival in St Louis, 'exhausted and feverish', Father De Smet received a letter from the Secretary of the Interior containing these words: 'You will please accept my thanks for the faithful and efficient manner in which you have discharged the duties entrusted to your care.'

It was Father De Smet's intention to return to the hostile Indians as soon as his health improved. In a letter from St Louis dated 21 September 1867 he wrote that:

> A large number of chiefs have invited me to visit them and seem
> disposed to make peace, but the winter is too far advanced and I
> am too weak to undertake the journey of over 3,000 miles. I
> must put it off until next spring.

In 1867–8 a new Peace Commission was set up. The Peace Commission consisted of the most distinguished officers of the United States Army, those who had just brought the Civil War to a close. It included five Generals – Sherman, Harney, Sanborn, Terry and Sheridan. But realising that force of arms would not succeed in quelling the Indian tribes, it called on a middle-aged Jesuit, Father De Smet, to achieve what superior arms could not, a negotiated peace with the hostile, non-co-operating Indians. The leader of this non-co-operating band of Indians was Sitting Bull. In 1857 he had been elected war chief of the Hunkpapa tribe. The Hunkpapas were part of a much larger Sioux confederacy. The nation of the Dakotahs (Lakota) or Sioux was divided into a great number of tribes with distinctive names, numbering between

50,000 and 80,000 souls, roving over a far extended wilderness. The very name Dakotah means 'many in one'. It was the most numerous nation in the United States. Sitting Bull came to embody the spirit of Dakotah (Sioux) resistance to the *wasichu* (white man) threat. He led them in their war with the white men. His men had out-thought, out-guessed and outrun the finest American army on record, an army outnumbering them 100 to one.

While the tribes of the southern plains had accepted the Fort Laramie Treaty, the tribes of the northern plains, led by Sitting Bull, refused to sign. The whites must withdraw from all Sioux territory and cease travelling through it. If they would not leave peaceably he would drive them out. So long as these tribes, the most powerful in the plains, refused to sign, there could be no peace. Sitting Bull distrusted all *wasichus*. He wouldn't even talk to them. Except one – Black Robe, who found welcome where no other white man would dare to venture. Major General David Stanley wrote in a letter from Fort Sully, Dakota Territory, on 12 July 1864:

> The Reverend Father is known among the Indians by the name of 'Black Robe' and 'Big Medicine Man'. When he is among them he always wears the cassock and crucifix. He is the only man for whom I have ever seen Indians evince a real affection. They say, in their simple and open language, that he is the only white man who has not a forked tongue; that is, who never lies to them. Alone of the entire white race, only he could penetrate the cruel savages and return safe and sound.
>
> *C and R, p. 1585.*

The Indian Wars of 1864–5 had been bitter and costly. According to an estimate by General Sherman, the Army commander, the complete subjugation of the Indians by force of arms would cost the country $500 million, not to mention the cost in blood and lives on both sides. Rather than war, a peaceful settlement was sought.

On 30 March 1868, Father De Smet, in his sixty-eighth year and in broken health, left St Louis by rail to join the Peace Commission at Fort Laramie. But even as he prepared for his dangerous mission Sitting Bull was still leading attacks against white soldiers. In May 1868 he led a war expedition against Fort Buford at the mouth of the Yellowstone River. Rows of stacked firewood – the winter supply – were burned. He then attacked Fort Totten in the north east and then Fort Stevenson.

268

Father De Smet left St Louis by rail in the company of Generals of the Peace Commission. They went to Omaha via Chicago and thence to Cheyenne, on the North Platte, holding a council with some Sioux bands on the way. From Cheyenne they made a brief pleasure excursion to Sherman Pass across which the new Union Pacific Railway had but recently been built. The Commissioners then went to Fort Laramie while De Smet returned to Omaha to go from there to Fort Rice. At Omaha however, Father De Smet left the military 'top brass', as a Black Robe in the midst of military uniforms would be unseemly to the Indians. He decided he would travel the rest of the way alone. He took passage on the steamer *Columbia* for Fort Rice, a distance by river of 1,005 miles.

The Missouri River, muddy yellow, was at that time very low and progress was slow in consequence.

At old Fort Pierre or Sully, where 200 lodges were set up in a beautiful elevated plain, was a mixed camp of various tribes – Blackfeet, Sioux, Two Kettles, Brûlés, Yanktonnais, Yanktons, Sans-arcs, Minneconjous and Ogallalas. Father De Smet spent time with them, counselling the chiefs and instructing the people. He recalled that 'during all my stay with them they treated me with the utmost benevolence, affability and attention. I was surrounded from morning till night'. Finally, on 24 May, after thirty-three days of constant struggle with the current, sandbars and snags, the steamboat reached Fort Rice. Two of the Fort's sweeping bastions appeared to rest in the water which washed their bases, while a deep ditch and extensive morasses guarded its other sides and angles.

At Fort Rice Black Robe was greeted by a great number of Indians in fantastic accoutrements – their heads adorned with feathers and silk ribbons, in which red and blue predominated, and their faces daubed with the most varied colours. They were there to attend 'the great peace council'. They gave him a great ovation. They then conducted him to a lodge that had been prepared for him, where the great chiefs were anxiously waiting to learn the Government's intentions towards them. He assured them of the Government's peaceful intentions, but declared he could not conclude any negotiations before the arrival of the Commissioners. He devoted the following days to instructing the Indians, and 600 children received baptism. He also prepared the soldiers in the garrison to receive the Sacraments on the forthcoming day of Pentecost.

On 1 June Father De Smet announced that he was going to seek the hostile Sioux tribes in order to induce their chiefs to attend the conference. The hostile Indians lived on the far side of the Bad Lands in Powder Valley country, an immense, sterile plain, furrowed with deep undulations. Numbering over 5,000, they roamed about with the uneasiness and restlessness of wild beasts. The Indians at Fort Rice were astounded at such audacity, and wished to dissuade him. 'Black Robe,' they said, 'it will cost you your scalp.' But the missionary replied: 'Before a picture of the Blessed Virgin, Mother and Protector of all nations, six lamps are burning day and night during my absence, and before these lamps more than a 1,000 children implore heaven's protection of me.' Then the Indians lifted their hands to heaven, exclaiming: 'How wonderful! How splendid! We want to accompany you. When will you start?'

'Tomorrow at sunrise.'

Chapter 16

In Search of Sitting Bull

At seven in the morning on 2 June 1868 Father De Smet set off for Sitting Bull's encampment, somewhere on the south side of the Yellowstone River, a few miles above the mouth of the Powder River. The morning air was bright and balmy but would soon be hot. Several prominent chiefs insisted on accompanying him. There were Running Antelope, chief of a large tribe of Hunkpapas, Two Bears, head chief of the Yanktonais, and also Bear's Rib, The Log, All Over Black, Returning Ghost, Red Cloud, Little Dog, Sitting Cow and White Gut. The chiefs and their tribesmen made an escort of about eighty Lakota and Yanktonais.

The cavalcade set a westerly course, following the direct path of the sun. Father De Smet soon settled to the rhythm of his horse's fast gait. That day they made twenty-two miles before encamping on the north bank of the Cannonball River, so called because of the 'balls' of stone that lined its bed. The next day they traversed rolling plains, the star-like blossom of the cactus, yellow, white and red, lending colour to the harsh landscape. That evening one of his escort by pushing his horse at top speed was able to run down an antelope. He used the stratagem of mimicking the cry of distress of a young fawn; when the animal stopped to look he lodged two arrows in its body. Lacking wood, they used bison dung, which, when dry, burns like peat, to provide a fire.

Next morning they were on the trail by five o'clock. Day after day they rode over undulating plains and immense high plateaux, completely without vegetation. The plateaux separating the waters of the Missouri from those of its great tributary, the Yellowstone, were 5,000 feet above sea level.

By 9 June they had been travelling for six days. They had found no trace of the hostile camps. Father De Smet sent four scouts –

Red Cloud, Little Dog, Sitting Cow and The Log – up country in search of them. He arranged with them a direction to be followed and camping-places to stop for several days in advance. He gave each of them a small charge of tobacco to offer as gifts, as invitations to a conference. A gift of tobacco, if accepted, would mean they could present themselves at the camp to talk. If the gift was refused, access to the camp would be forbidden.

On 16 June, as they travelled, they became aware of a tiny puff of yellow dust on the eastern horizon, billowing up from the dry soil, barely seeming to move, yet growing imperceptibly larger as it crept closer. Someone shouted '*Wasichus*' – 'whites'. What would white men be doing in hostile Sioux country? As the yellow dust cloud got closer it was possible to discern a troop of United States cavalry, in their sky-blue uniforms. Their drawn steel sabres glinted in the sunlight. Black Robe breathed a sigh of relief. Recently white soldiers under Colonel Chivington of the First Colorado Cavalry had massacred six or seven hundred women, children and old men at Sandy Creek, Colorado. Sioux penal law demanded that every Indian who had lost a member of his family at the hands of the white man was honour bound to avenge himself on the first white man he met. The Indians vowed vengeance in the way of white scalps.

The officer commanding the troop reined in his white charger. Sitting ramrod erect, as he had been trained to do at West Point, he saluted with his sword.

'Lieutenant Dixon, Sir! Second Dragoons, United States Cavalry, reporting for duty.'

Differing emotions gripped Father De Smet; first relief, then annoyance.

'What duty?' the silver-haired man asked, knitting his eyebrows.

'Protection, Sir,' the youthful lieutenant replied proudly, smiling.

De Smet smiled as he mused to himself what protection a troop of twenty-two white men would offer against 600 bloodthirsty Indians.

'But I must visit the Sioux on my own, alone. To be accompanied by other white men, especially United States soldiers, would completely compromise the entire operation.'

'I know, Sir,' the youthful lieutenant interrupted. 'The General said he was not going to be a party to suicide.'

As Father De Smet was considering a response to this unexpected

turn of events a *Sassakwi*, a war-cry, rent the desert air, bloodcurdling and chilling enough to make even the desert rocks tremble. An
Indian brave was pointing to the west. An Indian's sight was too
keen to be mistaken. On the horizon another dust cloud was visible,
growing in size as it approached. With understandable apprehension
Father De Smet awaited the on-coming Indians. They were now
within rifle range, riding with their heads low to the necks of their
ponies, screaming their war cry, their bison-hide war shields held
high. Despite his sixty-eight years of age De Smet sat tall in the
saddle.

A horseman, naked and riding bareback, reined in his horse.
With a touch from the riders knee the horse walked up to where the
pale-faces rested on their mounts. The lean wind-whipped warrior
was a man of wild and savage mien. He was joined by his fellows,
equally fierce warriors, their faces smeared with grease and char-
coal, their bodies painted with streaks of black, feathers above
their braided black hair. The warrior raised his right hand in salu-
tation, palm outward. He carefully scrutinised the pale-face dressed
in black. A metal object on Father De Smet's front caught his eye.
He looked at it carefully. A smile of recognition slowly spread
over his inscrutable face, exposing a row of strong white teeth that
would shame the purest ivory.

'How! How!' he saluted.

Black Robe returned the greeting with his own. 'How! How!'

The warrior intimated that Black Robe's gift of tabacco had been
accepted.

'*Tatanka – Iyotanka tahoksila*,' ('We are Sitting Bull's men'), he
announced proudly.

The warrior turned away from the priest and cast a gaze, beyond
contempt, on the young lieutenant of the Second Dragoons. There
was no greeting for him.

'Not you,' he indicated.

It did not take much time for the lieutenant to take on the import
of the Indian's message. The warrior then said something in his
Sioux dialect.

Mr Galpin, an old trapper who had lived with the Sioux Indians
for over thirty years, had been appointed by the Peace Commission
to act as interpreter. He came forward to interpret. The trapper and
the Hunkpapa got into conversation.

'No white man can pass beyond here,' the trapper relayed the
message. 'Only Black Robe,' he added.

The braves stared at the troop with unveiled hostility. Galpin repeated. 'Not you. You speak with a forked tongue. Only Black Robe speaks the truth.'

'Did you hear that, Father?' called out the lieutenant. 'He's calling me a liar. I've a good mind to cut down the savage.' His right hand reached for the hilt of the sabre that hung by his side.

Father De Smet mused over the word 'savage'. 'They are styled savages,' he had often said, 'but we may boldly assert that, in all our great cities, and everywhere, thousands of whites are more deserving of this title.'

At the same instant the Indian's right hand moved with cat-like alertness to the tomahawk in his girth. A single well-directed blow of the tomahawk would cleave the paleface to the brain.

De Smet sat with one hand over the other on the horn of his saddle.

Time hung for a moment. There was an ominous silence.

'Calm down, lieutenant,' De Smet advised. 'You had better return to your base.'

The lieutenant realised he was beaten. This was not the time for valour and heroics. Choosing discretion, he kneed his charger round. The rest of his troop of twenty-two men did likewise.

The chief, having restored his tomahawk to its usual resting-place on his body and tightened his girdle, intimated to Black Robe by the motion of a finger to move on. Sitting Bull's camp was three days' journey away. Hunched in the saddle Father De Smet rode off at a loping trot, the reins slack, letting his horse find its own pace. Behind his saddle, wrapped in a blanket, were his few belongings. The party vanished in a cloud of yellow dust.

As the sun hastened behind the peaks and darkness closed upon the desert, Father De Smet mused over the events of the day. The 'red Indian' was right. He and his fellow tribes-people had every reason to distrust the word of the white man. So many times they had been lied to, tricked and cheated.

Chapter 17

The Big Powwow

Led by Sitting Bull's emissaries Father De Smet and his escort rode out of the dark canyon into the brightness of the cloudless western sky. Below them stretched the sun-blackened plains of the Montana desert: vast, lonely, uninviting. On the horizon lava mountains, like low grey clouds, some capped with snow, stood sentinel. On they rode through a maze of treeless, grassless buttes, rugged cones, turrets, pinnacles and ridges.

They reached the sandy valley of the Poplar River where they camped under some willows and cottonwoods near a pool of green and stagnant water. All next day was spent in crossing high rolling plains in which cactus and absinthes flourished. They camped on the Big Sandy, a tributary of the Poplar. Finally on 19 June, after crossing a plateau about twelve miles wide, they reached a line of hills that hemmed the Powder River. They topped out on a rise, drew rein on the crest, and rose in their stirrups in amazement. From the vantage point on the knoll they saw stretched before them a flat plain, a large expanse of red-brown desert, sprinkled with the sparse silver-green of the sagebrush, and carved through with rivers. The valley lay quiet under the sun. Below their dramatic overlook lay the Powder River, its bed wide and sandy but not deep; its glimmering waters like a quiet mirror on the landscape.

Some four miles off in the Powder River bottoms Father De Smet beheld a detachment of 500 warriors coming across the plain towards them. He describes what follows:

I immediately unfurled my standard of peace, which was a banner with the holy name of Jesus on one side, and on the other a picture of the Blessed Virgin surrounded with a halo of stars. Believing it to be the United States flag, the Indians halted, and

appeared to be holding a consultation. The four head chiefs rode
up at full gallop and hovered about the banner. But as soon as
they learned what it represented, they shook hands with me and
signalled to their warriors to approach. They all drew themselves
up in a single line and we did the same. Then the two lines
approached each other. On both sides rose cries and shouts of
joy. I was moved to tears by the reception these pagan sons of
the desert gave me.

C and R, p. 910.

Then followed, according to their custom, the exchange of presents
– horses, weapons, garments.

The four head chiefs surrounded Black Robe with their mounts,
acting as a guard of honour against any perfidious attack. By the
penal code in force among the Sioux every Indian who had lost a
member of his family at the hands of a white man was obliged to
avenge himself on the first white man he met. As Father De Smet
acknowledged: 'Well, there were a good many of them in this position at the time of my arrival among them.'

Preceded by Black Robe's 'standard of peace' they trotted off in
the direction of the main camp, which was ten or twelve miles
away and consisted of nearly 600 lodges. The smoke of Indian
cooking fires rose out of the haze. Once across the Powder River
close military order was formed. Twenty *akicita* warriors, sturdy,
bronze of face and sinister of eye, warriors specially selected to
maintain discipline in the tribe, added their protection to Black
Robe's presence. As they neared the camp, scores of colourfully
painted warriors, savage in appearance, with trailing head-dresses,
buckskin breech clouts and long plaited braids, which danced as
they moved, came out to meet them. Plumes of eagles and other
birds adorned their long hair and even their pinto ponies had them
in their manes and tails, mingled with silk ribbons of various
colours and scalps captured from the enemy. Black, yellow or blue
streaks covered their naked bodies. Each warrior was armed with
a bow and quiver of arrows tipped with flint or jasper. Each
carried a *puggamaugun* or war-club of hard wood fastened to a
girth of deerskin and a stone knife. In addition to this some carried
the ancient *sheegwan* or Indian lance, consisting of a long pole
about six and a half feet long, with a spear of flint firmly tied on
with splints of hard wood, bound down with deer sinews. They had
been sent as a welcoming party by Four Horns, great chief of the

Hunkpapas. Four Horns shared his authority with Black Moon, his great orator, No Neck, and Sitting Bull, the *generalissimo* of the warriors and long in the highest councils of the tribe. The authority of a chief was maintained by physical superiority more than any moral superiority he might possess.

At the entrance to the camp Father De Smet was met by Sitting Bull, resplendent in all his war decorations. He rode his horse like a warrior, head erect, face expressionless. He had only been home in his encampment a few days from yet another war expedition. He was a tall, proud, powerfully built Indian, about thirty-five years of age. He combined the dynamism and drive of relative youth with experience in war, the hunt and the political and spiritual leadership of his people. He had a large-boned intelligent face, a low forehead, narrow, piercing eyes, a flat nose and thin lips and a jaw showing great determination. His black hair, braided on one side with otter fur, and allowed to hang loose on the other, reached to his shoulders. The centre of his scalp gleamed with a heavy streak of crimson paint. In his hair he proudly wore a single white feather upright, a symbol of his bravery, his first coup, when only aged fourteen, in his fight with the tribe's traditional enemy, the Crows. The first coup – striking an enemy with a coup stick – called for more daring than slaying them from a distance. A second feather red, in his hair signified a wound sustained in battle. He wore a bearskin belt, another symbol of bravery, given to one vowed to higher daring, who can now never retreat in battle. He wore an ermine skin on his shirt, his leggings were fringed with scalps he had taken and there were wolf-tails on his moccasins. In his right hand he proudly carried a lance. The sturdy ash staff was seven or eight feet long and tipped with an eight-inch notched iron blade. Blue and white beads covered its entire length; an eagle feather fluttered from its base. The lance had been presented to Sitting Bull by his father, along with a shield made from bison hide, as a gift on the occasion of his first coup. Four eagle feathers hung from the circular frame of the shield, signifying success in all four directions.

Sitting Bull was so named because on the day of his birth, in 1831, near the mouth of the Grand River, a bison came and seated itself a few feet from the *tipi* (wigwam) in which he first saw the light of day. The bull is characterised as an animal possessed of great endurance; when brought to bay it will plant itself immovably on its haunches to continue fighting to the death. Sitting Bull's name was well chosen.

Amid great excitement Black Robe entered the Hunkpapa camp. The Sioux lodges and wigwams, made of bison skin strapped to towering lodge poles, each housing eight to ten individuals, had brightly decorated exteriors. They were painted in wavy red, yellow and white lines, or decorated with figures of horses, deer and bison, moons, suns and stars. You could tell the different tribes from the markings on their *tipis* and the trappings on their horses. The lodges were grouped round a large 'medicine' lodge. In the centre of the lodge was a high pole, on which all the chiefs and braves hung their medicine bags, containing their idols, arrows, quivers, and trophies won from enemies, especially scalps. On important occasions, such as 'powwows', as now, a large fire was built in the centre of a wide level stretch of ground in front of the lodge. Here the 'medicine man' would go through his incantations praying for the success of the venture in hand. As the cavalcade advanced, the entire population of 4,000 to 5,000 Indians turned out to shout greetings and participate in the welcome.

With Father De Smet's standard in the vanguard, the cavalcade drew up at Sitting Bull's lodge in the centre of the village. As throngs of people pressed in from all sides Black Moon ordered the *akicita* to disperse the crowd. Sitting Bull ordered Father De Smet's paltry luggage be carried into his own *tipi*. Father De Smet entered the *tipi*, which was guarded by a band of *akicita*. The *tipi* was large, made of seventeen fine bison hides, with painted representations of Sitting Bull's exploits in war depicted round the walls. On caribou antlers hung a powder horn and bullet pouch.

Father De Smet had not drunk clean, clear water for days. He picked up a gourd dipper, dipped it into a hide bucket and quenched his thirst. He later wrote that 'hunger and weariness had by now taken possession of me'. Some *suc-ca-tush* (cracked corn and beans) was prepared for him and he then took a 'little nap' without delay. Though surrounded by 5,000 Indians, sworn enemies of the white man, he tranquilly fell asleep, wrapped in his Jesuit cloak, in the full assurance of the good faith of Indian hospitality. A guard kept watch over the venerable white man.

Later that evening, the four chiefs, Sitting Bull, Black Moon, Four Horns and No Neck, entered the *tipi*. Black Robe opened his eyes. A man holding a blazing knot of pine provided light. With Galpin as interpreter Sitting Bull spoke slowly and quietly in the name of his tribe and with great conviction and authority.

Black Robe, I hardly sustain myself beneath the weight of white men's blood I have shed. The whites provoked the war; their injustices, their indignities to our families, the cruel, unheard-of and wholly unprovoked massacre at Fort Lyon [where Chivington commanded] of six or seven hundred women, children, and old men, shook all the veins which bind and support me. I rose, tomahawk in hand, and I have done all the hurt to the whites that I could. Today thou art among us, and in thy presence my hands fall to the ground as if dead. I will listen to thy good words, and as bad as I have been to the whites just so good am I ready to become toward them.

C and R, p. 912.

The massacre at Fort Lyon referred to above is known as the Chivington massacre. In June 1864 Governor Evans of Colorado had sent out a circular to the Indians of the Plains inviting all friendly Indians to come into the neighbourhood of the forts and be protected by United States troops. In consequence of this proclamation 600 Cheyenne, after refusing to join the warring tribes, sought refuge near Fort Lyon and begged protection of the whites.

After a time they were requested to move to Sand Creek, about forty miles from Fort Lyon, where they were still guaranteed 'perfect safety' and the protection of the Government. On 27 November, Colonel J M Chivington, a member of the Methodist Episcopal Church in Denver, and Colonel of the First Colorado Cavalry, led his regiment by a forced march to Fort Lyon and fell upon this camp of friendly Indians at daybreak. The chief, White Antelope, always known as friendly to the whites, came running towards the soldiers, holding up his hands and crying 'Stop! Stop!' in English. When he saw that there was no mistake, that it was a deliberate attack, he folded his arms and waited till he was shot down.

(Jackson, p. 344.)

Father De Smet referred to the event in a letter headed 'On Board the Steamer *Ontario*, Fort Benton, 10 June, 1866'.

Chivington ordered the massacre (children, women, and old men included) of several hundred Indians, who had come to make a friendly visit to the post, according to their habit of many years' standing. All the papers were full of it and the frightful atrocity was fully exposed; still the monster found admirers and defenders, and still wears his epaulets. This is one case among a thousand. Is it surprising that the victims of such cruelties and oppressions, having no recourse to any laws for justice, rise furious, dig up the tomahawk and make their appeal to their quiver and scalping-knife, as their last and only resort for the remedy that is denied them elsewhere?

C and R, p. 1201.

Not content with taking life the soldiers subjected their victims to unspeakable outrages. One lieutenant killed three women and five children with his own hands, and took savage pleasure in scalping them.

In Major Wynkoop's testimony, given before the committee appointed by Congress to investigate this massacre, is the following passage:

'Women and children were killed and scalped, children shot at their mothers' breasts, and all the bodies mutilated in the most horrible manner. The dead bodies of females profaned in such a manner that the recital is sickening, Colonel J M Chivington all the time inciting his troops to their diabolical outrages.'

(Jackson, p. 351.)

Lieutenant Craven, in his evidence, stated that Colonel Chivington in conversation said, in the hearing of many, that he believed it to be right and honourable to use any means under God's heaven to kill Indians that would kill women and children.

One of the chiefs said to Father De Smet: 'If it had been any other man than you, Black Robe, this day would have been his last.'

Complying with Black Robe's request, the chiefs convened a great council for the next day, when Black Robe would inform them of the Government's proposals, and the warriors would decide if they should send a deputation to Fort Rice to treat for peace with the Commissioners.

Early in the morning of 20 June, men and women began preparing the place for the conference. This space covered nearly half an acre and was surrounded by a series of *tipis*, composed of twenty-four bison skins each, which were suspended on long pike poles. Ten *tipis* were joined to form one huge single council lodge. Father De Smet's banner of the Holy Virgin was hoisted in the centre, near bison robes spread on the ground as seats. On one side a seat covered with fine bison skin was prepared for Black Robe. At noon *akicita* ushered the priest and the interpreter, Galpin, to the bison robes and seated them to face Black Moon and Four Horns, the principal spiritual and political leaders of the village. First entered the principal leaders, in their flowing head-dresses of goose and eagle feathers, dyed in shades of yellow, green or vermilion. The eagle's feathers of a paramount chief cascaded down from his proud head. All wore their hair in long braids, hanging down on either side of their proud, aristocratic faces and falling well below their shoulders. Following came the 'one-feather' braves and the young bucks of the tribe. Behind them, in the lodge, partly uncovered to expose the interior, 500 Hunkpapa warriors had arranged themselves according to the several bands comprising the village. In front of them, behind Black Moon and Four Horns, sat the war chiefs – Sitting Bull, White Goat, No Neck and Gall, who could whip the braves into a frenzy. Pressing the warriors from behind, with order imposed by the *akicita*, the old men, women and children formed a dense mass of absorbed spectators. The air became stifling. A 'medicine man' of superior standing, in a simple costume of softest, whitest, doeskin, made his way to the 'medicine' lodge. He lit the fire in front of the lodge with a burning brand. When all the tribe had taken their places, ranged in a circle, Black Robe was solemnly introduced by Four Horns and Black Moon.

The council was opened with songs and dances, noisy and joyful, in which the warriors alone took part. They yelled and struck their mouths, at the same time performing leaps of all descriptions, now on one foot, now on the other, always at the sound of the drum and in perfect time, pell-mell, without order, turning to the right and left, in every direction and in every shape, all at once. Then there was that deliberate pause, that grave and meditative silence, that always preceded a conference. Not a syllable was uttered, scarcely a look cast aside. For a minute the whole assembly sat mute. Then Four Horns, an eagle-plumed head-dress over his hair, shining and black, like the plumage of a raven, his body adorned in profusion with wampums, gorgets and bracelets, embroidered leggings and moccasins on his legs and feet, rose. Full of the dignity of his office, he advanced with a slow and noiseless step towards the calumet, the emblem of savage brotherhood and union, which hung from a tripod in front of the *tipi*. He took down the calumet, wrapped in bison calf wool and red flannel. The wooden stem of the pipe, which signified peace, truth and mutual trust, sheathed in bird skins and ornamented with eagle feathers, was decorated with porcupine quills and the neck feathers of a mallard duck. In time of war the calumet and all its ornaments are red. Sometimes it is partly red and partly of some other colour. By the colour and the manner of displaying the feathers, a person acquainted with their practices knows at first sight what are the designs or intentions of the nation that presents the calumet. The pipe was filled and lit from a flint. Smoking the calumet forms a part of all Indian cere-monies. It is a sacred rite that they perform when they prepare themselves to invoke the Great Spirit. On all great occasions, in their religious and political ceremonies, and the great feasts, the calumet presides.

Holding the calumet to the front, stem upright, his right hand on the polished red catlinite bowl, he pulled on the pipe gravely. Four Horns solemnly presented its first fruits, its first puffs to *Wakantanka*, the Great Spirit (Mystery), or Master of Life, possessed of all-encompassing power, imploring his light and favour to aid the tribe through all its tribulations. All Indians admit the existence of the Great Spirit, a Supreme Being who governs all the important affairs of life. Then he presented it to the Sun, the author of light and heat, then to the earth and water, by which they are nourished. He then directed a puff to each point of the compass, begging of heaven all the elements and favourable winds. Four Horns then passed the pipe to Father De Smet who did like-wise. Anyone who refuses to smoke from the calumet is excluded from taking part and is obliged to withdraw. To refuse to accept the calumet, as between two different tribes, is equivalent to a declaration of war. On the other hand, to accept it is always, among the Indians, a sign of good harmony, fraternity and mutual charity, ready to aid one another in case of need. It was then passed mouth to mouth, from chief to chief, in order of rank, which each taking several puffs. Clouds of smoke soon filled the lodge. When the ceremony of the calumet was finished, Chief Black Moon rose. With the grave and austere demeanour of a chief, he addressed Black Robe in a low, tremulous voice, filled with sombre power.

Speak, Black Robe, my ears are open to your words. When I see you here in my lodge, I feel glad as do the ponies when first the green grass comes to the hills at the beginning of the year. My heart fills with joy that we can talk together as friends, for I have no wish for trouble with my white brothers, least of all with you who speak to me here, my friend.

C and R, p. 100.

All this was done with the greatest gravity and amid a profound silence. Silence is a virtue among the Indians.

Father De Smet rose to his feet. Complete silence continued. As was the custom in a gesture of friendship, Black Robe threw his arms upwards towards heaven, implored guidance from on high, and then let them fall impressively on his chest. A murmur of welcome 'Huh!' answered his salute.

For an hour he laid before them the motives that had brought him among them, which could only tend to their happiness. He had come only to end this cruel and unfortunate bloodshed. He spoke of the dangers with which they were surrounded, and of their weakness beside the great strength of the whites. The harm done by the war had been terrible, and the crimes committed on both sides abominable. The Great Father desired that all should be forgotten and buried. Today his hand was ready to aid them, to give them agricultural implements, domestic animals, men to teach them field-work, and teachers of both sexes to instruct their children, and all this was offered them without the least remuneration or cession of lands on their part.

What he beseeched was a Christian forgiveness and forbearance alien to the concept of vengeance so deeply embedded in the Sioux way.

'And now,' he concluded, 'in the name of the Great Spirit, and in the presence of your chiefs and braves here assembled, I conjure you to bury all your bitterness toward the whites, forget the past, and accept that hand of peace which is generously extended to you.'

Gesturing towards his flag he declared:

'The banner before you is the sacred emblem of peace, and never before has it been carried such a distance. I will leave it with your chiefs as a guarantee of my sincerity, and as a continual reminder of my wishes for the happiness of the Sioux tribes.'

No one interrupted the Black Robe as he spoke. Father De Smet heard the tribe suck in its breath with satisfaction and then break into a murmur. When he had done Black Moon rose. After passing the pipe once again he responded.

Before speaking he thoroughly weighed his words. He spoke slowly and cautiously to add to the solemnity of his words. He spoke in a deep guttural voice, since the meaning of Indian words is much governed by emphasis and tones.

Back Robe, your words are plain and good, and filled with truth. I shall lay them up in my memory. Still, our hearts are sore. They have received deep wounds.

These wounds have yet to be healed. A cruel war has desolated and impoverished our country; the desolating torch of war was not kindled by us; it was the Sioux east of us and the Cheyennes south of us who raised the war first, to revenge themselves for the white man's cruelties and injustice. We have been forced to take part, for we too have been victims of rapacity and wrong doing. Today, when we ride over our plains, we find them spotted here and there with blood; these are not the blood-stains of bison and deer killed in the chase, but those of our own comrades or of white men, sacrificed to vengeance. The buffalo, the elk, the antelope, the bighorn, and the deer have quitted our immense plains; we hardly find them any more, except at intervals, and always less numerous. May it not be the odour of human blood that puts them to flight? I will say further – against our will, the whites are cutting up our country with their highways; they build forts and arm them with thunderers [i.e. cannons]. They kill our animals, and more than they need. They are cruel to our peoples, maltreat and massacre them without reason, or for the slightest cause, even when they are searching for food, for animals and roots to nourish their wives and children. They cut down our forests without paying us their value.

We are opposed to having these big roads, which drive the buffalo away from our country. The soil is ours, and we are determined not to yield an inch of it. Here our fathers were born and buried. We desire, like them, to live here, and to be buried in this same soil. We have been forced to hate the whites. Let them treat us like brothers and the war will cease. Let them stay at home; we will never trouble them. To see them come in and build their cabins revolts us, and we are determined to resist or die. Thou, Messenger of Peace, thou hast given us a glimpse of a better future. Very well; so be it; let us hope. Let us throw a veil over the past, and let it be forgotten.

I have only a word more to say; in the presence of all my people, I express to you here my thanks for the good news that you have announced and for all your good counsel and advice. We accept your tobacco. Some of our warriors will go with you to Fort Rice to hear the words and propositions of the Great Father's commissioners. If their words are acceptable, peace shall be made.

C and R, p. 916.

Then he took his seat. All applauded the words of Black Moon.

Then Sitting Bull rose. He repeated the pipe ritual. As tribal war chief Sitting Bull spoke on behalf of the warriors. His oration was not as convincing as Black Moon's. He seemed keener to say what Black Robe wanted to hear than express his true feelings. After invoking the aid of the Great Spirit, he stated that for four years he had led his warriors in 'bad deeds', but only because he was 'pushed forward'. Now he welcomed Black Robe and hoped he would succeed in his quest for peace. Hunkpapa emissaries would return with Black Robe to meet with the white commissioners. Whatever they agreed in Council, 'I will accept and remain hereafter a friend of the whites.' Sitting Bull then shook hands with Black Robe, and with Mr Galpin, the old Sioux trapper who had interpreted, and with his Sioux wife Matilde Galpin (Eagle Woman). This was a mark of high respect for Eagle Woman, who was the offspring of a Hunkpapa–Two Kettle union, which gave Galpin great credibility with the Sioux. Sitting Bull returned to his seat.

But hardly had he sat down when he sprang up again, saying he had forgotten a few things in his speech. He then poured out an afterthought that all but annulled his former speech. He wanted all to know that he did not propose to sell any of his country. He declared upon his *wampum* belt (equivalent to an oath) that he was no *witko* (fool) who would let the whites take their land. No more land should be ceded to the whites. His two other conditions for peace were that the whites should abandon their forts, 'as there was no greater source of grievance to his people'; and they must respect the trees. The whites must stop cutting his timber along the Missouri River. 'The oaks have resisted the storms of winter and the heat of summer and, like ourselves, they seem to draw from them new vigour.'

Amidst a chorus of 'hows', Sitting Bull resumed his seat. Taking an eagle plume from his head, he smoothed his solitary tuft of hair. Then he fanned himself with a large hawk's wing.

Sitting Bull's speech was followed by speeches from Two Bears and Running Antelope. They touched on the same matters as Black Moon and pronounced in favour of peace. The council lasted four hours. The Indians were indifferent to time. They would talk, however long the time, till they reached a consensus.

At the close of the council the chiefs begged Black Robe to leave his banner of peace with them as a souvenir of the great day of the council. He did so, expressing the wish,

That this banner on which are embroidered the name of Jesus and the image of the Blessed Virgin might be for all a pledge of happiness and safety. For a last time I recommend the tribe to the protection of Mary, *auxilium et refugium Indianorum*, as she was anciently in Paraguay, in Canada, everywhere and forevermore.

C and R, p. 917.

A standard bearer was chosen. The honour fell to a distinguished warrior, covered with scars, named Gall. He had a remarkable story to tell. He had been arrested by American soldiers, on a charge of stealing horses. On the road to the prison at the fort, the soldiers thought or feared that he intended to escape, and they ran him through the body twice with bayonets. He fell, bathed in blood, but being still conscious, he feigned death. They trampled him and kicked him, covering him with bruises. To finish their cowardly and cruel work upon their prisoner, they thrust a third bayonet through his neck, and at last threw him into a deep ravine. Here he lay unconscious for quite a while, entirely naked, on the drifted snow. When he came to himself, it was already far into the night. He got up, and walked about twenty miles, the snow red with his bloody tracks. When he reached the timber, on the bank of the Missouri, he found a fire, at which he warmed his limbs, stiffened by the cold. The hope of life returned to him then, and he implored the Great Spirit to 'take pity on him and preserve him'. He then quenched his burning and feverish thirst and washed off from his body the clotted blood that covered it. In the hope of meeting someone, he continued to drag himself on. After travelling some miles farther he discovered an Indian lodge. It was that of old

Peter Padanegricka, who treated him like a veritable Samaritan. When it was daylight, his host conveyed him on a stretcher to the main camp, where he was received with all the honours of a great warrior. Upon hearing his tale of the soldiers' cruelty and seeing his wounds, the rage of the warriors knew no bounds, and a great number of unhappy whites fell victims to it. In less than a year Gall himself set out on his war of vengeance, and returned to camp amid acclamations, with seven white scalps on the end of his lance.

The council ended with a song that roused the echoes of the hills, and a dance that made the ground tremble. Father De Smet was glad to get out of the lodge and breathe the pure air of a cool and refreshing summer evening. Upon his return to his lodge, he found it invaded by a clamouring crowd of mothers with their babies in their arms, and followed by their other children. He at once came to them, and they crowded around him with a rare trustfulness, very unusual among Indian children, to offer him their little hands. The mothers were not satisfied until he laid hands upon the heads of all the babies and little ones, when they withdrew contented and happy.

Father De Smet and the Galpins slept in Sitting Bull's lodge, with all the other chiefs present, the *akicita* guarding outside.

The next day, 21 June, Father De Smet set off on his return journey to Fort Rice where three commissioners designated to carry the Fort Laramie Treaty to the upper Missouri Lakotas (Sioux) were anxiously awaiting the results of his efforts.

Repeating the ceremony of his arrival, all the chiefs, led by Sitting Bull and an escort of *akicita* rode with him to the Powder River. Also with Black Robe's party was a small delegation of eight deputies chosen by the council. The Hunkpapa leaders were not too hopeful that peace on acceptable terms would materialise from the talks at Fort Rice. That is why neither Four Horns nor Black Moon, still less the war leader Sitting Bull, intended to go to Fort Rice. But so as not to displease or disappoint Black Robe they sent this delegation of eight lesser chiefs, headed by Gall. Several warriors also accompanied the party, among them a venerable old man. He had come to the camp to shake Black Robe's hand and to express his happiness at seeing him again. On his breast he wore a copper cross, old and worn. This was the only religious token Father De Smet had seen in all the camp, and it filled him with joy and emotion. He questioned the old man to know from whom he had received this cross.

'It was you, Black Robe, who gave me this cross. I have not laid it aside for twenty-six snows. The cross has raised me to the clouds among my people. If I still walk the earth, it is to the cross that I owe it, and the Great Spirit has blessed my numerous family.'

Black Robe asked him to explain further, and he continued. 'When I was younger, I loved whisky to madness, and at every chance I would get drunk and commit excesses. It is now twenty-six snows since my last wild orgy. I was stupid and sick from it. Just then I had the good fortune to meet you, and you made known to me that my behaviour was against the will of the Master of life and offended Him grievously. Since then I have often had opportunities; my friends have sometimes sought to induce me to join them in their illicit enjoyments, but each time this cross has come to my help. I would take it between my hands and would recall your words and invoke the Great Spirit. Ever since we first met I have renounced drink, and have never touched a drop.'

C and R, p. 913.

Struck by this heroic perseverance, Father De Smet wanted to baptise the old man, but there was not time to instruct him. The intrepid neophyte at once proposed to join the caravan, happy in the thought that when they camped he could receive instructions from the Black Robe. At the end of eight days he was made a Christian, and with a soul overflowing with joy, he returned to his tribe.

At Powder River Sitting Bull gave a brief address recalling the pledges he had made the day before. He shook hands with Black Robe and was about to wheel his horse away when the priest stopped him. He removed his black weather-beaten hat and lifted off a silver crucifix that hung from his neck. He presented it to Sitting Bull. The Indian chief was completely taken by surprise. He gazed at the precious metal object in his hands with disbelief. Then a large grin spread around his face.

Both smiling, the two men separated and went their different ways. De Smet looked back once. Sitting Bull and his men were still on the bank of the Powder River. They did not leave until Black Robe had successfully crossed over the muddy waters.

Though nearing seventy, Father De Smet could still put fifty miles of hard country behind him between dawn and dark. They travelled, however, an average of thirty-five to forty-five miles every day. The weather was fine and favourable and bison and antelope were abundant. On 25 June Father De Smet sent a missive from Box Elder camp via Chief All Over Black to inform the commissioners at Fort Rice of the success of his mission. Father De Smet was a peacemaker. But he was a missionary too. On the journey he conferred the holy sacrament of baptism on some sixty small children and five adults of advanced age. On 30 June they made a solemn entry to Fort Rice where, to a huge reception accompanied by volleys of gunfire, they were received with demonstrations of the liveliest joy by the peace commissioners, the army officers and thousands of Indians, proudly wrapped in their mantles, their heads ornamented with feathers and ribbons, their faces daubed with vermilion, who had come to meet him. Major-General Stanley, who was there, described the event.

> The warriors formed a long file and marched with true military precision. It was a really remarkable spectacle, though little in accord with the tastes of the good Father, who does not love the sound of trumpets and the glare of parades.
>
> (Letter to Archbishop Purcell, Fort Sully, July 12, 1868.)

The Great Peace Council took place on 2 July. Fifty thousand Indians, Hunkpapas, Blackfeet, Yanktonai, were represented. It was the greatest council that had been held on the Missouri in fifty years. The treaty was read. The agenda called for each chief to make a speech, then sign the treaty already negotiated with the Lakotas at Fort Laramie. The presiding Generals made solemn promises to the Indians that if they would lay aside their arms, the Government would respect their rights, provide for their livelihood, and treat them as friends. Then the representatives of the tribes spoke in turn, beginning with the standard-bearer of the Hunkpapas.

Gall (identified as Man-that-Goes-in-the-Middle), stocky, powerful, with intense eyes, large flat nose and thick lips, gave a speech which contained no hint of an understanding that the commissioners expected him simply to sign a document that had already been worked out, no hint that he even fathomed the nature of a treaty. Tearing aside the calico that covered his chest, revealing the scars of his many wounds, he declared: 'The whites ruin the country; if we make peace the military posts on this river must be removed and the steamboats stopped from coming up here.'

Having set his own conditions for a treaty, Gall sat patiently while twenty other chiefs made their speeches. Then, with the treaty laid on the table, he marched to the front and touched the pen, i.e. made his mark.

The treaty that Gall had so innocently signed addressed no fundamental grievances of the Hunkpapas. The Government had agreed to abandon the Bozeman Trail forts, a matter of interest but not vital to the Hunkpapas. Altogether ignored were the detested forts of the upper Missouri, the steamboats, and whites in general. In blustering language Gall had asserted that all must go or there could be no peace. Yet he signed a treaty of peace that said nothing about any of these matters.

When the Hunkpapas consented to make peace, the assent of the other tribes was assured. On condition of an adequate indemnity, the Sioux were to cede to the United States their reservations in Kansas and Nebraska, but they were to demand the exclusive possession of the lands north of the Niobrara. The ceded lands formed a Great Sioux Reservation – all of which later became the state of South Dakota, lying west of the Missouri River. Here the government would establish an agency, issue clothing and rations for thirty years, build schools and educate the Indians and teach them how to support themselves by farming.

Upon these conditions the treaty was signed. The Jesuit priest, alone and unarmed, had achieved what the entire United States Army could not. The next day Commissioners distributed presents to the Indians – tinselled trinkets, bright beads, strips of cloth, yards of calico – who then dispersed, each one rejoicing over a reconciliation which he believed to be lasting.

The Generals who negotiated the peace wished at once to acknowledge their debt of gratitude, and immediately after the signing of the treaty they presented an address to Black Robe, enumerating the eminent services he had rendered the United States.

We are satisfied that but for your long and painful journey into the heart of the hostile country, and but for the influence over even the most hostile of the tribes which your years of labour among them have given you, the results which we have reached here could not have been accomplished. We are well aware that our thanks can be but of little worth to you, and that you will find true reward for your labours and for the dangers and privations which you have encountered in the consciousness that you have done much to promote peace on earth and good will to men; but we should do injustice to our own feelings were we not to render to you our thanks and express our deep sense of the obligations under which you have laid us.

Wm. S Harney, Major General and Indian Peace Commissioner.

John B Sanborn, General and Commissioner.

Alfred H Terry, Major-General and Commissioner.

C and R, pp. 921–2.

A few days later (12 July) Major-General Stanley was to write:

I am persuaded that this is the most complete and the wisest of all the treaties thus far concluded with the Indians of this country. Without doubt the fulfilment of the provisions of this treaty will assure peace with the Sioux. But whatever may be the result, we can never forget, nor shall we ever cease to admire, the disinterested devotion of the Reverend Father, who, at the age of sixty-eight years, did not hesitate, in the midst of the heat of summer, to undertake a long and perilous journey across the burning plains, destitute of trees and even of grass; having none but corrupted and unwholesome water, constantly exposed to scalping by the Indians, and this without seeking either honours or remuneration of any sort; but solely to arrest the shedding of blood and save, if it might be, some lives and preserve some habitations to these savage children of the desert, to whose spiritual and temporal welfare he has consecrated a long life of labour and solicitude.

C and R, pp. 1587–8.

But the humble missionary did not tarry to listen to praise. On 4 July, appropriately Independence Day, he started back home. He first visited several tribes encamped near Fort Sully, where he baptised all the young children. He also gave a retreat for the Catholic soldiers there. He then went on to Fort Leavenworth and St Mary's Mission. He arrived back in St Louis on 20 August 1868, ill and exhausted. The heat of St Louis was intense and oppressive. Deaths from heat-stroke were a daily occurrence.

291

On 28 August he wrote to Father Terwecoren,

This letter may well be my last. My health is very much under-
mined in consequence of the fatigues of my late painful journey
of about 6,000 miles, but still more by the shocking heat that we
have suffered for three months past. In proportion as I advance
in age, heat becomes more and more insupportable to me.

   After a few days spent among the Potawatomies of Kansas, I
found myself really, as you might say, demolished, panting with
open mouth for the slight breeze, hardly able to stir the little fine
leaves of the acacias which surround and shade the Mission of St
Mary's. This was on the 29 of July. Every one was languishing.
I was under a burning sun, with the thermometer ranging from
104° to 109° in the shade, and up to 130° in the sun. I shall, I
doubt not, feel the effects for a long time; but, let us be patient,
and hope!

C and R, p. 900.

Black Robe was too modest a man to voice abroad the dangers and
sufferings he underwent on his lone mission to the hostile Sioux or
to boast about the peace he succeeded in bringing about between
the Indians and the whites.

   Fortunately we have a letter written by Major-General David
Stanley to Archbishop Purcell of Cincinnati, dated 12 July 1868, in
which he details the events Black Robe would not mention himself.
This letter is given in Appendix 1.

Chapter 18

A Last Encounter

At the end of the Peace Conference at Fort Rice in 1868 Two Bears, head chief of the Yanktons said in his speech:

> When we are settled down sowing grain, raising cattle, and living in houses, we want Father De Smet to come and live with us, and to bring us other Black Robes to live among us also. We will listen to their words, and the Great Spirit will love and bless us.
>
> *Lavaille, p. 359.*

Time and again the Sioux had clamoured for Black Robes. Father De Smet's Superiors approved his project for founding a mission among them. But men and money were lacking. Father De Smet was called on to make another journey to Europe. There was another reason for sending Father De Smet to Europe. For three years he had been threatened with loss of hearing and Father Coosemans, his Provincial, wished him to consult 'some good old Belgian doctor'.

On 21 November 1868 Father De Smet left St Louis for New York. On 25 November he embarked on the *City of Baltimore* for Europe. This was his sixteenth crossing of the Atlantic. Some days before reaching Liverpool the boat ran into a violent storm, during which he fell on deck and broke two of his ribs. He did not receive proper attention until he landed several days later.

On 11 December he left Liverpool for London, from where he travelled to his home town Termonde. Here he remained for the rest of the year.

He spent the first five months of the year visiting the principal places in Belgium, Holland, France and England. As Vice-

293

Provincial he met several VIPs in Europe. Even after twenty years spent among the savage tribes of North America he remained ever a gentleman of polished manners and address.

On 12 June he took his farewell of the Fathers of Notre Dame College at Antwerp and sailed once more for America. He reached New York on 29 June 1869. Three days later he left for St Louis, where he arrived on 4 July. The energy and activity of a man of his years was truly amazing: in sixteen months he had travelled 15,000 miles. On his return to St Louis he was obliged to keep to his room for several weeks, and abandon his journey to the Sioux.

In a letter to his nephew Paul and his niece Augusta, dated 7 October 1869, he wrote:

My health leaves much to be desired. The heat of July and August has been very oppressive and I continue to be under the general influence of a general languor and feebleness. I have a more and more sincere and serious conviction that my end is near. Do not forget me in your good prayers.

C and R, p. 1536.

The following autumn, however, he managed to make 'two good trips', one of 1,200 miles, the other of 800 miles. In October 1869 he accompanied as far as Omaha six Sisters of Charity who were going to the Blackfeet. In November he made a visit to St Mary's Mission. In December he travelled to Chicago and Milwaukee on church matters.

By June of the next year he felt strong enough for travel again. On 1 June 1870 he set out from St Louis for the Upper Missouri to see about establishing a mission among the Sioux. He went as far as Grand River. This was Father De Smet's last visit to his 'children of the desert'. How many times in the last thirty years he had gone up the Missouri. Every wigwam brought back consoling memories: thousands of children baptised, enemies reconciled, suffering relieved, and souls enlightened in the mysteries of faith. The Black Robe's arrival among the tribes was signalled by lighting great bonfires on the mountains. His journey was a continual, triumphant march. Everywhere he could see the beneficent results of the peace negotiated two years before by himself. The Sioux were living on most friendly terms with the soldiers at the fort; in the reservations they tilled the soil, were clothed by the Government, and received weekly rations of flour, meat, coffee, and sugar. From all directions the Indians flocked to greet 'the great Black Robe', and declared their desire to remain faithful to the Fort Rice conventions.

At St Ignatius' Mission he met Father Grassi, an Italian, who had replaced Father Hoeken. He had collected material for a hospital and a boarding school. But Sisters were needed to develop this work. Father De Smet appealed to the Sisters of Providence of Montreal, and they responded promptly and eagerly. Before the year was out they were installed and ready to receive pupils and care for the sick.

But of all the tribes, the Coeur d'Alènes, formerly the most ferocious of all the Western tribes, were distinguished by their devotion to the Church. The wild mountain deer had been tamed to become gentle lambs of Christ. 'During the fifteen years I have known them,' writes Father Joset, 'never has their faith been so ardent as now. I am convinced that if we had sufficient means, these Indians would out-rival the Paraguay missions.'

A letter from Father Grassi stated:

The Coeur d'Alènes fast nearly every Saturday in honour of the Blessed Virgin, a fast more rigorous than ours, for it is not broken till sunset. To prepare themselves to celebrate worthily the feast, some wear belts of thorns, others flay themselves with briers, and others again retire to the forest in order to observe complete silence. There they pray and work, only returning to camp for the prayers said in common. Everything is referred to the missionaries, who are obliged to restrain, rather than excite their zeal. A chief of a neighbouring tribe witnessed the charity that animates these Christians and wished to remain, saying, 'this mission is a paradise'.

(Letter from Father Grassi, *Catholic Missions*, 1870, p. 251.)

But while missionary affairs were progressing well, Father De Smet could not but fail to see the portents of a coming storm. He noted with great apprehension the vast changes then sweeping over the country as a result of the discovery of gold in Montana. He thus refers to this important matter:

It is impossible to overestimate the dangers which, just at this time, are threatening all the mountain tribes, through the approach of the whites, the ease with which liquor, so fatal to the Indians, can be obtained, and the accompaniment of all the vices and excesses of our modern civilisation; especially as understood and practised by our American pioneers. These things must be seen to be appreciated and believed.

C and R, p. 83.

It seemed certain that the lands cultivated by the missionaries would be seized by the invaders and the Christians exterminated or driven into the arid mountain defiles. The most tolerant of the Government agents says in his report, 'The red man must disappear before the approach of the white man. The question is, how can this be accomplished with the least suffering to the Indians and the minimum of expense to ourselves.'

Father De Smet was no doubt saddened by what was happening. In 1846 he must have anticipated that the seed he had sown in Oregon would grow into a mighty harvest. Now, as he passed over the country again, he found it occupied by a new race, the hunting grounds of his neophytes filled with settlers; the Indians struggling in vain for their lands and being rapidly huddled together on small reservations. The whole opportunity for a great work had gone in the twinkling of an eye. The work of the missionaries among the Indians was confined to a few small localities.

But Father De Smet never abandoned hope.

Although the abuse of whisky has demoralised the Indians, through God's mercy a large number of the faithful have escaped corruption, and show the same desire to hear the word of life and approach the Sacraments.

Lavaille, p. 313.

He was delighted to find Father Ravalli, one of the noblest men that ever laboured in the ranks of the Church in Montana, rebuilding the long-neglected mission in St Mary's Valley. But if Father De Smet saw much to fear for his Indians, he also saw much to hope for in the new field opening up in this region. Where there used to be one Indian he saw that there would soon be a hundred settlers, and the Church began at once to establish missions in the little mining towns, thus laying the real foundation of its present prosperous condition in Montana.

With the approach of autumn he turned his steps homeward. After leaving the mission of St Ignatius on 8 September, he visited the mission of the Sacred Heart on 18 September and Fort Vancouver on 8 October. He sailed from Portland on 13 October, stopped at Victoria, Vancouver Island and reached San Francisco on 21 October. During this journey he visited about 20,000 Sioux, and administered baptism to 400. His resolutions were made; a mission should be opened the next spring.

On 29 March 1871, he wrote to his relatives in Belgium:

Today I begin my annual retreat as a preparation for a long journey to the Indian tribes of the Far West. Two Fathers will accompany me, and we intend to establish a mission for the Sioux. The head chiefs of the tribe are expecting me, and I have just written to inform them of my plans and to ask them to prepare a cabin for us in their camp. I send you the names of these chiefs; they are my intimate friends, and you, too, will love them for my sake, I am sure, and will pray for their conversion.

But the long-cherished project was destined never to be realised. His failing strength was not equal to the labour involved. On 25 June Father De Smet left St Louis for Europe, to solicit more funds and more new Black Robes. He returned to America in April 1872.

In October 1872 Fathers Giorda and Guidi invited Father De Smet to visit their Rocky Mountains missions. In his reply of 27 October the old missionary replies that he 'will gladly make the journey if my health permits. However, I must add that the doctor who attends me gives me very little hope and calls me a bird for the cat.'

For two years the Sioux had been expecting Father De Smet to come and found a mission among them. In October 1872 a deputation of chiefs arrived to remind him of his promise.

There were wide smiles of joy as the two parties recognised each other.

'Hello, Black Robe,' said the tall Yakima chief, dressed in all his chiefly regalia. 'I'm Ignace,' he added, smiling a wide smile.

'Ignace! Yes, of course,' said Black Robe. 'Yes, I remember very well.'

They sat down and began talking.

'So what brings you to this big city?'

'We have no Black Robe. We have come to ask you to come to us, to visit us, to send us a Black Robe.'

'But what happened to Father Caruana?'

'He is no longer with us. The agent banned him from the reservation. They have put a Protestant in his place. We don't like him or his squaw. The other day he tried to bribe me to change to his religion.'

'Really?' queried Father De Smet, though without much surprise in his voice.

The background to events such as that described by Ignace was as follows.

On 5 December 1870 President Ulysses Grant, who had been inaugurated President the year before, announced to Congress that all Indian agencies would be handed over to the religious denominations that had established missions among the Indians. The religious denominations would nominate the agents in the reservations. The Indians would no longer be imposed upon by government functionaries who enriched themselves at their expense.

The Catholic Church congratulated itself upon President Grant's 'peace policy', since the greater number of the agencies had been evangelised by its missionaries, and they numbered over a 100,000 neophytes among the Indians. The Protestant sects numbered less than 15,000 adherents. Great was the astonishment three days later, therefore, to learn that a Jew had been appointed Superintendent of Indian Affairs in Oregon. From that instant Catholics knew what to expect from promises of the Government.

In January 1871, Secretary of the Interior Delano, consulted the episcopacy upon the choice of a representative to nominate Catholic agents. Father De Smet was proposed by the Archbishops of Baltimore, New York, Cincinnati, and St Louis. Called to Washington, the veteran missionary found himself in the company of about thirty ministers of the Reformed Church, likewise summoned to give their advice on the means of civilising the tribes. They claimed the lion's share in the partitioning of the agencies. 'Neither my presence, nor my demands on behalf of the Catholic missions, produced any effect. The plan for civilising and evangelising the Indians had already been decided upon by the President and approved by the Senate.'

Afterwards it was learned that instead of forty nominations to which the Catholics were entitled, only eight had been accorded to them, the remainder being divided among the different sects. The President favoured especially his coreligionists, the Methodists, granting to them a third of the agencies.

The superintendent of Indian Affairs began the discharge of his new functions by making over the Catholic schools and churches to his Protestant friends, and, in the case of the Yakimas, forbade Catholic missionaries to enter the reservation. At one stroke, 80,000 Indians, without being consulted, found themselves torn from the Church. In a letter to a colleague, 11 February 1871, Father De Smet complained: 'In the whole of this affair the Indians have not been consulted as to the religion they desire to belong to.'

But this was not all. Large sums of money due to the Indians in exchange for their lands were held by the Government, and the interest on this was used for the upkeep of the schools. Henceforth this money would be expended on the salaries of Methodist, Presbyterian, and Quaker schoolteachers, employed to teach the children of Catholic Indians. In this manner did the Government repay the services rendered to their country by the Catholic missionaries.

A journalist wrote at the time:

If it be true that the Indians are condemned to annihilation, should they not at least be allowed to choose the faith in which they wish to die? Baptised and instructed as Catholics, the Indians have been divided between the various denominations, and the missionaries, who collected money in Europe for evangelising these poor Indians, are now expelled from the missions they founded. Incredible as this seems, documentary proofs of this condition of things are now in the hands of General Grant. It is horrible to think that these Indians, who had immortal souls as well as the Negroes lately set free, are divided into bands and placed under ministers of every denomination, regardless of their own wishes and convictions.

New York Freeman's Journal, December 14 1872.

Nor were Father De Smet's missions spared. In the Rocky Mountains the Flatheads were the only tribe that had a Catholic agent. The missionary in charge had to cover a distance of ninety miles to visit his flock. The Quakers established themselves in the Kansas 'reductions', and were guilty of shameful extortion. 'One can scarcely believe that such a state of things could exist in the republic of the United States, so much vaunted for its liberty,' wrote Father De Smet. With touching confidence that nothing could shake, he adds, 'We pray and hope that justice will be done.'

Not content with praying, the intrepid veteran redoubled his efforts; he exerted himself to obtain men of recognised integrity for the posts at his disposal.

On 27 March 1871, he addressed to General Parker, Commissioner of Indian Affairs, a long account of the situation, notably in Montana, Idaho and Washington territories. The Nez Percés, a tribe almost exclusively Catholic, were handed over to the Presbyterians. The chief of the Spokanes was threatened with imprisonment for having tried to restrain the licentiousness of his tribe. The Catholic agent among the Blackfeet had been replaced by a sectarian as debauched as he was malicious. In Dakota, where the Sioux clamoured for Black Robes, all the agencies but two had been given to Protestants.

Recalling the services rendered by his fellow-missionaries, Father De Smet demanded for them the right to pursue their apostolate unhindered:

> For thirty years we have laboured among the benighted tribes of the Far West with only the view of promoting the knowledge of God among them and adding to their temporal welfare. We have divided with them the little means placed at our disposal, and often have we joyfully shared their poverty and privations.
>
> *Lavaille, p. 365.*

Four years before, General Parker had owed the success of his office among the Sioux to Father De Smet, and common justice required that he now accede to the priest's request. But for the moment the Indians were quiet, so why consider a priest whose services were no longer necessary? The letter remained unanswered. For a year Father De Smet repeated his requests to Washington. He wrote to the Secretary of the Interior.

> All that the Catholic bishops and missionaries aim at, in this country of religious liberty, is to be allowed their rights, in accordance with their call from above, to evangelise the Indians who have received them with joy, and not to be turned out of the missions where they have laboured for years with zeal and fervour for the welfare and salvation of the Indians, as has been the case in several sections.

Like his colleague on Indian Affairs, the Secretary of the Interior did not deign to reply to the grievances of a sick Jesuit.

The Indians found it difficult to get along with their new masters, and felt like orphans since the departure of the Black Robes. They sent frequent messages to the Great Father in Washington, entreating him to give them back their Catholic agents, their priests, and their Catholic schools. Such petitions received scant recognition at the White House, the religious convictions of the Indians being of as little importance in the eyes of the Government as compared with their lives and property.

But despite persecutions, the Catholic Indians, with but few exceptions, remained faithful to the Church. In fact, had it not been for the restraining influence of the priests, matters would have boiled over into bloody revolt.

Father De Smet hoped to visit the Sioux in the spring of 1873. On 18 February, he wrote to the Catholic agent at Grand River,

I hope the approaching spring may be of some service in regaining my lost strength and general health. In regard to my prospects of seeing the Indians later in the spring, it is difficult to determine beforehand and under my present dispositions. Should there be any prospect on my part, I shall certainly inform you in due time.

A month later he wrote again:

Captain La Barge's boat (*De Smet*) is advertised for Benton, and will leave St Louis on the 12 of April. My room is kept ready and at my disposal. Should my health permit I shall gladly undertake the trip. I had of late a very severe attack of sickness. I am again convalescent and in good hope.

Lavaille, p. 384.

But those who saw the old priest daily did not share his illusions. He could scarcely get out of the carriage. He soon realised he must abandon all hope of leaving St Louis. His heart was crushed with disappointment, and in the following words he assures the Sioux of his prayers and that he will always keep them in mind. To their agent he wrote: 'I sympathise sincerely with my good Indian friends, who have been very severely visited by sickness this last winter and lost many of their dear children. I pray for them daily that the Lord may have pity on them and take them under His holy protection.'

All his life Father De Smet made a study of the Indians. They were his absorbing interest. He studied their origin, their tribes, and mode of life, but above all their religious ideas. Before Longfellow had embodied in his 'Hiawatha' the ancient traditions of a race doomed to extinction, Father De Smet had collected their simple legends, in which one discerns their belief in a Creator, the fall of our first parents, the deluge, the dispersion of mankind, and in a divine Mediator who intercedes for us with the 'Master of Life'.

He also collected material that would one day be of value in a history of the missions. In fact the very last letter he ever wrote (St Louis University, 12 May 1873) was devoted to this subject.

Reverend Dear Father War

Please let me know the exact dates of St Mary's Mission and when established on Sugar Creek?
When on Kansas River?
When was the convent built?
In my sickly moments I collect materials which may be of great service for the future history of the Missouri Province.
Pray for me.

In May of 1873 there had been much activity at the University of St Louis, such as repair work after the hurricanes and thunderstorms that had battered the country. At the end of the month there was excitement again – but from a different source: a visit by a VIP.

At the Priest's House the Rector greeted General Parker.

'Where's Father De Smet?' asked the General.

The Rector was surprised the General did not know. He put him in the picture. 'Father De Smet has gone to his reward.'

Disbelief flashed across the General's face. 'You mean he's dead?'

Father Rector nodded. 'It was last week,' Father Rector elaborated. 'His good friend Captain La Barge was launching a new steamboat. This new boat was to be named *De Smet*. Father De Smet was asked to bless it. He felt he had to, despite not being well. How could he disappoint an old friend? The ceremony took place on 13 May. Upon returning home in the evening he was taken quite ill and grew rapidly worse. The next day, after saying

Mass, he said to the server: "This is the end, I shall never again ascend the altar." He suffered from Bright's disease, chronic inflammation of the kidneys. To this was added severe haemorrhage. A painful operation was performed. While it brought temporary relief, his weakness increased daily. On May 20, 1873, he asked that the last sacraments be administered to him, which he received with touching piety and perfect resignation. Fathers O'Neill and De Blieck tell us that from that time on he seemed oblivious of earth and thought only of eternity. The end came at 1.45 on the morning of May 23. We buried him a few days later.'

It was the very last thing the General wanted to hear. By now the injustices against the Indians had risen to such a pitch that war was imminent. As in 1868, the Government had hoped to call upon Black Robe's services as a mediator.

The situation facing General Parker and the United States Government was of Homeric proportions. The Indians were an omnipresent threat: now their patience had come to an end. They had listened to too many broken promises, to too many lies, had been cheated too many times. They were on the warpath.

The Sioux tribes had been given many promises that their lands would be safe from white invaders. The United States Government guaranteed to the Sioux possession of the Bad Lands, north of the Niobrara River. A few years later gold was discovered in the Black Hills (*Paha Sapa*), that rose 4,000 feet from the yellow plains in the western one-third of the Great Sioux Reservation. Fifteen thousand miners invaded the country and took complete possession of it, despite the fact that the 1868 Peace Treaty recognised those lands as belonging to the Sioux. Again and again the Indians appealed to Washington without redress.

In 1869, a commission set up by President Grant to report on Indian conditions, had this to say:

Every means that human ingenuity can devise, legal or illegal, has been resorted to for the purpose of obtaining possession of Indian lands. The history of the Government connections with the Indians is a shameful record of broken treaties and unfulfilled promises. The history of the border white man's connection with the Indians is a sickening record of murder, outrage, robbery, and wrongs committed by the former, as the rule, and occasional savage outbreaks and unspeakably barbarous deaths of retaliation by the latter, as the exception.

After the Sioux massacre of 1862 the Winnebagoes were driven from their homes in Minnesota. The Government robbed them of their lands on the grounds of offering them a 'permanent home'.

The Indians were removed to 'reservations' on absolutely barren land, where there was no possibility of growing anything; no hope of them ever becoming self-supporting; kept of necessity in the hopeless condition of paupers. They were forcibly expatriated from Mankato down to St Peter's, to Fort Snelling, thence down the Mississippi to the Missouri, thence up the latter river to their new 'reservation', a total distance of 1,000 miles. Overland it would have been 300 miles.

In 1868 some government officials ordered the Red Cloud and Spotted Tail tribes to move away from their land on White Clay Creek. Mr Hayt, the Commissioner of Indians Affairs came to tell them how much better off they would be away from White Clay Creek.

> When he rose to speak, Chief Spotted Tail sprung up, walked towards him, waving in his hand the paper containing the promise of the Government to return them to White Clay Creek, and exclaimed, 'All the men who come from Washington are liars, and the bald-headed ones are the worst of all! I don't want to hear one word from you – you are a bald-headed liar! You have but one thing to do here, and that is to give an order for us to return to White Clay Creek. Here are your written words, and if you don't give this order, and everything here is not on wheels inside of ten days, I'll order my young men to tear down and burn everything in this part of the country! I don't want to hear anything more from you, and I've got nothing more to say to you:' and he turned his back on the Commissioner and walked away. Such language as this would not have been borne from unarmed and helpless Indians; but when it came from a chief with 4,000 armed warriors at his back, it was another affair altogether. The much-terrified Commissioner wrote the order then and there. In less than ten days everything was 'on wheels' and the whole body of these Sioux on the move to the country they had chosen to go to.
>
> *Jackson, pp. 183–4.*

In the summer of 1873 the railhead of the Northern Pacific Railway touched the Yellowstone River and the town of Bismarck sprang up on its eastern bank. Across the river a fine new fort was built – Fort Abraham Lincoln – in which General Custer's Seventh Cavalry were billeted.

This was adding insult to injury. Sitting Bull determined to fight the railway. At a ceremony on Rosebud Creek in 1869 Sitting Bull had been elected war chief and leader of the entire coalition of tribes that formed the Sioux nation. His horsemanship in battle was faultless. Without slackening speed he could dive over the side of his horse and remain clinging to the saddle-horn and one stirrup. While in full gallop he would swing up a large war bow and fit an arrow to it. In the 1870s the Sioux began acquiring rifles and pistols. The Winchester and Henry repeating rifles were especially prized. They were far superior to the old trade muskets that fired powder and ball and lacked accuracy. The United States Infantry were armed with long-range rifles. War with the well-armed whites demanded equally sophisticated weapons. The knife-pointed war clubs, and tomahawks, the bows and arrows would no longer suffice.

At daybreak on 17 March 1876, with the temperature 50° below zero and thick icy fog hanging over the valley, white soldiers on white horses stormed into a Sioux village, pistols popping. The Indians tried frantically to escape from their *tipis* fastened tightly against the sub-zero cold. In their sleeping robes scantily clad men, women and children ran in all directions to escape the horsemen. Men grabbed their weapons and ran to their horses only to find that the soldiers had already seized half their number. The women hovered together, like statues of despair, clutching their babies and children. Half the village was destroyed. Death was everywhere, and in its most horrific and disgusting aspects. Sorrow beclouded every brow. The Indians were left destitute on the snow in the bitter cold. Short on clothing, food and shelter they made for Powder River, where Sitting Bull had his camp on the west bank of the river.

Sitting Bull and Crazy Horse had agreed to fight only a defensive war. Their soldiers would fight only if directly assailed, only if their women and children were threatened. Now the whites had provoked them into an offensive war.

On 16 June 1876, Little Hawk's scouts dashed into the village, shouting to alert the camp that white men were approaching the Rosebud River. Young men painted and clothed themselves for battle, checked their arms and secured their best horses.

On 17 June 1876, as the sun rose over the big bend of the Rosebud, Sitting Bull and Crazy Horse rode with their young men to confront General George Crook. The Indians called him 'three stars' because he wore one star on each epaulette and one on his hat. He rarely wore uniform; instead he wore a canvas suit and a cork helmet. He preferred a mule to a horse and wove his forked blonde beard into braids tied behind his back. That day his men were unsaddled, and even though in enemy territory, had taken no precautions against a surprise Sioux attack. The General played whist with some of his officers while soldiers brewed coffee.

Sitting Bull, armed with rifle, bow and arrows, and daubed with red paint, led the attack, mounted on his horse Bloated Jaw. Crazy Horse, without feathers, in just a white shirt, his hair flowing loose behind, and armed with a lance, was there too. They won a crushing victory.

Some days later, 25 June 1876, in the valley of the Little Big Horn, the village drowsed in the hot afternoon; the women carried out their chores in their *tipis*, others bent through the river bottom digging wild turnips or picking berries, while children splashed in the cool waters of the river. Suddenly all hell broke loose. Women on the bluffs east of the river had sighted blue-uniformed cavalry in Reno Creek. The village exploded in pandemonium. Men rushed to paint themselves for battle and get their ponies.

Great clouds of dust rose up over the valley as Lieutenant Colonel Custer's Seventh Cavalry charged down the valley, shouting his favourite battle tune 'Gary Owen'.

The Seventh Cavalry, with its 750 men, formed the bulk of General Terry's force of 1,000. The Indian horses raised their own dust as they rode out to meet the attack. Sitting Bull and Crazy Horse rode into the attack, to the sound of pounding hooves, eagle-bone whistles and the warbling tremolos of women yelling encouragement from the western hills. That day hundreds of men saw the sun for the last time. General Custer, along with seventeen officers and over 300 soldiers, was massacred. The dead lay naked on the ground, to be torn asunder by beasts or to bleach in the rain.

This defeat was a terrible United States disaster. For the Sioux and the Cheyenne, never had they triumphed so spectacularly.

Sitting Bull commented: 'I feel sorry that too many were killed on each side. But when the Indians must fight, they must.'

The Government wanted to end a costly war. Overtures were made to Sitting Bull. This was his reply: 'Tell them at Washington if they have one man who speaks the truth to send him to me, and I will listen to what he has to say.'

They had had one man – Black Robe. But he was now dead, as General Parker had found out to his dismay.

In 1877 the search for new hunting grounds drove Sitting Bull and his tribesmen to cross the border into Canada, where he could rely on justice and protection of the 'Mounties', the Red Coats.

In October 1877 General Terry led a delegation to Canada to persuade Sitting Bull to return to the United States where everything would be fine for himself and his people. Sitting Bull was there in a dark shirt with white dots, black leggings with broad red stripes down the sides, a blanket draped loosely over his shoulders, handsomely beaded moccasins, a cap of box fur with a badger tail over long unbraided hair and a quiet ironical smile.

General Terry rose to speak. 'It is time for bloodshed to cease,' he said. 'You can return to your country and friends.'

Sitting Bull smiled broadly. The Indians sat with inscrutable countenances and puffed methodically on their pipes. Sitting Bull laughed at yet another lie. When Terry said they could return without arms, Sitting Bull interrupted and ordered Terry not to say any more words, but simply to go home and to leave the Sioux with their red-coated friends.

A wry smile must have issued from a Black Robe looking down on the proceedings.

Black Robe was buried in the little cemetery of the Novitiate at Florissant, at the foot of the grave of Father Verhaegen, who had come to this place with him fifty years before.

In 1878, on the fifth anniversary of Father De Smet's death, a fine bronze statue (nearly fourteen feet high) of the great missionary was unveiled in Termonde (now Dondermonde). He is represented in his priestly robes, in the attitude of moving forward, an eager expression on his face. In his right hand he carries a crucifix, in the other the symbol of peace, an olive branch.

When news of Father De Smet's death reached Europe his example and his 'Letters' persuaded hundreds of young men to offer their services for his missions. The number of vocations rose dramatically.

Appendix 1

Letter of Major General David S Stanley, US Army, to Archbishop Purcell of Cincinnati

Fort Sully
Dakota Territory

July 12, 1868

H G Monseigneur Archbishop Purcell:

Monseigneur

Herewith I send you a testimonial which the Peace Commission, lately sitting at Fort Rice, has given to our well-beloved missionary, Father P.J. De Smet.

Probably you are informed in regard to the work of this commission during the last year. In the month of May of the current year the commission succeeded in convoking Fort Laramie, on the Platte River, a certain number of chiefs belonging to the most formidable and most warlike tribes. The Hunkpapas, however, still refused to enter into any arrangements with the whites, and it is unnecessary to say that no treaty with the Sioux was possible, if this large and hostile tribe was unwilling to concur in it. In this condition of affairs, the Reverend Father De Smet, who has consecrated his life to the service of the true religion and of humanity, offered himself, despite his great age, to endeavour to penetrate to the hostile camps and to use his influence with the chiefs to induce them to appear before the commission at Fort Rice. As the letter of the members of the commission will inform you, there is reason to believe that his mission has been wholly successful.

I could give you only an imperfect idea of the privations and dangers of this journey, unless you were acquainted with the Great

Plains and the Indian character, which is naturally inclined to vengeance. Father De Smet, alone of the entire white race, could penetrate to these cruel savages and return safe and sound. One of the chiefs, in speaking to him while he was in the hostile camp, told him, 'if it had been any other man than you, Black Robe, this day would have been his last'.

On leaving Fort Rice, Father De Smet had to direct his course straight west. The enemy had pitched his camp a little above the mouth of the Yellowstone River, near Powder River. The distance to be travelled, going and coming, was 700 miles. The country is a barren desert. Nothing in the way of vegetation is to be seen save sagebrush, the *artemisia* of the plains. No buffalo are to be found except along the Yellowstone, where they are very numerous.

The Reverend Father is known among the Indians by the name of 'Black Robe' and 'Big Medicine Man'. When he is among them he always wears the cassock and crucifix. He is the only man for whom I have ever seen Indians evince a real affection. They say, in their simple and open language, that he is the only white man who has not a forked tongue; that is, who never lies to them. The reception that they gave him in the hostile camp was enthusiastic and magnificent. They came twenty miles to meet him, and the principal chiefs, riding beside him, conducted him to the camp in great triumph. This camp comprised more than 500 lodges, which, at the ratio of six persons to the lodge, gave a total of 3,000 Indians. During his visit, which lasted three days, the principal chiefs, Black Moon and Sitting Bull, who had been redoubtable adversaries of the whites for the last four years of the war, watched constantly over the safety of the missionary; they slept beside him at night, lest some Indian might seek to avenge upon his person the death of some kinsman killed by the whites. During the daytime, multitudes of children flocked to his lodge, and the mothers brought him their new babies that he might lay his hands on them and bless them.

In the gathering of the Indians the head chiefs promised to put an end to the war. Sitting Bull declared that he had been the most mortal enemy of the whites, and had fought them by every means in his power; but now that Black Robe had come to utter the words of peace, he renounced warfare and would never again lift his hand against the whites. The chiefs delegated several of the principal warriors, who, in company with Father De Smet, arrived at Fort Rice on the 30 of June.

The arrival of the Reverend Father with the Indian delegation gave rise to great rejoicing among the friendly tribes at the fort. They escorted him thither with great ceremony.

Not in fifty years, very likely, had there been seen so numerous an assembly in our country as that which had come together at Fort Rice. The interests at stake were far above anything that our friends can imagine. The first chiefs or representatives of nine bands of the Sioux nation were present. I do not think it necessary to mention the strange names of these different bands, which are besides for the most part unknown to you; suffice it to say that the tribes represented at the meeting cover with their habitations an extent of territory equalling in area six times that of the State of Ohio; and any one who is at all acquainted with the Indian question, is aware that no peace with the Indians can be worth anything if it does not comprehend the Sioux, who are the most numerous of all the tribes with which we have had to treat down to this day, and the most warlike as well, and the one that has had the most to complain of on the part of the whites. The treaty signed by all the principal chiefs now needs only the sanction of the Senate to become a law.

I am persuaded that it is the most complete and the wisest of all the treaties thus far concluded with the Indians of this country. Without going into details, by the provisions of this treaty the Indians are to be abundantly provided with victuals, clothing and agricultural and mechanical implements. No money payments have been stipulated, as unfortunately money excites the covetousness of more than one and often converts commissioners, governors of territories, superintendents, agents and traders into a band of thieves. Without doubt the fulfilment of the provisions of this treaty will assure peace with the Sioux. The importance of this result will be understood, if it is considered that a distinguished general (Sherman) stated, last fall, that a war undertaken with the object of exterminating the Indians of the plains (and he thought it would have come to that extremity) would cost the country $500,000,000. I will say in passing that this method of pacification seems to me altogether too much like violence.

But it is time to close this long letter. Whatever may be the result of the treaty which the commission has just concluded with the Sioux, we can never forget nor shall we ever cease to admire, the disinterested devotion of the Reverend Father De Smet, who, at the age of 68 years, did not hesitate, in the midst of the heat of summer, to undertake a long and perilous journey, across the burning plains, destitute of trees and even of grass; having none but corrupted and unwholesome water, constantly exposed to scalping by Indians, and this without seeking either honours or remuneration of any sort; but solely to arrest the shedding of blood and save, if it might be, some lives, and preserve some habitations to these savage children of the desert, to whose spiritual and temporal welfare he has consecrated a long life of labour and solicitude. The head chief of the Yanktonnais, Two Bears, said in his speech: 'When we are settled down sowing grain, raising cattle and living in houses, we want Father De Smet to come and live with us, and to bring us other Black Robes to live among us also; we will listen to their words, and the Great Spirit will love us and bless us.'

David S Stanley
Major General. United States Army.

C and R, pp. 1584–8.

Appendix 2

Funeral Oration for Father De Smet

Father De Smet's death caused a deep grief in St Louis where he had made his home for fifty years. His funeral was one of the largest ever held in that city. The funeral oration was given by Bishop Ryan.

Yes truly, in the tent of the poor Indian as in the heart of our populous cities, people will speak with love and respect for a long time to come of the Reverend Father De Smet . . .

This zealous priest busied himself for a half-century, with the most perfect purity of intention, in the service of God, in saving souls, in propagating the glory of the Master of heaven and earth:- what a noble life! And think that he expended his strength on behalf of the poor Indians, those outcast, disinherited children of the desert. Almost the whole of his life was passed in the civilisation of the wild and nomadic Indians. It was for their sake that he so often visited Europe, in quest of auxiliary missionaries and of financial and other aid, needed for the establishment and maintenance of missions among the red men . . .

I once heard some one say in my presence to Father De Smet, 'But, Father, how is it possible for you to be so contented among these frightful savages?' 'Frightful savages?' he replied. 'You don't know what you are saying. You do not know those simple, kindly people. I have met more savages in the great cities of America and Europe than I have ever seen in my life in the plains and deserts of the United States.'

'I have been in a position,' said our dear friend, 'to appreciate these poor Indians. A band of them once came to me to receive holy baptism. I gave them the proper instruction, and made them children of heaven. Then they besought me earnestly to come again to them the following year, and I promised to do so. I returned at the appointed time, and as they showed an eager desire to approach the sacraments, I asked them what faults they had been guilty of since my last visit. They looked at me with astonishment and a kind of stupor, and said, "do you suppose Father, that after all the benefactions we have received from God, those of creation, redemption, the knowledge of the true son of God, Jesus Christ, and you coming to us, do you suppose that we would be so wicked as to offend the Lord and appear before you charged with sins or crimes?" You see, brethren, those unhappy Indians were hurt, at the thought that any one could think them capable of ingratitude toward God.'

A man who works for God has no other object than God; his works are all manifest, they bear the stamp of sincerity; he goes forth full of light and truth; his conduct can be known and judged by all the world. It was thus that when the red man of the forest saw Father De Smet, he judged favourably of that countenance upon which such frankness, honesty and innocence were imprinted. The Indian felt instinctively drawn toward this man of God, whose behaviour was dictated by no motive or self-interest. The savages understood perfectly well that the zealous missionary came among them, not to make a fortune, not to win renown or acquire standing, but purely to labour for the salvation of their souls. This is why they instantly understood whatever the Father said to them; they read in the features of the worthy priest the uprightness of his life, and they fell prostrate at his feet; they implored the aid of his sacred ministry, and asked to be taught. It is a remarkable thing, brethren; Father De Smet never needed, so to speak, but to show himself, and on the instant a current of active sympathy was established between him and those he approached. The red men felt themselves fascinated by his gaze, by his expressive speech and his masculine energy.

C and R, pp. 1592–9.

Bibliography

Catlin, G, *Illustrations of the Manners, Customs and Conditions of the North American Indians*, 2 Vols, H G Bohn, London, 1857.

Chittenden, Hiram Martin and Richardson, Alfred Talbot, *Life, Letters and Travels of Father De Smet Among the North American Indians 1801–1873*, 4 Vols, Francis P Harper, New York, 1905.

De Smet, Pierre-Jean, SJ, *The Oregon Missions and Travels over the Rocky Mountains in 1845/6*, Edward Dunigan, New York, 1847.

Hunt, Norman Bancroft, *The North American Indians*, Brian Todd Publishing, London, 1991.

Jackson, Helen Hunt, *A Century of Dishonour: A Sketch of the United States Government's Dealings with Some of the Indian Tribes*, Little, Brown and Company, Boston, 1909.

Lavaille, E, SJ, *The Life of Father De Smet SJ (1801–1873)*, Loyola University Press, Chicago, 1915.

Lewis, Merriwether, and Clark, William, *Travels to the Source of the Missouri River and across the American Continent to the Pacific Ocean in the years 1804, 1805, and 1806*, 3 Vols, Longman, Hurst, Rees, Orme and Brown, London, 1815.

Sage, Rufus B, *Life in the Rocky Mountains 1820–1875*, Arthur H Clark Co., Glendale, California, 1956.

Taylor, Colin F, *The Native Americans*, Salamander Books Ltd, London, 1991.

Utley, Robert M, *The Lance and the Shield. The Life and Times of Sitting Bull*, Pimlico Press, London, 1998.

Waldman, Carol, *Atlas of the North American Indians*, Facts on File Publications, New York, 1985.

Washington, Irving, *A Town on the Prairies, 1835–1851*; *Astoria, 1838*, University of Oklahoma, 1964.